FRENCH CATHEDRALS

LE PUY

FRENCH CATHEDRALS

MONASTERIES AND ABBEYS
AND SACRED SITES OF FRANCE

BY

ELIZABETH ROBINS PENNELL

ILLUSTRATED
WITH ONE HUNDRED AND EIGHTY-THREE PICTURES BY
JOSEPH PENNELL
ALSO WITH PLANS AND DIAGRAMS

NEW YORK: THE CENTURY CO.

TO FRANCE
THE FIRST FRIEND OF AMERICA
THE COUNTRY WE HAVE
LOVED FROM THE
BEGINNING

CONTENTS

v

LIST OF ILLUSTRATIONS

vii

AT TOULOUSE AND ALBI

AN ALBERT DÜRER TOWN: ROCAMADOUR

NOTRE-DAME AND OTHER CHURCHES IN PARIS

CHARTRES—THE HOUSE OF PRAYER

ST. JULIEN OF LE MANS

"IN THE PERIL OF THE SEA": MONT ST. MICHEL

NOTRE-DAME OF LAON

ST. ETIENNE OF BOURGES

AMIENS: "THE PARTHENON OF GOTHIC ARCHITECTURE"

NOTRE-DAME OF ROUEN

WHERE KINGS WERE CROWNED: RHEIMS

A MAGNIFICENT FRAGMENT: BEAUVAIS

INTRODUCTION

I

It is many years now since our first visit to a French cathedral, made through no mere whim of the tourist, nor odd chance of the traveler, but because J., who had just finished a series of drawings of the English cathedrals for "The Century Magazine," was asked to begin a second of the great churches of France. The work, before it came to an end, carried us north and south, east and west, from one cathedral town to another; it kept us in each sometimes for weeks, sometimes for months; it spread over eighteen years, so that we got to know them all with an intimacy that visiting them for pleasure alone could never have given us.

France, in the earliest days of our cathedral journeys, was an undiscovered country. The tide of travel swept across it to Italy or to Switzerland, and few stopped by the way, except for the inevitable holiday in Paris, a winter on the Riviera, or perhaps a round trip to the Châteaux of Touraine. When we cycled, as we usually did, we had the hard white road between its lines of poplars to ourselves, and, as a rule, only the commercial traveler shared the friendly inns and their good dinners with us. Day after day passed in the little towns without our hearing a word of our own language spoken. In the cathedrals we seldom met any but natives. The motor had not as yet driven the cyclist off the road, nor the Touring Club regulated inns which understood so well how to regulate themselves. There were no competing series of Handbooks to Cathedrals and Guides to Medieval Towns to impose new responsibilities upon the tourist, no color prints and picture post-cards to cheapen the beauty of the land, no *Entente Cordiale* of hypocrisy, but in France a healthy, honest hatred of the foreigner, especially of the Briton. Books had been published about the cathedrals, of course. Viollet-le-Duc had issued his huge "Dictionnaire" years before, and Fergusson his big "Illustrated Handbook"; Prosper Mérimée had made the "Notes" of his official journey among historic churches, and Freeman had written much upon the subject. But their books and others like them were for the architect, the student, the government. The most popular authority on cathedrals, as I remember, was Parker, and Parker refused to see purity and perfection in Gothic architecture outside of England—what would he have thought of those new authorities who are more apt to deny even the existence of Gothic architecture outside of France? Ruskin and William Morris were influences to reckon with, and both were alike in their admiration for France and their reverence for the work of its architects. Ruskin could never look unmoved at a French cathedral "lifting its fair height above the purple crowd of humble roofs," nor Morris smell without a thrill the mingled odor of beeswax, wood-smoke, and onions that greeted him on landing in the home of the "glorious churches" he loved. But even Ruskin and Morris were slow to rouse this enthusiasm in others. Out of the hundreds who hurried to spend Mornings in Florence, or study the Stones of Venice, to hardly one did it occur to break the journey in order to see how nobly Laon crowns its hilltop, or Rheims broods, sphinx-like, over the plain. If the tourist strolled to Notre-Dame in Paris as a tribute to Victor Hugo, if he got off between trains at Amiens because he had read "Our Fathers Have Told Us," or at Rouen because it was convenient on the way from Dieppe, he felt that his duty to the cathedrals of the country had been more than done.

For us, therefore, wandering in a "fairyland of travel," there was something of the joy of the discoverer when the forgotten cathedral town, to which work was our guide, turned out to be "the most picturesque place in the world," something of the pride of the pioneer when we settled down and made ourselves at home in it. We were generous enough not to keep our discovery always to ourselves, not to allow the cathedral to remain neglected for a while longer, nor the tide of travel to sweep by unchecked. It is on our conscience now that we did not, for often the result of our description in print was an invasion of the place described. At this late day letters still come to us asking for information about Le Puy because of our article on that town in "The Century" eighteen years ago. The landlord of more than one little old hotel has assured us that we helped to make his fortune, and to raise his prices. And so we feel the responsibility for our share, however small, in bringing about the recent popularity of France with the tourist, and the consequent loss of much that made it charming in the old days when we first knew it.

II

OUR choice of cathedrals and the order of our visiting them depended, not upon haphazard, but upon a scheme carefully prepared, though not by ourselves. Mrs. Van Rensselaer, who had written a book on the English cathedrals, planned a second on the French, with reference entirely to her own interest in the subject and the value of the examples she selected in the history of architecture. After the first few chapters, however, she abandoned the work, and as I had been to the cathedrals with J., who was making the drawings in the order she suggested, I undertook it in her place. I think, on the whole, it was an advantage to have a route mapped out for us. We should not have known where to begin nor where to stop had not some such restriction from outside been put upon us. Left to ourselves, we should not have wanted to omit one cathedral or important church, and a lifetime would not suffice for the study of them all. As time went on, the scheme was altered and modified, why or how it does not matter now, for our work was in no way affected. But at the beginning we kept scrupulously to the route, and, as it was planned according to architectural history, it was the cause of our seeing a great deal more of France and learning a great deal more about its cathedrals than we might had we followed the more direct lines of travel.

This architectural route took us first, and as long ago as the late eighties, to the cities of Provence: to Avignon, Arles, St. Gilles, to the old Romanesque churches with the mark of Rome strong upon them and a breath from the East warming them into fresh and richer flowering, that are not the least of the wonders in the land of Mistral and Daudet—the land of the olive and the vine. Provence, at all events, was a good beginning and sent us the more hopefully to the other centers of Romanesque in France—to Périgueux, Angoulême and Poitiers in the old kingdom of Aquitaine, to Caen in the far north, to Clermont-Ferrand, Issoire, and Le Puy in Auvergne, to

Toulouse in Languedoc.   Disappointment may have awaited us in some few of these churches where the restorer had been before us, but many were marvelous beyond our expectation, while always the loveliness of the French country and the charm of the French town colored and heightened our pleasure. Then followed the great Gothic churches, and we wandered from Albi to Paris, from Bourges to Beauvais, from Chartres and Le Mans to Laon and Rheims, from Amiens to Rouen. There were interruptions, our original plan held us more lightly, we kept less faithfully to its architectural order, and at times we added to it ourselves; for instance, going to Mont St. Michel for no better reason than because we knew it must be one of the chief marvels of all.   Then there were intervals when we stayed away altogether from cathedrals, and years passed before the series was completed, so that it was virtually only yesterday when we reached the last cathedral on the route mapped out almost a quarter of a century ago.

III

THE outline of the route, as I have given it, will explain the vast extent of France over which it compelled us to travel. Except Brittany, Touraine, and French Flanders, there were few parts of the country where it did not take us, as a rule by as roundabout a way as possible.   We should have been unobservant, indeed, if, from our cycles, we had not found out for ourselves the variety there is in the beauty of France, where the traveler by train was then accustomed to see only monotony. The contrast between the Romanesque of the South and the Romanesque of the North was not stronger than the contrast between the olive gardens of Provence and the apple orchards of Normandy, or between the watered meadows of Poitou and the volcanic peaks of Auvergne. Gothic did not pass through more varied phases than the shifting landscape as we rode from the poplared lagoons of Picardy to the sun-steeped shores of the Tarn, from the plain of La Beauce to the vineyards of Champagne, from the lonely sea-girt abbey on its hill to the very heart of Paris, the capital. We journeyed to see cathedrals, it is true, but we saw as well the country of which they are the glory.

This was the beginning of our love for France: for its well-ordered landscape, which has the style and distinction of its architecture; for the pale skies of the North and the *Midi's* brilliant sunshine; for the people, with their thrift, their industry, their intelligence, their courtesy, their charm—the most industrious people in the world, though the virtuous Briton loves to deplore their idleness and frivolity; for the towns, always individual in character and picturesqueness; for the life in these towns, as well-ordered as the landscape and the architecture. The splendor of the churches we visited seemed to us no less because, in a comfortable little inn close by, the cloth was laid for us at noon and again at night with as excellent a meal as we could wish, because beds there were soft and linen fresh, because somewhere not far from the old gray walls was a garden with clipped alleys and shady groves for us to rest in, because we were surrounded by people with the sympathy to understand our work and the manners to respect it; because every-day industry could be occasionally exchanged for the gaiety of feasts, dignified by tradition, and animated by the joy in them of the only men and women I know who can work and play with equal zest.

IV

BUT the cathedrals were, after all, the end of our journeyings. Like Stevenson, we never wearied of them; they were our "favorite kind of mountain scenery." It was for the first glimpse of their towers upon the horizon that we watched from train or cycle, or later, alas! motor; it was to see them near that we hurried at once on our arrival in town or village; it was within their walls or under their shadow that most of our time was spent.

If we could not easily follow our route without learning much of France, neither could we wander from one great church on our list to the next without beginning to understand the development which converted the Roman basilica into the Romanesque church and, in its turn, the Romanesque church into the great Gothic cathedral, which made piers and arches aspire ever higher and higher, statues become more delicately wrought, windows let in a richer light, ornament flower more flamboyantly; without, in a word, beginning to appreciate the perfection in the architecture, the unity of so many noble parts in one noble whole, to which the French cathedral owes its supremacy among the Christian churches of the world. There may be at times richer color in the Italian, deeper solemnity in the Spanish; the English minster may borrow greater tenderness from the peace and seclusion of its green inclosure. But none approaches the French in the dignity and grandeur that befits the house of God, in the harmony without which the work of art is not complete, in the human sympathy, expressed in its inexhaustible ornament, which appeals to the people and tempers their awe with love. Though we also learned that this perfection was based upon science, that the laws of thrust and balance meant more in its development than the shining of Seven, or any number of, Lamps of Architecture, we were only the more impressed. Ruskin, for years, set everybody to seeking in a building the last qualities that should be looked for in it—virtue and vice, truth and falsehood, right and wrong—and the enthusiasm he kindled was for ethics, not for art. He only succeeded in preventing his devoted disciples from seeing cathedrals as they are. Viollet-le-Duc, on the other hand, could write of architecture architecturally and yet with such eloquence and ardor that even the layman, in reading, must get some dim glimmering of the romance there is in the logic of growth, and borrow some of his enthusiasm for architecture not as a branch of ethics, but as an art and a science. There are cathedrals where I cannot remember him with patience, though, unfortunately, there is no forgetting him, so wholesale was his destruction of the old work that he might substitute his own. When, however, it comes to reading about cathedrals, there is no authority I would less willingly dispense with, and he and Professor Charles H. Moore, and the appropriate articles in the "Dictionary of Architecture and Building," will do more to put the mere lover of cathedrals like myself in the right spirit for understanding the science of cathedral-building than all Ruskin's Chapters on Morals.

To live intimately in the cathedral atmosphere was, I found, to be no less stirred by the cathedral's associations with the past —with the faith that was its inspiration and the saints who were its guardians, with the battles fought and the blood poured out for it, with the kings it made and unmade, with the miracles worked under its roof and the people who used nave and transept as their own. It is as full of history as of architecture, with so many sides to its beauty that it is easy to understand why Hawthorne, coming like ourselves from a country younger far than Gothic or Romanesque, found the cathedrals the only things that quite "filled in" his ideals of the Old World. Architecture has been called a "distinctly political art," and in France it is never so truly, if unexpectedly, political as in the cathedrals. When I came to them straight from those of England, nothing struck me so much as their position in the town. The English minster is shut in from the vulgar crowd by its close, and has the air of belonging as exclusively to "the gentry" as the mansion in the big park, to which the public are admitted as a privilege, not as a right. The French cathedral opens directly on the street, surrounded not by the respectable residences of deans and canons, but by the houses and shops of the people who often made of its outer walls a prop, or a support, for their own, and of its nave a place of meeting—the Union Square or Hyde Park of their day. They sold their butter, poultry, vegetables, flowers, meat, crockery, and old rags at its sculptured doors, and carried their daily business even to within the sacred precincts. The cathedral became the center of the town and the town life, the most truly democratic institution in the most democratic of countries, the headquarters of the only possible Socialism; very human in its dignity and as simple in its grandeur. The greatest of the great cathedrals of France belong to the period when the communes, one after the other, were fighting for their freedom and winning it, and as Viollet-le-Duc explains the architectural side of their development, so Thierry, in his "Lettres sur l'Histoire de

France," gives the clue to the civic side, and, indeed, I know of few books of such absorbing interest to the wanderer among cathedrals. There are many others that can supply more detail. Innumerable little volumes have come out of late years on the Medieval Towns and Cathedrals of France, while every cathedral has its special historian whose treatise, often as dry as it is learned, can be had in the local book-shops. Nor, for the sentiment of the place, can you overlook such writers and artists as Huysmans and Pater in Chartres, Ruskin in Amiens and Rouen, Hugo in Paris, Henry James at almost every stage of his "Little Tour in France," and Robida all over the land. All are to be read and seen. "A church is a piece of history," Stevenson says, but it is not everybody who can master it without help, or who would understand unaided why "the historical use" of cathedrals is one of their dignities, why they are the "only witnesses, perhaps, that remain to us of the faith and fear of nations."

It would be strange if during my many summers in French cathedrals I had not gained some knowledge of their history and construction, stranger if this knowledge did not keep me from attempting to pose as historian or architect when writing of them. For the more I learned, the more I realized that it is only after years of study and of technical training that the most ardent lover of cathedrals can become a technical authority. In my love and admiration for them I am not to be outdone by anybody, and I do not believe that the ability to see and feel their beauty is a matter of technique. It is a matter of knowing how to see them, though it is still true that only the artist or the architect should ever write technically of his art. So it should be made quite clear at the start that the following pages have no other object than to express whatever little fraction may be expressed in words of my own impressions of the beauty of French cathedrals, of their might and majesty and meaning. To myself these impressions were deep and vivid, and there are churches, as there are men, who seem to impose upon one the necessity, or at least the desire, to record the effect made by their personality, or individuality, in the course of long and close intimacy. Besides, such an attempt would, in a measure, help to pay the debt of gratitude I owe them for the pleasure they have given me—a pleasure that it will be impossible for them to give in precisely the same way, if at all, to anybody in the years and generations to come. For the day has dawned that, with its waning, will see the beauty of French cathedrals, as we of our time have known them, fade and pass away.

V

FRANCE is, of all countries, the most conservative, for the people who have the secret of the enjoyment of life are in no haste to lose it. I used to think that the blue blouse of the men and the white cap of the women might pass for symbols of constancy, or conservatism, so sure was I that the pleasant things they stood for would resist all change. Summer after summer I would return to the charming, well-ordered town, the friendly, comfortable inn, the courteous people, the joyous feasts, to find them as I had left them. But when I return now, I come everywhere upon the trail of the innovator. France, I do believe, has changed more in the last few years than in the whole century before, and one of the most immediate causes of the change is the motorist. It has been said that the motor-car has restored the romance of travel; it would be truer to say that the motorist has destroyed it forever. A quarter of a century ago —I have not forgotten—Ruskin was saying the same thing of the cyclist. But the cycle brought back freedom to the traveler without demoralizing the countries through which he passed. The cyclist, as a rule, did not carry his customs and habits with him wherever he went, nor scatter gold by the way, for the good reason that he usually was too modest a traveler to impose his demands upon anything, and had not the gold to scatter anywhere. To be a cyclist was not to be a millionaire. But to motor means money, and money recognizes only one standard of comfort and insists upon maintaining it. Already, before the motor was heard of, money had reduced the large towns of the Continent and the large hotels to one level of dull uniformity; soon money, with the motor, will have worked the same disaster in all the smaller towns and all the little inns. The cyclist took things as he found them, asking of his Touring Club only to reduce the cost of life for him as he rode; the motorist will have nothing remain as it is, but clamors for the latest fashions in plumbing and upholstery, and for his own hours, and his own *menu,* his own table at meals, and he raises the scale of living as he goes. A peep into an inn which has managed to evade his tyranny, and he flies to the next, where the jug of hot water is ready, the art of cutting thin slices of bread and butter for the five-o'clock is practised, and the same meal is served that is now of obligation in every big hotel from London to Rome, from Paris to Vienna. He does not know that it is just in the old-fashioned inn he disdains that the traveler who does know is sure of an excellent dinner and a good bottle of wine, a comfortable bed at night, and, most likely, a cheerful landlady and gay talk at the *table d'hôte*. But the Ritz and the Plaza are the motorist's ideal, it is only in them he can take his ease—he would not exchange a liveried flunky for all the cheerful land-ladies of Europe. The motor gives to the traveler who can afford it the opportunity to see the world as it never was seen before, and the motorist is fast making the world not worth seeing at all. I do not pretend to explain why it is that a thing in itself so admirable should have such a disastrous effect upon the average man or woman who uses it, but that it does is a fact. The worst of it for France is that not only the English and Americans have discovered the country in their destructive flight, but also that particular type of Frenchman who is afflicted with Anglomania and has become the most intolerant and snobbish of them all.

It may be said that hotels have nothing to do with cathedrals and that I write from too material a standpoint. But for us—for J. and me, that is—the hotel did have much to do with ca-thedrals, since we did not rush through the towns, but lived in them. Besides, the change in the inn is typical of the change going on all around it. The good white road is deteriorating until its present condition is becoming a national problem. Peace has gone from the little towns. The horn of the motor plays the *Ça ira* of the new revolution, and the pace of life must quicken to its tooting.

Perhaps the motorist cannot do the cathedrals of France any actual harm. His motor gives him time only to glance, if even he does as much as that, at "these solemn old churches," for he is always in the hurry that, where they are concerned, seemed a crime to Hawthorne. They are threatened, however, by a more serious danger. If I had to choose between two evils, I should prefer even the motorist to the restorer. The work of restoration dates much further back than our time. The cathedrals were Historical Monuments before ever we visited them, and the State had taken them under its protection. Wherever we went, almost, Viollet-le-Duc, Abadie, or an architect of lesser fame, had been already, and already left his mark. Churches like St. Front at Périgueux, St. Pierre at Angoulême, St. Servin at Toulouse, faced us in various stages of brand-newness. At Le Mans, at Laon, we have had to lament the destruction accomplished between our first journey and our last. To hardly a cathedral have we gone and not found it partially hidden under scaffolding, to hardly one could we go now and not find scaffolding covering some part of it, within or without. Indeed, the business of repair is carried on at such a rate that the cathedral I visited yesterday will rarely be found as I left it by the visitor of to-morrow.

If the restorer were content to restore literally, his interference would be less fatal. But to him restoration means rebuilding, re-creating. He pulls down the old to replace it with a new of his own fashioning, with his version of what he thinks the original building ought to have been and certainly never was. Once a French architect told me, pointing to a Romanesque doorway in a Gothic church, that if he were in charge he would tear the whole church down and restore it to the Romanesque of the doorway. To prop and support weakening walls and piers, to prevent the cathedral from tumbling into a heap of ruins, is one thing. It is quite another to turn it into a new building, scraped and smoothed and cleaned, and the work of yesterday sacrificed to the imitation of to-day. Architects pulled down without scruple in the earlier centuries, but it was to build up something of their own which, though it might be inferior in beauty or dignity to the building they sacrificed, had still the character of their age. There are cathedrals in which, because of this continual pulling down and putting up of parts, you can trace almost every step in the development from the most primitive Romanesque to the most debased Rococo, and if the harmony of the whole suffers a loss, at least the value of the historic record is increased a hundredfold. Hardly a cathedral in France was absolutely completed within one architectural period and is architecturally perfect. It has come to be a common saying in every well-appointed guide that, for perfection, the spires of Chartres, the nave of Amiens, and the choir of Beauvais should be united in the same church, and the French have gone so far as to realize their ideal of the perfect cathedral in composite photographs where you may see, for instance, Beauvais and Chartres, or Rouen, Rheims, Chartres, and Troyes combining to produce a west front beyond reproach. But the imperfection had the merit of being genuine, even beautiful in its way, an essential part of the cathedral's experience and life. The restorer destroys it for his idea of a perfection that never existed. He adds nothing of his own, fills no gap in history, but turns the building into a hybrid that belongs neither to the present nor the past, that, as an architectural expression of his own period, has not a shadow of the value of the sky-scrapers of New York or the smoking chimneys of Pittsburgh. Nor is it only the beauty of the old work he destroys forever, but all the beauty that Time, with the changing of the seasons, has brought to it. The French cathedral, as William Morris wrote of St. Mark's in Venice, was always beautiful and, from the first, meant to grow more beautiful by the lapse of time, and it became eventually not only a work of art, not only a monument of history, but a piece of nature. The restorer strips its stones bare of their history and wipes away the color and tone and texture that Nature lavished upon it through the centuries.

I see no possibility of his hand being stayed. The great churches of France are the property of the State, whose care for them is paternal. They might, for all we know, have fared as badly had this care been left to the Church, but then they would have run less risk of degenerating into "specimens." Now that Church and State in France have broken the old ties and ceased to work together, the cathedral is more than ever at the mercy of a government that has the same genius for order as its people, and that will see to the careful overhauling and classification of its buildings according to the best archæological and architectural authorities. The student may profit, though I doubt it, but the people will have been robbed, and the cathedral, once warmed and illuminated by Faith, will become bare and empty, and the chill of the deserted house will greet you at its door. To go to Mont St. Michel as it now is, abandoned to tourists in summer, in winter to sea-gulls, is to foresee the fate of many of the churches where men and women have prayed for centuries and where the art of France reached its full perfection. As the years go on, one has, I know, a way of looking at the past through a kindly glass that magnifies it, giving it at once a larger and a finer scale. But I think there is another reason besides the passing years for my sadness to-day when I go to France and find its good roads ruined, its provincial towns invaded, its little inns aping the manners of big hotels, and the cathedrals I have loved growing neat and cold and lifeless: both the art that made them and Nature that took them for her own, dishonored. However, all the beauty of the country and its churches has by no means disappeared as yet. There remain corners that the motor has not reached. There is still time, though it threatens to be short, for those who would feel the charm of France and rejoice in the splendor of its old cathedrals.

THE authors wish to express their indebtedness to Harper & Brothers for their courtesy in permitting them to reprint the chapter on Rocamadour, with its illustrations, together with several pictures on Toulouse previously published in *Harper's Magazine*.

It is interesting in this connection to state that the French Government has acquired for the Luxembourg the other drawings which illustrate this volume.

CHAPTER I

ROMANESQUE AND PROVENÇAL SUNSHINE

FRENCH CATHEDRALS

CHAPTER I

ROMANESQUE AND PROVENÇAL SUNSHINE

I

IF I had myself planned the original route of our cathedral journeys, I could not have made a better beginning. For our list of churches opened with those of Provence, and to Provence we went first at midsummer, and so saw the churches first in hot Provençal sunshine.

It is the way to see them first—the way to see them always, if possible—and, often as I have returned, this is the season I have chosen. Provence is unlike every other country in the world, and it is never so entirely itself as in the summer. For me it would always have charm, even when the *mistral* in winter turns it bleak and gray. But, like a garden, it flowers in full beauty only in the light and in the heat. Provençal life is an outdoor life. The color of the Provençal earth is dull until the sun warms and fills it. Provençal architects were artists who knew the effect of strong light and shadow on carven surfaces of stone. The sun is the explanation of everything "down there," the real reason for the gaiety of the people, for the golden glow of the landscape, that, without it, would be grim and arid, for the olives on the hillside and the ilex at the farmer's door, for the low red-tiled roofs and the aromatic herb-scented

3

air, and so also for the luxuriance and the glory of the architecture when it is most completely Provençal. The richest sculptured portal is the richer for the sunshine, the dark of nave and choir the darker for the glare without. From the beginning, the sun has worked with the architect to give both the big cathedral and the little village church a character personal to the land and the people.

The Romanesque of Provence, where perhaps this character expresses itself most strongly, is unlike the Romanesque of every other part of France. It belongs to the period when Provence was still very near to Rome, still very far from the countries of the North, and politics and history can be made to account for the difference. But, if I could never discover in Provençal Romanesque a suggestion of the architecture of penance and contrition that all Romanesque ought to be according to Huysmans, I did not have to go to books and musty records for the reason. I found it much closer at hand in the quality of the Provençal sunshine. Nothing could be sad in that radiant land, which in memory I see now as I saw it the first burning August I came there, the white cities ablaze in the heat, and, in their midst, the church with the shadows lying black and brilliant upon its shining walls.

II

At Avignon, the cathedral in this vision of sunlight rises from a rock well above the windy town. I had seen a little of Provence before coming to Avignon. I had made myself familiar with *les antiquités,* as the Provençal calls the Roman ruins of which he is so proud, by watching the modern bull-fight in the old arena, by sauntering in the footsteps of the Félibres between the tombs and cypresses of the Alyscamps, the old Elysian Fields, at Arles, by wandering from Orange to St. Chamas. It was the pleasantest object-lesson possible, the easiest way to learn that the country was Roman before it became Provençal. The ruins have been so intimately appropriated by the people that there is nothing of the archæological specimen or antiquarian bore about them. Dumas, I believe, said of one Provençal town—Arles—that it was the Mecca of the archæologist.

PORCH OF THE CATHEDRAL OF NOTRE-DAME-DES-DOMS, AVIGNON

But Arles conceals the fact successfully from every one who is not on archæology bent. The "antiquities" are as much a part of the Provençal life of to-day as the beautiful Arlésienne in cap and fichu, as the well-built *gardien* of the Camargue or stalwart fisherman of Martigues. I never thought of looking to them for instruction, but there was no looking at them at all, and then going to Avignon, without understanding how short a step it is from Roman architecture to Romanesque in Provence.

The western porch of the cathedral of Notre-Dame-des-Doms, I have read, was built by Constantine, and again I have read that it is no older than the oldest of the Crusades. I know that before it the definition Gallo-Roman loses its learned sound and seems inevitable. Even those who are not trained architecturally are more apt to see the resemblance of the design to Roman work than the difference from it, especially if other towns with Roman remains have been already visited.

The cathedral was founded by Martha, the sister of Lazarus, who came to Provençal shores with the two Maries, and who, among her numerous good deeds, conquered the dragon of Tarascon, the terrible Tarasque, leading him like a lamb by the ribbon from her neck. She dedicated the cathedral at Avignon to the Blessed Virgin, who was then still living, and heard, no doubt, of the success of Martha's mission to be busy about many things in Provence as in Palestine. But the building as it stands is later in date than the porch, and in the interval between them the architect had got much farther away from Rome. I cannot say it appeals to me as powerfully as many another cathedral of France, but this is easily explained. In the first place, noble as is its position on the Rocher des Doms, between high palace and high garden, with wide steps leading in a fine sweep to its door, and its tower lifting the huge modern statue of Our Lady aloft into the sunshine, it does not altogether hold its own against the big, heavy mass of the Palace of the Popes, belittled though this mass be by the wants and necessities of the modern barrack into which it has been turned. In picturesqueness and association the cathedral has rivals in the town's towered, battlemented walls, and the rivalry here might be more formidable but for the passing of Viollet-le-Duc; in the desolate ruin opposite at Villeneuve-les-Avignon; even—for me at least—in the broken bridge of St. Bénézet, the little Provençal shepherd boy who, seven hundred years ago, startled Avignon by his miracle of architecture, just as that other little shepherd boy was later to startle Flor-

THE TOWER OF ST. TROPHIME FROM THE CLOISTER, ARLES

ence by his miracle of painting, and over whose bridge I, too, have often passed and danced with all the world, in the song sung on gray days and winter evenings in my old convent home so far away as Philadelphia.

The interior of the cathedral has fallen upon evil times. The two popes and the army of cardinals buried within its walls cannot make up for the character swept from it by centuries of alteration, desecration, and restoration. As I write this, however, I reproach myself, and wonder how I can find fault. For the group of great buildings on the Rocher des Doms, as you see them from the town below or the country beyond, would not compose so well without the cathedral and its tower, while I know of few things in Provence lovelier than the wide valley, and the Rhône winding through it, and the distant purple hills, as you look out upon them from the terrace, or platform, in front of the old west porch. Indeed, I am sure, no matter how good other reasons might be, that my enthusiasm was less at Notre-Dame-des-Doms, in Avignon, only because it was so much greater at St. Trophime, in Arles.

Who has not seen Avignon, the city of the popes, has seen nothing, Daudet once wrote. But were I forced to choose between them, I should rather see Arles, though it had never a pope to brag of. I confess at once that I cannot speak without prejudice of the cathedral of St. Trophime, which, as I recall it, is inseparable from golden summer and autumn days when Arles was *en fête,* and the *farandole* unwound its gay length through the near streets and squares, and bulls were fought in the neighboring arena. No other church in all Provence is so beautiful in my eyes. The statuesque Arlésiennes, busily bargaining before it on market days, are not statelier than the rows of saints and the Christ, with angels, apostles, and mystic beasts in attendance, who guard the door, as if against the dreadful dragons and crawling creatures who creep and twist here and there among the decorations. The story of judgment, of virtue

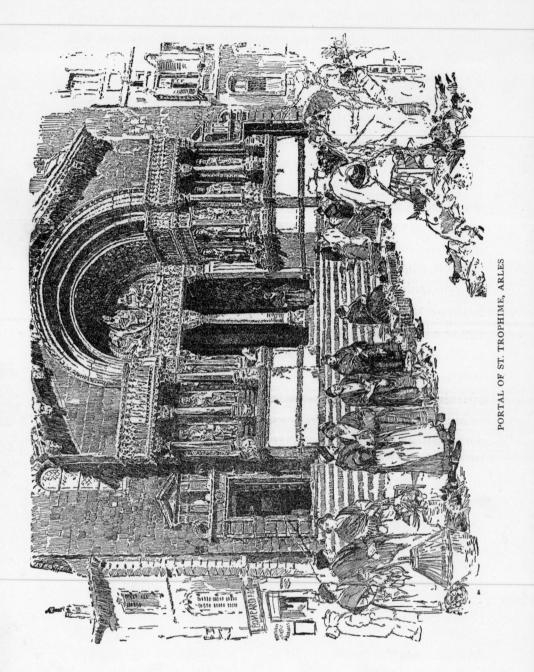

PORTAL OF ST. TROPHIME, ARLES

and sin, of reward and punishment, is nowhere else set forth with greater grace and strength to be read by people, who, in those old happy ages, were spared the evils of what we call education. Time has dealt gently with the sculptures, toning them into the new beauty it is in its power to give, and preserving them from its worst desecrations. St. Trophime perhaps it was who worked the miracle and let the porch at Arles escape when, to right and left, statues were broken and defaced by heretics and by Republicans, all deliriously determined to win immortality for themselves by their excesses of vandalism. He was a saint the Arlésiens must have had very good reason to respect and love. For they made him their special patron, handing over to his care the cathedral that had first been dedicated to St. Etienne, and bringing his body from its tomb in the little church of St. Honorat, at the end of the Alyscamps, and burying it in the larger church which ever since has borne his name; nor is it on record that St. Etienne ever manifested any ill will to the Arlésiens for a fickleness that might have irritated into vengeance a less holy saint than he. I hesitate to say which impressed me the more in the porch of St. Trophime: the effect of richness in the decoration before I stopped to study out the detail, or the elaborate splendor and inexhaustible imagination this detail revealed when it came to be studied. And no matter at what hour I might happen to be in the *place* which it shares with the *Hôtel de Ville* and the Museum and an obelisk in honor of I hardly know what, when this *place* was deserted or when it was filled with the noise and chatter of the market, in the morning as in the evening, in sunshine as by moonlight, it seemed to me that this was the hour, and this the effect for which architect and sculptor had worked so surpassingly well together.

I believe that, in point of time, the gap between the porch at Avignon and the porch at Arles is not so wide as between the earlier building and its Roman models, but in beauty and sentiment they are as the poles apart. I can fancy the architect of

FROM THE PORTAL OF ST. TROPHIME, ARLES

(RENAISSANCE TOWN HALL)

Notre-Dame-des-Doms at home in ancient Rome, but never the architect of St. Trophime. He, as man and artist both, was not Roman but Provençal. As the American of our generation is the product of many races in a land foreign to all, so the Provençal sprang from the chance mixture of Phenician and Greek,

Roman and Gaul, with a touch of the passing Saracen and Goth
and Frank. The race thus created was practically distinct
from those that had gone to its making, and to it, more than to
other people of the South, joy was the secret of life and of
beauty, whether beauty was expressed in the passing gaiety
of the hour or in the art that
endures. Moreover, by this
time, the Provençal had been
to the Holy Land, his own
people were in Antioch, he
had seen the great doorways
of Syria. The grace he gave
to the porch at Arles is far
removed from the severity of
Roman arch and gateway
which, after it, struck me as
ponderous. But the new race
could not get rid of all traces
of its origin. It is to this day

ON THE STEPS OF ST. TROPHIME, ARLES

Greek in the beauty of its women; architect and sculptor in
the twelfth century were Roman in the structural design of the
porch of St. Trophime, and the classic fall and folds of the
draperies of the saints: though only kindly saints of Provençal
origin would have come down, as they did once in the moonlight, to say Mass for the little girl who had trudged up from
the country to hear the holy rite in St. Trophime, had arrived
too late, and had cried herself to sleep at their feet, as is told
in the prettiest legend I know of the cathedral. The Provençal
brought a new element, structural as well as legendary, to his
building, which made it neither entirely Roman nor yet entirely
the Romanesque of the rest of France. St. Trophime has none
of the heaviness, the almost brutal strength of the Norman's
work in the North, none of the riotous extravagance of ornament that breaks out in many an early church of Aquitaine. It

is never barbarous, for the Romanesque architects of Provence were never barbarous, but the decoration is refined and elegant, well balanced in its elaboration, sharing the characteristics of the people who have no rivals in gaiety, but need none to teach them the virtue of self-restraint.

Architect and sculptor, when their work was finished, must have seen that it was good, for the porch is the only decoration they gave to the façade of St. Trophime, which, for the rest, is small and insignificant. The whole building seems the smaller because of the scale on which the Roman architects built in Arles, and it is of the greatest simplicity. It has no intricate buttressing and forest of pinnacles as in later Gothic, no touches of color as in the Romanesque of Auvergne, no chapel-encircled apse nor cluster of cupolas. And the cathedral is well shut in by surrounding buildings, only giving an occasional unexpected glimpse of the quiet walls, the low roof, and the central tower, as you wander through the narrow streets or in the cloisters or among the Roman columns and broken stones to the east. When you pass beneath the Christ over the door into the cool dark of an interior, all Romanesque

DETAIL OF THE PORTAL OF
ST. TROPHIME, ARLES

except for the flamboyant Gothic of the choir, the effect is bare
and therefore restful, without the excitement of golden domes
or flaming shrines or intricate carving, and the light is dim and
shadowy in the nave and the lofty narrow aisles.   When the
Provençal sun shines and the town in its dazzling whiteness
hurts the eyes, this simplicity, sometimes dismissed as somber
dullness, has a serenity, a tranquillity,
that is a prayer in itself.

Architect and sculptor let their fancy
loose again in the cloisters to the south
of the cathedral.   There is no lovelier
spot in Arles than the little sunlit square
inclosed by arcaded walks, where you
are no longer overwhelmed by the mystery of the Sacred Presence and the
obligation of solemn ceremonial, and
where the gray stone blossoms into
ornament as exquisite as that of the
west porch.   I could have asked no better thing of it than this loveliness, but
the student who prefers a comparative
study will find that as well.   For two
sides only are Romanesque.   These are
the most richly decorated, with clustered

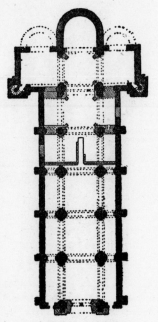

PLAN OF THE CHURCH OF
ST. TROPHIME, ARLES

FROM CORROYER'S "ARCHITECTURE
ROMANE"

saints to serve as piers and with capitals so sumptuously
wrought as to make everybody, save the student, who looks at
the other two sides of a later date and style, regret more than
ever the coming of the Gothic architect to Provence, where he
was and must ever seem a stranger.

Arles may not suggest "the opulent town," "the little Rome
of Gaul," it once was.   It has not succeeded in maintaining its
episcopal dignity, and its archbishop now must live at Aix.   Mr.
Henry James complains that it has not even a "general physiog-
nomy," nor any architecture except St. Trophime.   As you

NORTHEASTERN ANGLE OF CLOISTER, ST. TROPHIME, ARLES

wander through its quiet streets, between the little white houses, almost every one with the green curtain at the door and the bird-cage hanging beside it, its aspect is as provincial as the name the Romans gave to the whole province. Still, it has its "antiquities," its great arena and theater, the tombs of the Alyscamps, and here and there a bit of old Roman or Gallo-Roman work let into the modern house, to keep its history and traditions in countenance. At the near little town, or village, of St. Gilles, however, I could never see any suggestion, except the old abbey church, of the larger horizon and of the greater past I know it must have had when Crusaders, and Knights of St. John, and Counts of Toulouse were matters of fact in its every-day life. It is now so unimportant as barely to call for mention

THE CLOISTER, ST. TROPHIME, ARLES

in the guide-book, and as it offers but the one sight to the sight-seer, it is not much bothered by tourists. Roman ruins in Provence are much more of an attraction than an old abbey church in a place as dull and placid as St. Gilles was as I remember it. The dullness—or it might be more exact to borrow Mr. Henry James's word at Tarascon and call it "vivid sleepiness" —was broken only by the daily arrival of the diligence between Nîmes and Arles, and, on one memorable occasion as we sat at the café after dinner, by the tinkling of many bells and the passing through the moonlit streets of shepherds with their flocks on the way to summer pastures on the hills who might have strayed, for all we knew, straight out of a poem by Mistral or a tale by Daudet.

The church, however, makes up for a great deal. Its west

SOUTHERN DOORWAY, PORTAL OF ST. GILLES

porch, no less than the west porch of St. Trophime, represents the triumph of Romanesque in Provence, and represents it much more floridly and with much more of the East than of Rome. Time has not treated it as kindly, it has been neglected, because all St. Gilles has been neglected and allowed to dwindle into so insignificant a place that you can only wonder how Knights of St. John ever came to make it their headquarters, why Counts of Toulouse ever thought it worth claiming for their own. When I first saw the church, green things grew from its crumbling walls, some of the statues were defaced and broken, scaffolding over one bit foretold the repair that means destruction. But it was beautiful in age and neglect, and as I should rather see it than all restored to the brand-newness of the modern architect. It has three doors instead of the one at St. Trophime, and the sculptor worked with a freer hand. Here, too, the saints stand in serried rows, and the decoration is alive with mystic beasts and monsters; here again the lessons of religion are carven for the faithful to read. Architect and sculptor had strayed further from Roman models, but to their work they brought the same "little more" that makes the great portal, like the porch of St. Trophime, such worlds away from other French Romanesque, and as Provençal in character and charm as the beauty and dress of the women grouped about the steps on every market morning.

The porch is worthy of the rich and worldly Knights of St. John, worthy of gallant Crusaders, of powerful lords from Toulouse, but the church behind it is by comparison small, and as shabby and forlorn as Albigensian heretics, followed by Huguenots in their worst fury of fanaticism, and Red Republicans in their first throes of liberty, could make it. I could never look at it without marveling anew why St. Trophime, only a couple of miles away, should have been so successfully protected against the same foes. In the little green town garden to the east of the church of St. Gilles, you may see the bases of the piers where nave and choir should be and are not, and these survivals of a past grandeur would seem sad in the general abandonment if the garden were not so charming in the sunshine, with the old stones making pleasant cool spaces amid the warm green of trees and shrubbery. All St. Gilles was pleasant to me, though tourists have been sometimes warned of its decay and dirt, and at the little inn, the name alone of the landlord

2

THE PORTAL OF ST. GILLES

when I stayed there was a recommendation, for he was an uncle
of Alphonse Daudet, whose mill is within a walk of the town,
and whose "Letters" written from it cannot be quite forgotten
so long as any one is left to feel the spell of Provence. Altogether, though St. Gilles has an air of having gone down in the
world and dragged the abbey church with it, though at moments its abandonment might seem more cruel than the entire
desolation of Les Baux, my days there were full of the life and
color of Provence, and the sunshine in which a more abandoned
town would be stirred into gaiety and a less noble church transfigured.

III

I KNOW few countries as overburdened with the romance of the
past as Provence. It has its classic tradition, its medieval tradition, its papal tradition. Its independent cities were as tena-
cious of their rights, which means of their character, as the
Italian. It had a title to give that could add to the glory of the
crown of France, and, when the time came, mad patriots to help
in the destruction of that crown, as it was hoped, for evermore.
It had its troubadours and courts of love, its knights and crusaders and tourneys. It was, in a word, a land which busied
itself during untold centuries in making history and legend.
And yet, few countries preserve the past so zealously simply to
subordinate it wholly to the present. It is everywhere in Provence as in the little garden at St. Gilles, where the old work of
hundreds of years ago is adapted to the use or ornament of
to-day. If there is sign of decay now and then in the towns,
there is none in the people. Their life is as full, active, and intense as ever, and they have taken care that the outside world
should know it. At Avignon, on that high platform at the
cathedral door, when I looked down to the spacious valley of
the Rhône, unrolled like a map for my benefit, popes and cardi-

nals, kings and knights, even Petrarch and Laura vanished before the Félibres, feasting in the Ile de la Barthelasse and dreaming—loud enough to drown all other voices—their dream of the new-old Provence of which they were the prophets.   I would have exchanged all the papal archives for Roumanille's "Librairie Provençale" below in the Rue St. Agricol.   In the Alyscamps, or rather everywhere, at Arles, there was no escape

IN THE CHOIR, ST. GILLES

from the insistence of their call to the country and its beauty, and the call was as loud in town after town, in village after village, where they talked volubly for all the world to hear. The speech, customs, feasts, games, dress—everything of the past has been entirely merged into the present, until the relics or ruins of earliest ages shake off their age, and Roman arena and Romanesque church become as essential to modern life as if they were built but yesterday.

This is why Provence, venerable in years, seems so young.

FROM THE CENTRAL DOORWAY, PORTAL OF ST. GILLES

If there were no Baedeker, it might never occur to those who love it that it could date back further than Mistral and Daudet. Mistral, "mighty as the north wind's blowing," has extolled the beauty of the country as troubadours extolled the beauty of the ladies they served. Daudet has put into words the charm of Provence as no one ever did before his time. If he is not read as he was twenty or thirty years ago, it would be a pity. Neither

Thomas Hardy in Dorset nor Cable in Louisiana ever expressed with such force, because with such sympathy, the spirit of the place he knew and cared for above all others, nor showed it so tenderly in its weakness and its strength. Some old countries and towns are oppressive in their age, and redolent of the charnel-house. Indeed, to my surprise, I note that some travelers have found the beauty of even Provençal towns like Arles "profound and melancholy." But this I cannot understand. For the Provence I know has not outgrown its youth nor outlived its gaiety, and its churches at Avignon and Arles and St. Gilles never degenerate into mere examples of Gallo-Roman or Romanesque—into mere architectural fossils—but are part of the grace and gaiety of life as it is lived to-day "down there" in the sunshine.

CHAPTER II

ROMANESQUE AND RESTORATION IN AQUITAINE

CHAPTER II

ROMANESQUE AND RESTORATION IN AQUITAINE

I

THE journey to Périgueux lay through a beautiful, tranquil country, with sluggish streams and lines of poplars winding across meadows all white and gold in the springtime, and here and there low rocky hills to break the monotony of green and blossom. The tranquillity seemed to have taken possession of Périgueux itself when I arrived in the late twilight. Shops were shut; work was at an end; the town was as entirely at peace as if nothing could ever again wake it from its slumbers.

It was another thing in the morning. The *place* below my windows in front of the hotel was a mass of booths and merry-go-rounds; the *place* behind the hotel was a mass of cattle. When I went out I had to force my way through crowds of horned beasts, market-women, shrieking merchants of everything, peasants in blouses, natives as wide-awake as if they would never let the town go to sleep again, and I found silence only when my first walk ended in the little square that opens out before the north door of the cathedral of St. Front.

Let me say at once—for it must be said, and disagreeable things are best disposed of without delay—that my first feeling before this north door was one of disappointment, which grew more acute the more I saw of the cathedral. Architecturally,

27

St. Front is, or was, one of the most interesting cathedrals in France: a Byzantine church in the far West, so like St. Mark's of Venice in size, and ground-plan, and clustered domes, and everything save ornament, that many think it must have been the work of architects who knew either Venice or Constantinople, or perhaps both. In those remote ages, though it is hard for us who depend on railroads and steamship companies to believe it, the romance of trade brought distant parts of the world almost as close together as they are to-day. One commercial line of travel for Venetians and Greeks was across France from Provençal ports to Périgueux and to Limoges, where there was a Venetian quarter just as there is an Italian quarter now in New York. At Angoulême there was a colony of Greek priests as there are still Armenian fathers at Venice. If priests followed in the train of commerce, there is no reason why architects should not as well, or why the reports they spread of the marvels at home should not have sent French architects to Venice and Constantinople to study in the best schools of architecture of the time, precisely as the present fame of the *Beaux-Arts* draws American students to Paris. At all events, the builders of St. Front forgot the basilicas of the Romans in Aquitaine, after which an older church had been modeled, and, retaining a portion of this church, they built up a new one on a scale becoming the Benedictine Abbey at Périgueux—for St. Front was not originally the cathedral— and as like as they could make it to Santa Sophia and St. Mark's. But, curiously, they are said at the same time to have so modified their Byzantine model, or to have strayed so far from it, that in their arches could be seen the first promise of the transition which was to lead eventually to the great Gothic of the North. Altogether, from what I have read of St. Front as it was not much more than half a century ago, I should have supposed it the church of all others worth watching over, treasuring, and preserving, as the canvas of the early master, however black-ened and stained, is preserved, or the rare book, however tattered the leaves.

During ages, I know, it was not the fashion to take care of anything architectural, but St. Front, left to itself and time, fared better than when, with the turn of the tide, fashion forced the State and architects and scholars to active interest in the churches and cathedrals of France. Other French churches may have suffered no less from restoration, but I have seen none where the restorer was so uncompromising in his measures as Abadie at St. Front. The old church was absolutely destroyed, pulled down to the ground, or, so they say at Périgueux, blown up by dynamite that he might be the more unhampered when he finally got to work on his new building, designed according to his idea of what tenth- and eleventh-century architects should have made theirs. The cathedral now is as much Abadie's work as the Sacré-Cœur on the hill of Montmartre: "deprived of its value in the history of art," Parker says, nothing more than a "modern church studied from a Romanesque original," in the words of the "Dictionary of Architecture." Worse to me is the loss of pictorial interest and picturesque associations. The interior is simple and spacious with, at certain hours, a pleasant effect of light and shadow, though there is too much light for the fine solemnity usual to an old Romanesque, or Byzantine, church, while there is none of the color or splendor of St. Mark's: so bare and cold and empty an interior, indeed, that I was astonished to see the priest at the altar and the people at prayer. The domes, which were always a distinctive feature, may now be correct in number, piers and arches may be correct in proportion and in their manner of performing their structural duties—correct, that is, if Abadie's conception of Byzantine in France is accepted. But St. Front is nothing more than a copy, and not even a copy, the authorities will tell you, with the merit of blind fidelity to the original, for it seems that the special differences from the Byzantine models, which were its chief interest, have disappeared. For the sake of sham correctness, for a technical perfection, that may never have existed, character was deliberately and irreparably cast aside.

Before the north door, I was conscious of little save the tedious symmetry of the mason's work; I could grow no more enthusiastic when I passed into the cold and dull interior. As I wandered there disconsolately, a polite old man fell upon me and undertook—unasked—to play my host in the cathedral. He remembered it as it was before the coming of Abadie and, for my consolation, was amiable enough to describe it as then no less bare of ornament and color than now. I am afraid that, in his politeness, he either perjured himself hopelessly, or else, despite the love he professed for the cathedral, he had no sense of the beauty and quality of age, though he bore his own so gracefully. However, he realized that my interest was all in the old St. Front, and he took me out of the south door to show me, high up

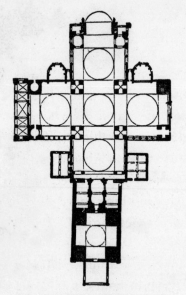

PLAN OF THE CATHEDRAL OF
ST. FRONT, PÉRIGUEUX

Within its walls, the diameter of St. Front, exclusive of the remains of the Early Christian church, is 176 feet, and the height of its central dome is 84 feet.

above, some of the original capitals and a carved corbel built into the modern wall, he did not seem to know why, and a small space of the old stonework put back, apparently, to emphasize the difference between it and the new. It was such a pitifully small survival that I do not believe I was as grateful as he expected. The vandalism struck me as the more sweeping because of the contrast when I turned from the door and looked down upon the town as I could see it here, stretching away to the south, for St. Front stands on much higher ground. The group of shabby old houses with their weather-worn, tempest-tossed

INTERIOR OF THE CATHEDRAL OF ST. FRONT, PÉRIGUEUX

tiled roofs, saved for my pleasure because of their shabbiness
and decrepitude, were, in their color and confusion, far more
picturesque than the colorless, correct building towering above
me, while far beyond them my eyes were carried to the hills
which cannot grow shabby and decrepit, and which no Abadie
will ever have the power to touch. My guide did not lose hope,
but took me next to the porch, like a long court, at the west end,
with bits of old sculptures set in the walls, and a door opening
into the cloisters which had been converted into a workshop for
masons. Their litter of ladders and planks and pails made the
few old Byzantine capitals and broken arches seem the more
disconsolate and forlorn. I suppose that already nice neat
cloisters have emerged from the workmen's mess, that the low
wall, with railing, then just begun, runs all round the west end
and the part of the south side it was destined to inclose, and
that this little corner, too, has become with the rest sadder far
than the saddest of all sad bare ruined choirs where late the
sweet birds sang.

By this time the old man was sharing my disappointment as
if he were personally responsible, with such evident distress
that I was tempted to perjure myself and admire, just to relieve
his mind. For the honor of himself and Périgueux, he led me
down to the river, where there were some old timbered houses
and the wreck of a Renaissance hotel, where St. Front was so
far away that its brand-newness was not quite so aggressive, and
where, as the restorer could not tamper with the little hill on
which it is built, I had still the pleasure of seeing it rise majes-
tically, as a cathedral should, above the houses huddled about it,
and could say so with no risk of dishonesty or deceit. He also
insisted upon conducting me along a narrow street and showing
me the delightful thirteenth-century façade of an old convent,
for he was determined before we parted to convince me that
Périgueux was not swept completely bare of the relics of its
tremendous past. There he left me, but not without many

apologies: he was *dans le commerce* and could not stay longer; and, when I thanked him, he assured me it was his pleasure—it was nothing—*"tous les Périgourdins sont comme ça!"* And he lingered to direct me to the church of St. Etienne in the *Cité,* which I really would find ancient, and to the Roman ruins not far from it.

I dwell upon the kindly old man because he went far to help me through my bitterest experience in any French cathedral. He, in his friendliness, would have reconciled me to St. Front if anybody, or anything, could. It seemed only right in return to follow his directions, and I went to the ancient church of St. Etienne in that part of Périgueux called the *Cité,* for the excellent reason that it was the city of Vesuna for some time before the city of Périgueux was dreamed of, and then it was Périgueux for some time after the little hamlet that sprang up about the great Benedictine Abbey was known as the Faubourg of Puy-St.-Front. St. Etienne was the cathedral in the beginning and for long years, and only in the seventeenth century gave precedence to St. Front. In its present degradation, it evidently has not been thought of sufficient interest to restore seriously. I found it outside very tumbled down and disreputable, and inside an extraordinary medley of Byzantine domes and Rococo altars and ornament, with the dust of ages lying thick over everything and producing as surprising effects as the London grime works upon the exterior of St. Paul's. Within and without, the church was as picturesque as St. Front doubtless was before it fell into the clutches of the restorer, and the one result of my visit was to add to my original disappointment in the cathedral. After St. Etienne, keeping to the old man's directions, I walked to the Roman arena, the merest fragment compared to the amphitheaters of Provence, and to the Roman tower of Vesuna, surrounded by a tiny garden, then one riot of roses. Here my obligations ceased, and it was in the course of my own idle dawdling through the fair that I came by chance to a *place* where the statue of Montaigne looked to the merry-go-rounds and acrobats and dancers and side-shows, as if for proof of how much better it is to be second or third in Périgueux than first in Paris.

The fair lasted throughout my stay. When it was question of amusement, the people showed no tendency to idleness. There was the note of the *Midi* in their gaiety, their noise, their exaggerations, in the cheerful way the waiter at the hotel pronounced everything "magnificent," from St. Front to the cattle market at our door. But it was very different from the *Midi* of Provence, where the people throw themselves into work with equal energy. "We are of the *Midi,* here in Périgord," a native informed me one evening at dinner. "We are gay, not like the people of Angoulême, whose gaiety is that of Cognac: ours is the gaiety of the Truffle. We are reproached by all other Frenchmen for being too fond of pleasure. As soon as evening comes, we stop work, we shut our shops, we are off to amuse ourselves. We work only to live, and we live to make the most of whatever amusement life, which is very short, can give us."

This philosophy pleased me and explained many things in the town that I had not understood, but it made the destruction of the cathedral seem the more wanton and therefore the more melancholy. Its natural fate in an easy-going town like Périgueux would have been to grow old in peace and beauty, and to bear Time's sorrows with dignity. The passing of the restorer there strikes me as no less barbarous and unjustifiable than the passing of the Protestant who raided it of old. He has done every bit as much harm, and worked as great a sacrilege, for St. Front was of the utmost importance in the history of architecture, and to-day it is important only in the history of Abadie.

II

WHATEVER influence the builders of St. Front were destined to have on the architecture of France, it was nowhere felt so immediately as in the near churches of Aquitaine, and among these in none with so much distinction and preëminence as in the cathedral of St. Pierre at Angoulême.

The same beautiful, tranquil country stretches about Angoulême, and in the town there is already a touch of the *Midi*, though not so strong and irresistible as in Périgueux. I came to Angoulême the first time from Poitiers, and the whiter houses and flatter roofs, the tiles, the greater number of green shutters as I drew to the end of my journey spoke plainly of the approach to the South. I saw promise of the South, too, in the handkerchiefs worn instead of caps by the women in the town and near country, and I heard it in the soft, caressing voices of the people and their encouraging superlatives. The *"magnifique"* of Périgueux was *"superbe"* at Angoulême. *"Madame, Angoulême c'est une ville superbe,"* they told me at the hotel, where I was urged to hurry without delay to the ramparts and satisfy myself that the views it provided were *"tout à fait épatantes."*

The exaggerations of the *Méridional* always reconcile me to the truth, however short it falls, and there is no denying that Angoulême falls very short of being superb. For a town of much history, Roman, Frankish, English, and I hardly know what, for a town of more romance, associated as it is with that most romantic of royal houses, the house of Valois, with one famous Balzac, who was born there, and with another and more famous who made it a scene in his "Comédie Humaine"—for a town with all these attractions, Angoulême is singularly inexpressive. Its streets cross each other so regularly at right angles that it looks like a French version of Turin or Philadel-

BENEATH THE TRANSEPT TOWER, CATHEDRAL OF ST. PIERRE, ANGOULÊME

phia, and I never knew it to be stirred by the gaiety that redeems the commonplace of Périgueux, perhaps because I never chanced to be there at the right season. I always happened to find it as busy with grim labor problems as London, its energies concentrated in a battle between employers and workmen from the paper factories and foundries who clamored for their rights, chief of which was Sunday as a day of rest. However, if the town itself failed to justify the people's "superb," I could not complain of the views, which were an exaggeration even of the adjective bestowed upon them. After I had seen everything to be seen in the town, I was almost inclined to agree with Freeman that, "except we went on purpose for the view, we should hardly go to Angoulême at all." For there is no question that if Angoulême has disposed of whatever distinction it must have inherited from the past, it is now, as ever, in possession of a most noble and commanding site. It is built on a hill, fairly steep, well isolated, and once strongly fortified as it needed to be. There is little left of the old walls, but their place all round the high plateau is taken by a walk shaded with trees, opening out into circular terraces and little groves, and overlooking a wide stretch of country which changes with almost every step you take; here the Charente or the Anguienne flowing between low or poplared banks, here a wooded space, far off the hills, everywhere white houses gleaming from out the green of plain or wood, and close to the hill the great factories and barracks that have made the fortune of the modern town.

The walk, no matter where you begin to follow it, must, sooner or later, bring you to the cathedral of St. Pierre, which stands close to the ramparts and rivals St. Front in majesty of position. My experience in Périgueux was repeated in Angoulême. St. Pierre was as grievous a disappointment as St. Front, for both churches have fallen before the same enemy. A cathedral rose from this very spot on the hill of Angoulême long before the Byzantine church of Périgueux was built. But,

3

as happened to most churches of that date, it was burned to the ground. For the rebuilding, either because faith was more ardent or money more plentiful, wood was replaced by stone, while to seek a model there was no further to go, for people influenced by a colony of Greek priests, than to Périgueux and to the wonderful abbey church on the banks of the Isle. As the years went on, the new cathedral of St. Pierre, which had varied from its model in some particulars, was added to, enlarged, changed somewhat in plan, given a more ornate façade, worked over and made ever lovelier, and of all who lavished their zeal and devotion upon it, none was more zealous and devoted than Bishop Gérard in the twelfth century, by which time the design and detail borrowed from St. Front had been not a little modified. After this came the usual vicissitudes. Like almost all other cathedrals, St. Pierre was the victim of local feuds and foreign wars, of slack bishops and ravaging Huguenots, of Gothic innovators and Renaissance pedants. Its story is the familiar cathedral story. But if it was raided and done up afterward, each raid and each doing up contributed a fresh chapter to the history recorded on its walls. By the middle of the last century, St. Pierre had come out safely from the changes and chances of time, not by any means the church that the eleventh-century architects could have recognized at a glance as theirs, but one in which every addition and every alteration told something of the facts and associations, the tragedy and ro-

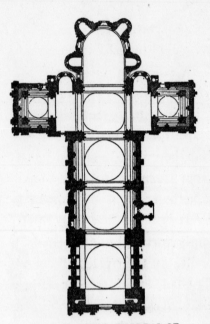

PLAN OF THE CATHEDRAL OF
ST. PIERRE, ANGOULÊME

The length of St. Pierre, outside the walls, is 266 feet, and its breadth across the transept 165 feet

FAÇADE OF THE CATHEDRAL OF ST. PIERRE, ANGOULÊME

mance, of the intervening years. Then, like St. Front, it fell to
the mercies of Abadie, who, once a church was in his hands,
never showed any mercy at all. Before I left Angoulême, I had
come to see in the whole town nothing but an architectural

CENTRAL LANTERN AND TOWER ABOVE THE NORTHERN TRANSEPT-ARM,
CATHEDRAL OF ST. PIERRE, ANGOULÊME

nightmare of a monument to his memory. The *Palais de Justice* is the work of his father. He himself built the *Hôtel de Ville,* and also St. Martial and St. Ausone over the ruins of the two old abbey churches; and he restored the cathedral, which means that he destroyed the past to substitute his conception of what it should have been.

ONE BAY OF THE NAVE, CATHEDRAL OF ST. PIERRE, ANGOULÊME

The west façade of St. Pierre, with its sculptures, is painfully new, only an old statue or two retained to suggest the richness of tone and texture which it required centuries to produce, but not more than a day to destroy. The central dome is no older, and the tower is rebuilt, with only the beauty of the composition, as they are seen above high garden walls and trees, to help you to forget their flagrant and undesirable youth. The whole exterior has become a tribute to the industry of the skilled restorer of modern France rather than to the genius of the old architects of Aquitaine. The interior is no better. It also is painfully new, painfully correct, to the regular lines neatly marked in the stonework of nave and choir, to the stations of the cross, to the monuments, the crucifix in the north transept, the very reliquary in the choir. Like St. Front, it has a simple spaciousness, and the pure light that floods it, and the shadows that pass through it with the passing hours, are restful to the eye and to the temper. But it has all the discomfort of the new, unlived-in building, so much so that I fancied the chill of it must penetrate to the poor shivering little souls of the children collected in the nave on certain afternoons to receive the religious instruction that the Church in France now provides with the fresh access of fervor born of persecution. Even if the restorer had succeeded in filling St. Pierre with the solemnity and religious atmosphere with which the modern Romanesque architect has filled the new cathedral in Westminster, it would not have been just the solemnity and atmosphere that I looked for at Angoulême. There I wanted, not Romanesque according to Abadie, or any other modern architect, but Romanesque as it managed to survive through the ages, through the turmoils and tribulations, through the neglect and the misplaced enthusiasm, that all helped to write history on its walls, as experience and tragedy write their tale on the face of the man who struggles and survives.

It might seem useless to have gone to Périgueux and Angoulême only to be disappointed when, on every side, were churches where disappointment would be impossible. But for the sake of their old importance they were marked on that architectural route which it was our business to follow, and I do not regret having gone to them, nor do I consider it a waste of time. For, having seen them, now that I give my impressions, I can refer to them as the strongest witnesses that could be summoned to testify to the evils of restoration. Their interest survives and always must in history, but they themselves are dead, and can no more be brought to life again than the old builders and patrons. There, where the old churches stood, stand the new cathedrals, cold and hard, "feeble and lifeless forgeries," warnings of the irreparable loss to France and the world if the restorer's hand is free to work his will.

CHAPTER III

FROM POITIERS TO CAEN

CHAPTER III

I

THE road climbs up into Poitiers with great promise of picturesqueness, and the town makes much, though not perhaps the most, of its position on the hill. It bears the responsibility of its historic name more lightly, and is a quiet, leisurely place, not so ancient in appearance as I hoped, full of peasants on market days, of soldiers and students at almost all times, and, when I was last there, often rudely disturbed by the horn of the motorist on his way from Paris to Bordeaux. Otherwise, it drowses peacefully through its days, as if content with the share it has already taken in shaping the history of the world.

As the churches were my immediate concern, I could hardly complain if they happened to be the most picturesque things in Poitiers, and to look the oldest. The town played so big a part in the past that its very name suggests, even to one with no more history than myself, the epoch-making wars and decisive battles of which it was the center, and the French and English kings, the saints and heroes and light ladies who, strutting their little day across it as across a stage, turned its history into romance. But Poitiers, though it cannot shake off the old memories, has got rid of as much of the evidence of the past as it could. Crooked as Angoulême is regular, straggling at ran-

dom up and down the hillside—"one of the worst built towns I
have seen in France, very large and irregular," was Arthur
Young's description in 1787—you would think it the place of all
others for odd nooks and forgotten corners. It has, however,
extraordinarily few to show. There are old buildings and
monuments, to be sure; it would be strange if there were not.
You can go right back to prehistoric times, if you choose, simply
by taking a trolley-car to the *Pierre-Levée* on the outskirts of
the town, the Druidical dolmen brought to Poitiers, one legend
says, by Ste. Radegonde, partly on her head and partly in her
apron, though what induced her to perform this feat of strenu-
ousness I have found nobody who could tell me; or, Rabelais
says, it was put there by Pantagruel for no more recondite
purpose than to serve as table when his fellow-students were
invited to picnic with him. I believe there are, somewhere in
the town, Roman ruins which I never saw. But I did see the
scale upon which Poitiers had to defend itself in later times, for
part of the walls and bastions of the old fortifications now support the terraces of the Blossac, that enchanting little garden
overlooking the green valley of the Clain. I also learned what
an excellent substitute the Counts of Poitiers had for steam
heat in their old castle, now the *Palais de Justice,* for before the
colossal fireplace of the *Salles des Pas Perdus* whole armies
might have warmed themselves. And I stumbled now and
again upon other houses built in the years when the wonder is
that fighting left Poitiers any time to build at all. But these
things make a meager showing for a town with so extravagant
an inheritance of history, and it is only right, by way of com-
pensation, that Poitiers has managed to preserve a finer series
of beautiful and historic old churches than almost any other
town in France.

What special Providence watched over these churches it
would be hard to say, though I am afraid it took the form of
centuries of neglect and indifference. I believe no older Chris-

tian church has survived in France until our time than the Baptistery, or *Temple de St. Jean,* so old that it is believed to have been a pagan tomb before it became, in the fourth century, a place of worship. It is much below the present level of the near streets, and has a pathetic look in its little hollow as if it had been dug out unwillingly from the lower historic strata to which it belongs. Its age is really all I could find to recommend it, and I had to examine it carefully to realize how old it is, for the restorer has been at great pains to rob it of every sign of its one recommendation. I know it has no small archæological value, but for me this is far exceeded by the Romanesque splendors of which it was the germ. I would exchange it willingly at any time for the church of St. Hilaire, or the tower of St. Porchaire, or the shrine of Ste. Radegonde, who is honored as she ought to be in Poitiers, a town she held in highest favor, performing for it many miracles besides that display of physical strength when she made it her gift of the *Pierre-Levée.* She is buried in the crypt of the church of her name, and her tomb is famed far and wide, pilgrims coming to it in crowds once every year. The persistence on all occasions of the old women who sell candles at the church door proves how rare it is for any one to cross the threshold and not to want to make her an offering; while the little marble tablets, each with *"Merci,"* or *"Merci, Ste. Radegonde,"* or *"Reconnaissance"* in golden letters upon it, have spread from the crypt up the stairs, and even to the choir walls, as further proof that candles are not burned nor prayers said in vain. The church has the religious atmosphere of all churches that inclose a holy shrine, and the restorer has not wholly succeeded in effacing the work of time. It is venerable in aspect, sunk, like the Baptistery, to a lower level than the streets, and it seems lonely and abandoned except at the season of pilgrimage, for the neighborhood, as I remember it, is one of the quietest and most deserted in the town. Ste. Radegonde was to me in many ways so interesting that I say less of it only because there is more to be said of two other churches of Poitiers: the cathedral of St. Pierre and Notre-Dame-la-Grande.

II

THE cathedral of St. Pierre may not rank with Notre-Dame-la-Grande in architectural importance, certainly it does not in picturesqueness, but it has plenty of character of its own. It stands half-way down the hillside, exposed to the winds which in Poitiers put the *mistral* of Provence to shame, so that I used to think all the streets, instead of one only, should be called *des Quatre Vents*. It is in the same quarter as Ste. Radegonde, a provincial calm prevails in the neighboring streets and squares, and about it there are many trees which to the north are arranged and clipped into a formal grove. Standing thus in the midst of green and apart from the busy quarters of the town, St. Pierre has much the same air of retirement as the English cathedral in its close, though few English cathedrals, if any, hide themselves so effectually. It is only when you wander toward the Clain, or on the Blossac, that you see how St. Pierre and Ste. Radegonde spring up like giants from out the cluster of pygmy roofs. The exterior is not so imposing when you are close to it. The very width of the fourteenth-century west front takes away from the height and, together with the low towers, makes it seem almost squatty. As I last saw the cathedral, scaffolding was spread partly over the west towers and the doors, and already spaces of staring new stone gave warning of the ravages the removing of the scaffolding would reveal. Some little of the old work had up till then escaped, enough to make me very grateful to the sculptors of the Resurrection over the door, for they were evidently men of tender heart and they spared the wicked the most cruel of the tortures of war sinners have had to endure for centuries in stone on the walls of many

CATHEDRAL OF ST. PIERRE, POITIERS

a Christian church. A gay grotesque here and a gaping gar-
goyle there were also unspoiled, but by now the scaffolding may
have, and most likely has, swept over them as well.

But St. Pierre reserves its character chiefly for the interior.
I cannot say it is character of the kind I like best in a Catholic

church. I can imagine no one going to the cathedral for the consolations, the solemnity, or even the terrors of religion. A great deal is expressed in the fact that Arthur Young, who had no patience with what to-day is prized as picturesqueness, found it "well built and very well kept" and almost the only thing worthy of notice in a town so little to his liking. But for the impression it has to give of white spaciousness without mystery, I know of no other cathedral that can be compared to it; "a daylight church," if ever there was one. It was built in the latest days of Romanesque, then on the point of developing into Gothic, but from other buildings of the same period I have never had just this sense, not of height, not of length, not of breadth, but simply of space. This comes, I suppose, from the height and width of the arches between the lofty nave and the almost equally lofty aisles, from the absence of triforium and clearstory, so that nave and aisles, as everybody from Murray up or down has said, look like one spacious hall, and from the great size of the windows in the aisles. The choir shares the spaciousness, is also without mystery, and ends not in the rounded apse of French Romanesque, but in the straight east wall of the English cathedral, a tribute to the power and influence in Poitiers of English kings, or rather kings of England. For neither Henry II, who founded the church, nor Eleanor of Aquitaine, his wife, who shared the good work with him, were English, though, like a certain type of Frenchman to-day, they had become anglicized by life in England and brought English fashions with them across the Channel.

Mystery is essential to the religious beauty of a church, and, in the frigid atmosphere of St. Pierre, faith flowers into fervor only at the shrine of Notre-Dame-des-Bonnes-Nouvelles. Nor does the clear, steady light falling through the ample windows reveal any flowering forth into decoration, except in the choir, where the thirteenth-century stalls are as elaborate as the rest of the church is simple, covered with a maze of carving, a laby-

NOTRE-DAME-LA-GRANDE, POITIERS

rinth of beasts and birds and strange beings, all little masterpieces, but none in my memory so masterly as a magnificent
centaur, a winged beast with female head, a horrible two-headed
monster, and a cat catching a mouse with a dramatic tenseness
and triumph that only the lover of cats, who had long observed
and studied their every movement, could render with such sympathy and truth.

I could appreciate the cold, bare beauty of the cathedral
though it awoke no emotion in me, but I was always glad to
leave it for Notre-Dame-la-Grande, the little Romanesque
church higher up on the hill, set down in the midst of the bustle
of the market, inseparable, as I recall it, from the most animated
business of the town, elaborately decorated, its stones tenderly
colored and crumbled by time, knocked about enough in the
course of the ages to have become the architectural record of
their passing, and not too obviously restored—the most beautiful and human little church in Poitiers, or, for that matter, in
France.

Its traditions are ancient: it also is supposed to have
had its origin in a pagan tomb, and is said to have been founded
by Constantine, and dedicated by Ste. Radegonde, who seems
never to have left anything in Poitiers alone when she could help
it, and the appearance of the old church is as aged as its traditions. Not that it gives the slightest suggestion of senility or
superannuation. On the contrary, it belongs to the present as
actively as to the past, as if it renewed its youth with each new
generation. The cathedral and Ste. Radegonde may hide themselves discreetly out of sight, but Notre-Dame-la-Grande shows
itself bravely in the market-place and becomes a part of it. I
never went there in the daytime that I did not find the open
space around the church crowded with stalls and booths under
huge umbrellas and vivid awnings, with peasants and peddlers
driving hard bargains, with chickens and ducks and geese cack-
ling and crowing and quacking their loudest, with an overflow

CATHEDRAL OF ST. PIERRE

everywhere of vegetables of every shape, color, and size, usually
in the background a mess of carts, horses, and dogs. Here,
anyway, Poitiers gave the lie to my description of it as quiet and
leisurely. Anything could be bought at the church door, from
a bit of ribbon or flannel, to a live goose or the cabbages and
turnips grown on the slopes of the hill below the Blossac. There
was no forgetting the intimate, homely relations Notre-Dame-

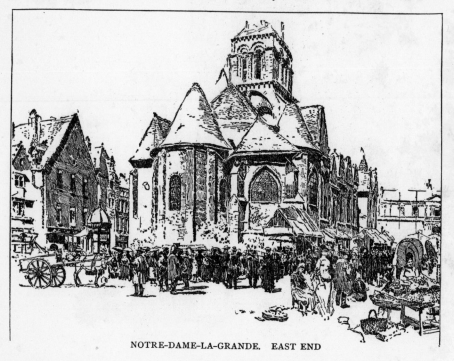

NOTRE-DAME-LA-GRANDE. EAST END

la-Grande has maintained with the people during centuries, true
to the Catholic policy which has ever been to make the faithful
at home in their churches. The student or archæologist might
object that the market interfered with his study of the old
fabric. But I thought the worn, yellowing walls more beautiful
when the umbrellas flaunted their gay colors below it. I found
the wonderful sculptures of the west front more wonderful as
I saw them over the crowd of people intent upon the commonplace affairs of daily life. The whole façade is one mass of
decoration; to a great bas-relief Mérimée compared it, and

NOTRE-DAME-LA-GRANDE. WEST FRONT

others have likened it to the carved panel of an ivory triptych.
It has the exquisiteness, the perfection, of the museum piece,
and is as delicately wrought as a jewel. Sculptures stretch from
the beasts that twist and writhe and curl and curve in the mold-
ings of the arched doorway, up to the mosaic-like surface of the
gable between the two little pepper-pot turrets. There is hardly
an inch of stone without carving or ornament of some kind.
And all this beauty blossomed under the sculptor's hand that

the façade might serve, not the great of Poitiers, but the lowly, the people to whom it was an open book, a Bible, in which to read the lessons of their faith. For centuries, as still to-day, peasants and peddlers, between the barterings and bickerings of the market, could look up there and get by heart the history of the Mother of God, following the drama scene by scene, from the first, where Adam and Eve play their rôles as graciously as if it were not their fault that ages later the Blessed Virgin was called upon, in sorrow and in suffering, to crush the head of the serpent, down to the homely scenes of the Visitation and the Nativity, told more realistically and dramatically than in any printed book, and so on to the end.

I wish the interior had come as well out of the test of time and the restorer. It has all the architectural elements of the beauty and impressiveness that one has a right to expect in a Romanesque church. The ceiling is low, the apse is rounded, the light drifts in dimly from the small windows in the aisles and from the central lantern. I was thankful that the light was so dim, for the restorer, bent on archæological accuracy and with his own idea of the original scheme of decoration, of which traces were discovered in the apse, has painted walls and columns all over with a checker-board pattern, varied by lozenges and acutely angled zigzags: an attempt, I have no doubt, to reproduce in paint the usual ornament in stone of the Romanesque sculptor, but the effect is like nothing so much as cheap linoleum. The color is an offense, and the restless pattern destroys the unity of the beautiful architectural design. The church may once, as it is thought, have been painted throughout, but the most primitive work could never have been so crude, and, in any case, only a somber splendor of color, such as the mosaics give to St. Mark's, could ever have replaced the natural color of the stone without discord. Toward evening checker-board, lozenges, and zigzags are softened in the kindly shadows, and I seldom went into the church except when services were

NOTRE-DAME-LA-GRANDE. CHOIR

held there after dark. It was my good fortune to be in Poitiers once during May, and eight was the hour for the Month of Mary. From the back of the nave, where lights were low and the kneeling figures all in shadow, I could then see no ugly detail of wall and column, but only the sanctuary and the golden glory of the altar, the priest, before it, holding high the Blessed Sacrament in its golden ostensorium, as he blessed the people. Then Notre-Dame-la-Grande was beautiful, solemn, and at peace.

III

It is a long step across France from Poitiers to Caen, but a delightful one to make for anybody with a fancy for strong contrasts. Aquitaine and Normandy are both parts of the same country, but they are as far apart in sentiment and standards as the North and the South must ever be. The meadows are as green and fresh, the springtime as full of blossoms, in Normandy as in Poitou, but towns grow grayer toward the North, and people less gay. I do not believe that Caen is larger than Poitiers, but it takes itself more seriously, appears to be less gifted with leisure, and gives itself more the airs of a big town. Busier I am sure it must be, close as it is to the sea, and engaged in commerce, and not, like Poitiers, devoted entirely to learning, though in its day known above all as *la Ville de Sapience*. Besides, though I doubt if it has more history, all it has is so familiar that a walk through the town is like nothing so much as going over in a new form one's earliest history lessons at school. For Caen is associated especially with William the Conqueror, and he is one of those figures in history, like Queen Elizabeth, or Henri IV, or Napoleon, or George Washington, whom we could not help knowing by name even if we wanted to.

As the towns differ, so do their churches. The Abbaye-aux-Hommes and Abbaye-aux-Dames, for which Caen is famed, were built at very much the same time as Notre-Dame-la-Grande, and not so very long before the cathedral of St. Pierre, but they seemed to me to have absolutely nothing else in common. The Norman brought the qualities that made him the man he was to his building, so that his churches, like himself, suggest above all else power and strength. In the struggle to live, it was long before he had much use for the graces and elegances either of life or of architecture. St. Etienne, the

ST. ETIENNE. WEST FRONT

Abbaye-aux-Hommes, has precisely the characteristics that a vigorous Viking of a man like William the Conqueror would demand. He it was who built it, and Mathilda, his queen, built La Trinité, the Abbaye-aux-Dames, and the work was not done

ST. ÉTIENNE. NAVE

for the pleasure of it, as I suppose was the case when William built his innumerable other convents and churches, but it was undertaken as a penance, imposed upon both by the Pope that they might thus expiate their sin in marrying within forbidden degrees of kindred.

The King's church was begun, the Queen's dedicated, before the Norman descent upon England. The history of their progress is characteristic. William was in the prime of his vigor, and as keen to conquer architecturally as in every other way. He pushed on the work in the precipitate, thorough fashion in which he vanquished his enemies, and the Abbaye-aux-Hommes was finished in less than fifteen years. The task was the easier because no time was wasted on delicacy or exquisiteness of ornament. Kingship for William was too uncertain and stern an affair to allow of dawdling over so superfluous a matter as decoration. The west front, with the gable between the two towers, in which authorities see the beginning of the splendidly flamboyant west fronts of later ages, is as simple and massive as the entrance to a citadel or castle. Inside, the church has a huge heavy beauty, and is less like French than English Romanesque, with its triforium and clearstory and low aisles, recalling Durham or Gloucester rather than Poitiers or Périgueux or Arles, and it is as grim as the background to the last grim scene in the Conqueror's life should be. You can see his tomb, or as much as has been left by generations of desecrators who pulled down and desecrators who built up, and, seeing it, if you know your history at all, you cannot fail to recall the horrible details of that last scene—the funeral procession of many monks but hardly a friend, the bursting forth into flames of a house as they passed, the haggling for money over the grave, the rough handling of the coffin, the disaster to the body so much too big for it, the wild flight of the congregation, and the hurrying of the monks trembling to their cells. Horrors stick in the memory, little as we want them to, and the associations with the mighty

King who was founder of the church seem to chill and pervade this massive interior. And it has been neglected, deliberately destroyed, and as deliberately restored, and in it I fancy religion must always have been stern and gloomy for the devout of Caen, with not a touch of the cheerfulness, the homeliness, of the South. St. Etienne seems to have preserved, perhaps cultivated, the penitential mood in which it was built. The exterior is as severe: a wild, bare rock of a church I thought it, seeing it

ST. ETIENNE—ABBAYE-AUX-HOMMES, CAEN.　EAST END

so soon after Notre-Dame-la-Grande, where the stone wilderness of the façade, in the sunlight, blossoms like the rose. But St. Etienne relaxes somewhat as you look up to the southern side, where the long, austere line of the building shows above many trees, or as you see it from across the fields, its gray spires high above the belt of green.

The Queen's church must have been taken in charge by the King, for it has many of the same qualities as his own, a masculine rather than a feminine church. But the building of it extended over a longer period, to ages when architects, even of

LA TRINITÉ—ABBAYE-AUX-DAMES, CAEN

the North, were more lavish of ornament, and brought greater grace and lightness to their design. La Trinité is a mixture of styles, the Norman force and vigor, by no means outlived, but already making certain concessions. It shows to less advantage from the distance, having an unimpressive sky-line, for its west towers are low and spireless, though now and then, from the street or the waterside in my wandering, I found it could group itself picturesquely with the near houses. I cannot say that I, personally, found it much more sympathetic than St. Etienne. Here, too, the restorer refuses to let you forget him. The church.—at least as I saw it—was divided into practically three, parts of it used by the Sisters and their patients from the near hospital, while the nave, now the parish church, was kept in just the condition of orderly emptiness that lessens my pleasure in the naked interiors of England. On occasions, a solemn ceremonial would fill it with animation and life, and I never liked it better than on a day of First Communion, when it was aglow with faith and warm with prayer. The exterior seemed also to borrow new color as the people came out after Mass, and everywhere the somber lines of the crowd were broken and relieved by white spaces of muslin dresses and fluttering veils.

Wandering farther through the town, I came to other churches, for there are so many that the number of their towers and spires has often led the traveler, who sees them rising from the low-lying town as he approaches it by road, to compare Caen to Oxford, the English city of spires. St. Pierre, St. Jean, St. Sauveur, and more than I can name, were always distinguished architecturally, but have been less cared for than the two abbayes of royal descent, and so have been allowed to tumble into picturesqueness, some indeed to tumble wholly from their religious uses. You do not go out in search of them, and for that very reason there is all the more pleasure in coming upon them by chance, all the excitement of discovery. Some are sadly battered, but to most neglect has given just the qualities which

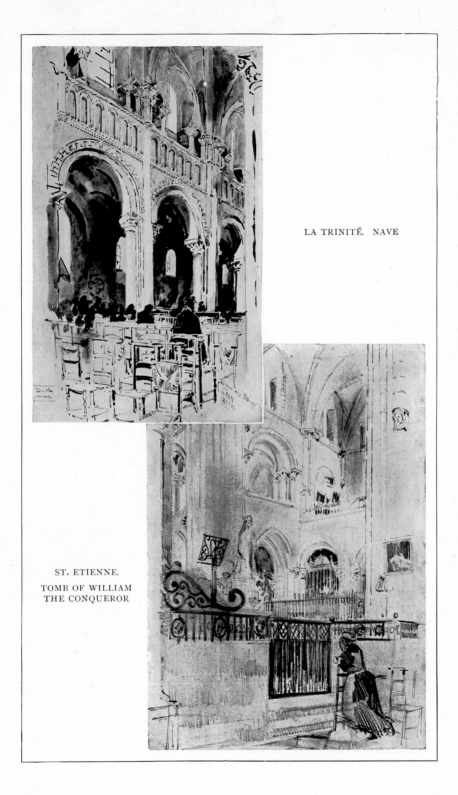

LA TRINITÉ. NAVE

ST. ETIENNE.

TOMB OF WILLIAM
THE CONQUEROR

I miss in St. Etienne and La Trinité. These two, however, are the center of Caen's great past, forever associated with the greatest figure in that past, and architecturally they are so typical in their Northern grandeur and grimness that they offer as suggestive a contrast to Southern Romanesque, as Caen itself offers to a Southern town. To go to them from the early churches of Provence and Aquitaine, then to leave them for the early churches of Auvergne, is to feel more keenly the wide gulf set between the architecture of the North and the architecture of the South, each beautiful, but each in its own strangely different way.

CHAPTER IV

THE CHURCHES OF AUVERGNE

CHAPTER IV

THE CHURCHES OF AUVERGNE

I

IT was a convenient habit of the older generation of travelers to keep their history at their fingers' ends, ready to produce at a moment's notice wherever they went. When Château-briand returned from Italy in 1805 and spent five days at Clermont-Ferrand in Auvergne, he had scarcely arrived before he was shedding his sentimental tear over it as the tomb of Masillon and the cradle of Pascal, and displaying an amount of knowledge about it that impressed me the more because, when I came to Clermont just a hundred years later, I thought it looked so little as if it ever had had any history at all.

Of course I knew it must have a past before I consulted Châteaubriand. I had stopped there not because it is the station for Royat, which is all Clermont now means to most travelers; not because the Gordon Bennett race was going to be held in a few days; but because it is a cathedral town, and I had never yet been to a cathedral town in France that was not so full of history there was no escaping it. But in the station with people taking and changing trains for everywhere, in the boulevard in front with trolley-cars and motors and soldiers coming out of whirlwinds of dust, on the long drive through shop-lined streets up to the *Place de Jaude,* in the huge hotel with its crowd of commercials, Clermont struck me as aggressively modern. As

the days went on, I stumbled upon plenty of signs of its venerable age, for Clermont, really, is not the least ashamed of being
old. On the contrary, it has done its duty by its past most
conscientiously. It has erected a monument to Vercingétorix,
whose cradle it was as well as Pascal's, and who was so fine a
hero I blush to think how long his name suggested nothing more
heroic to me than a street in Paris; it has its statue to Urban II
and its *Rue Godefroi de Bouillon,* as it should, for it is Clermont's distinction to have been the first town where the first
Crusade was preached; it has set up its tablet to Pascal on the
house where he was born; it has preserved its old churches, old
houses, old corners, old market-places, when they did not seem
too much in the way. But it has done all this with singular inef-
fectiveness.

There are only two things, besides its modern energy and
enterprise, that it insists upon your seeing. One is the beauty
of its position—among "the most beautiful in the world," Châteaubriand declared, after he had exhausted his memories and
had time to see the wonderful view which, at every turn,
Clermont commands of the great chain of hills almost encircling
its lower height, or of La Limagne, the plain stretching away
eastward and, in the August days, a sea of harvests; the other
is the cathedral of Notre-Dame, with its tall spires, standing
nobly on a high place in the center of the town.

II

VIOLLET-LE-DUC, as a mere accident in the career I wish were less
industrious every time I travel in France, did for Clermont what
Clermont, in six hundred years, had not been able, or had not
chosen, to do for itself. He finished the cathedral. It had stood
there, through the long centuries, a huge shapeless fragment,
with a nave too short by a couple of bays and with no west front

at all. That was how Châteaubriand found it, and not being particularly interested, he simply noted the fact and put it down to scarcity of money. But the cathedral was begun at a period— 1248 is the date—when scarcity of money was no obstacle to the builders of most of the great French churches. Nor could the enthusiasm at Clermont have been less than elsewhere, for Jean Deschamps, who designed the cathedral, is one of the few architects of his age whose name is remembered, as it scarcely would have been by people indifferent to his work. Auvergne's inclination to heresy was as little likely to have been the reason. Auvergne was at least orthodox enough to burn its Protestants at the stake and to send its Jansenists to Paris, and Clermont was one of the towns that remained Catholic through it all. The difficulty, more probably, lay in Clermont's mistake in ever having attempted to build a cathedral according to Jean Deschamps' design. For, perhaps because he was a Northerner himself or because he saw challenge to his talent and ambition in the achievement of the Northern architect, he planned his church in the Northern manner, the Gothic, as we call it to-day, which was an alien at Clermont, an importation from beyond the Loire. And it was an importation—a supply—for which there was no demand. Auvergne had already developed the Romanesque, common to all France south of the Loire, into an architectural style as distinct in character as its hills and valleys, and so accomplished that it is classed by the authorities among the perfected styles of Europe.

Had I not brought with me memories of Chartres and Paris, I should not have had the courage, nor the heart, to see anything save the beauty of the cathedral. As it was, I thought it extraordinary how well it comes out of the comparison and with what dignity it holds its own, in spite of Viollet-le-Duc's brand-new front, in spite of the extensive restoration going on while I was there, and in spite of that blackish-brown stone of which it, as well as the larger part of Clermont, is built: the volcanic stone

5

of Volvic, harsh in color and too hard to crumble and mellow with time into greater richness of surface. It is this stone that made Clermont seem a harsh, forbidding place until I had stayed long enough in it to get accustomed to a prevailing color so unlike that of the typical French town I already was delighting in. It oppressed me no less at Notre-Dame on my first visit, where, however, I learned at once how much there was to make up for it. I could never approach the cathedral, as it rises at the end of the busy, crowded *Rue des Gras,* the steps that lead up to the west doors adding to its height, without marveling at the unerring instinct for effect with which the old architects placed their big churches, for the idea was Jean Deschamps', if the execution is Viollet-le-Duc's. Nor could I leave it without marveling more at the way these west doors seem made to frame in the Puy de Dôme, where it faces the town from beyond the lesser slopes, its old crater now nothing but a harmless huge green mound against the sky. And the interior might be built of harsher stone, it might bear Viollet-le-Duc's hall-mark and the patches of his successors more obtrusively, it might have been cleared more thoroughly by the Revolution, and it would never cease to be solemn and splendid as long as so many of its windows retain the old glass. This glass is mostly of the same period as that of Chartres, when, as has been well said, the craftsman cared more to make a translucent mosaic of color than a transparent picture. Looking up to these window-labyrinths of twisted tracery and starry light, wandering through the shadowy aisles so noble in proportion, past the chapels where an old gilded reredos glimmered through the dusk, or an old fresco glowed in faint, faded color on the walls, or a richly carved old confessional invited to confession and made a luxury of penance, it seemed nothing short of ingratitude to find any fault at all. Beauty is not such a glut in the market nowadays that we can afford to be over-fastidious when it comes our way.

III

IF the cathedral were still more beautiful, however, it could not have quite the same interest in Clermont as the much more modest little Romanesque church of Notre-Dame-du-Port, which is now so shut in by the near streets and houses that you might think Clermont wanted to hide it. In the process of time,

CHURCH OF ST. AUSTREMOINE, ISSOIRE. FROM THE EAST

the surrounding level has been raised, so that the church now stands not only on lower ground than the cathedral, but, like St. Jean at Poitiers, in a little hollow of its own. Notre-Dame high on the hill cannot be forgotten, but you are almost at the door of Notre-Dame-du-Port before you see it, and indeed, if you start to go to it from the *Place de Jaude*, you may not see it at all unless you keep a sharp lookout. Châteaubriand, evidently, never discovered it, though he spared those few minutes from the view to the cathedral. Arthur Young, to whom agriculture anywhere left small time for architecture, would not have been bothered to look at a grimy old church in what must then have been the dirtiest part of a dirty town. Much more recent descriptions of Clermont cheerfully omit it from the list of "curiosities" to be visited. But fashions in dress have not been more capricious than fashions in art. It is not so very long since Gothic architecture to people of taste was barbarous. What wonder, then, if Châteaubriand, or Arthur Young, was not ashamed, as a pupil of Chautauqua might be to-day, to stay in Clermont and ignore Notre-Dame-du-Port altogether! And though Fergusson and Parker praised French Romanesque into some sort of recognition, though Richardson based his own fine art upon it and tried to popularize it in America, there are people who will still tell you that all Romanesque is stern and gloomy, the very La Trappe of architecture, to be feared, not admired. However, think what you will of Romanesque, believe it prison-like in its sternness or agree with me that its beautiful solemnity is an inspiration to prayer, you cannot deny to Notre-Dame-du-Port, when you see it at Clermont, the same sort of interest that the Roman temples have as you see them under Italian skies, or the little brick churches where the Dutch built them on the banks of their gray canals. For Notre-Dame-du-Port belongs to the country, it shows what the Auvergnat builder could do when left to himself; it is as essentially a native as the chain of Puys and the hardy men and women born and bred under their shadow. It has that character which, whether in the work of the artist or the architect, we have come to prize as the greatest beauty of all.

I had not to look more than once at the church to know that, if Clermont could shut it in, the restorer could not be shut out. He made his descent upon it during the last century, and Notre-Dame-du-Port, as it is now, is in a large measure his work.

The whole question of restoration is, I admit, a difficult one. The church, very likely, was far on the road to ruin when the restorer appeared. The eighteenth century started by taking too much care of the buildings it inherited from ages it despised, and it ended with the Revolution that saw in a church only a place to be dishonored. You can no more forget the Revolution in the churches of France than Cromwell and the Puritans in those of England. If Arthur Young, whose visit to Clermont was in 1789, had waited a few years, he would not have complained of the apathy of its citizens "at a moment when every bosom ought to beat with none but political sensations." He would have wished, rather, for a little more tranquillity to these bosoms, had he been in Clermont to watch the business-like sacking of the cathedral, or the bonfire they made, up there in the *Place de Jaude,* with the great silver lamps that had burned for centuries before Notre-Dame-du-Port, and the bodies of the faithful who had become saints in her service dragged from the broken tombs, and anything and everything sacrilegious hands could seize in the shrine of the Black Virgin, so long the patron and guardian of the town.

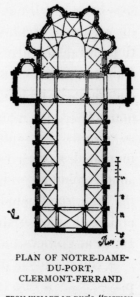

PLAN OF NOTRE-DAME-DU-PORT, CLERMONT-FERRAND

FROM VIOLLET-LE-DUC'S "DICTION-NAIRE DE L'ARCHITECTURE"

You can imagine the state of the church when "apathetic" citizens had got through with it, and no doubt, after the years of indifference and poverty that followed, it was an object of pity for the zealous restorer; no doubt he did what was to be done as scrupulously as he knew how— too scrupulously, that was the trouble. For some say Notre-Dame-du-Port was the first of the Romanesque churches of Auvergne, the model for the others, and the restorer, according to the ideal of restoration, was bound to show what it should have been as the perfect model, no matter how far short of perfection the work of the original builders and the centuries may have left it. His scaffolding was not removed until it was complete with the indispensable square inner porch; the central tower; the beautiful lines and curves of the apsidal chapels; here and there on the walls, the mosaics—the first touch of color at the first breath of the South; in a word, with all the characteristics by which the Romanesque of Auvergne may be known. But, though I do not always agree with Ruskin and William Morris, I am one with them in preferring the old church in ruins to the old church in the restorer's new version. How much of the work is and is not his, I leave it to the expert to say. At least, it is not so obvious when one enters by the south door with its broken, mutilated statues, while the interior—low, round-arched, with simple columns and elaborately wrought capitals, dimly lit by the high, small windows—is free from the geometrical designs and restless color that cover the walls and columns of Notre-Dame at Poitiers and St. Austremoine at Issoire.

A church, like a man or woman, ought to look the part it has played. No one would forgive the picture-restorer who smoothed out the wrinkles and tightened the skin of the old Philip in Velasquez's portrait. What I should like to see is Notre-Dame-du-Port wrinkled and faded in its architectural old age, not done up, with every trace of its long, vivid, and adventurous life wiped out. It goes back to the darkest of the Dark Ages. It was the cathedral before the more ambitious Notre-Dame on the hill was founded. The local saints of Clermont were its exclusive property, and the deeds that made Clermont famous were done at its threshold. It was in the open place, once just outside, that the cry *"Dieu le veut! Dieu le veut!"* rang out in response to the inspired call of Peter the Hermit; it was before the Black Virgin within that the vow to free Christ's sepulcher was confirmed, priests, monks, knights,

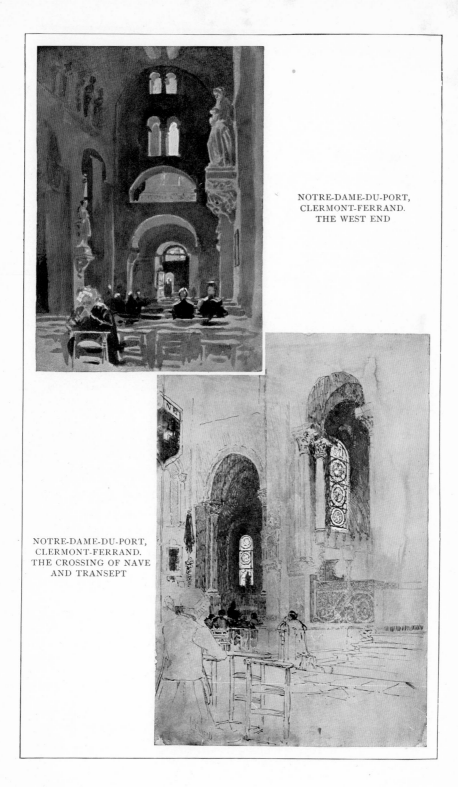

NOTRE-DAME-DU-PORT,
CLERMONT-FERRAND.
THE WEST END

NOTRE-DAME-DU-PORT,
CLERMONT-FERRAND.
THE CROSSING OF NAVE
AND TRANSEPT

NOTRE-DAME-DU-PORT, CLERMONT-FERRAND.   THE SOUTH PORCH

crowding in through the same south door which the beggars
hold so peacefully to-day: a swish of silken draperies, a clang of
armor over the transept pavement, down the winding stairs
from the sanctuary, into the holy of holies, the crypt where

Notre-Dame-du-Port—Our Lady of Refuge—has worked her miracles for centuries. That is what I am willing to believe her name means. People, with little sense of the fitness of things, say the name comes from that of the old *Place-le-Port,* just outside when the church was built, and the most important square in the town; others trace it to a Celtic origin. But why stray after definitions when never for a moment at Clermont have her servants failed to find in her their port, their refuge, from every evil? No waters at Mont Dore, or Royat, were as healing as the cool spring bubbling at her feet. It was always at her bidding that the sun shone when, after a season of rain, the grain was rotting in La Limagne, at her bidding that the first showers fell when the land was parched and shriveling under brazen skies. It was she who freed Clermont from pestilence. And when the Black Virgin of Chartres perished in the flames kindled by the Revolution, and Ste. Geneviève's ashes were scattered in the *Place de Grève,* and horrors untold were done from one end of France to the other and even at Clermont, Notre-Dame-du-Port saved herself for her people. A raid upon the crypt by pious women at night, a trembling flight through the streets made hideous by the new practice of Fraternity, a secure hiding-place guarded in patient silence by a faithful few—so the story goes. And there was another interval of peril, not more than thirty years since, when the statue again was stolen, no one will ever know by whom, or why, or how, though it is known that the black wooden face, wet with tears for the empty shrine, moved the thief to repentance, and the statue was brought back as mysteriously.

More touching as tributes than all these legends, though disastrous in effect, are the walls of the crypt lined with the little marble gilt-lettered tablets by which thanks for heavenly favors are now expressed all over France, and the array of little and big gold and silver hearts hung in neat festoons and symmetrical lines on old Romanesque columns that down here are painted to look like the sham marble of the cheap restaurant. If you come to the crypt in Huysmans' belief that Romanesque is the architecture of fear and penitence, your illusion will be further weakened by the presence in the sacred sanctuary of two little nuns, sweeping, dusting, changing the water in the vases, tidying up generally. I never failed to find them there, and though the crypt is as dusky a cavern as the Romanesque architect could make, with hardly any light, except from the lamps and candles lit by the faithful who bring their petitions and vows to Our Lady, these little nuns and the orphans in uniform, always at their heels, gave it a domestic air which, if not conducive to mystery, helps to explain one of the holds the Catholic Church has upon her children. The people are as out of place in an English cathedral as in Buckingham Palace; in a French cathedral or church they are as much at home as in their own cottage or garret.

IV

It is not until you have wandered over La Limagne and its encircling hills that you know what beautiful use Auvergne made of the architecture it developed for itself. Notre-Dame-du-Port is but one of its many Romanesque churches. Everywhere you find them. Even Royat, which you would not suspect of such an unprofitable weakness, can show an old fortified church as a foil to its hotels and casinos and baths. And if you travel farther, either by road or by train, it will seem to you as if the hills had been made for no other end than that every one of them might hold a little town or church upon its summit, as if fire had burned and rent and fashioned anew all this land, scarred by the memory as fiery of the sins and hatreds of dead men, only to create the picturesqueness which the modern traveler delights in. And there is scarcely a town or church on the top of a hill that is not the architectural reward for the

climb, though it is to Issoire, probably, you would be first di-
rected from Clermont by the architect who cares more for the
perfect design in the Romanesque of Auvergne than for the
chance picturesqueness of place.

Issoire is low in the plain, and so modern and decorous you
would call it commonplace, were not its commonplaceness the
result of as lurid a history as Auvergne has to tell. The first
town in which the voice of
Austremoine was heard when he
came to convert Auvergne, it
was to earn a reputation as "the
boulevard of Protestantism," in
the days when Catholics burned
Protestants, and Protestants
skinned Catholics alive with equal
alacrity. It practically vanished
during the Wars of the League.
Indeed, I have read that a monument was put up to mark the
place where it had stood. The
church of St. Austremoine must
have come out of the ordeal in
a sad state of disrepair, and could
hardly have been improved by
the Revolution, a couple of centuries later on. You must take
it from the restorer, with what
faith you may, that it was a
replica of Notre-Dame-du-Port,

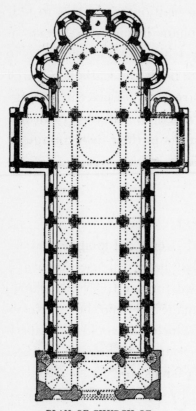

PLAN OF CHURCH OF
ST. AUSTREMOINE, ISSOIRE

differing little save in its greater size, in certain details in the
arrangement of the chapels, in the slight variations of the
sculptures on the outer walls. I thought it too well looked out
for, too obviously preserved as a "specimen," isolated in a little
place neatly cleared for it. The interior, as I saw it, was always

CHURCH OF ST. AUSTREMOINE, ISSOIRE.   NAVE AND TRANSEPT

deserted, and I was ready to believe the geometrical patterns, in dull dingy color schemes, on the old walls and columns had frightened away the devout, as well they might. On the whole, I got most pleasure from the wonderful capitals, more wonderful, I thought, than those of Notre-Dame-du-Port. They were not overlooked by the decorator, but the paint might be laid on with a thicker, more garish brush, and it could not bury the naïveté of the centaurs armed with bow and arrow, the warriors in chain-armor, to whose enigmatic presence there no one so far has found the clue, the Good Shepherd bearing the lost sheep on his shoulders, the grinning devil dragging his victims by ropes round their necks to hell. They are all amazingly full of character and expressive in their primitiveness, but not one is more amazing than that capital where the sculptor had the ingenuity to represent the Last Supper, with Christ and the Twelve Apostles at table, in such daring perspective that every figure, keeping its place in the composition, can be seen from below. Realism in decoration is not considered legitimate nowadays. St. Bernard objected to it on other grounds, denouncing the work of the Romanesque sculptor as barbarous and impious. But at Issoire and Clermont I could only be thankful that the artists' idea of what is wrong in art was not always in accord with ours, and that the Romanesque sculptor got through his task before St. Bernard thundered against his impiety.

This pleasure is also to be had at St. Nectaire, for which little village Issoire is the station, just as Clermont is for Royat. It is reached only by road, and most people have no other object in reaching it than to take the waters. But the church in the town, named after St. Austremoine's fellow-missionary, is as well worth seeing as Notre-Dame-du-Port, of which it is another replica, like it in all the features peculiar to Auvergnat Romanesque, even to the carved capitals; like it also in the opportunity it has offered to the restorer. But it has a beauty that Notre-Dame-du-Port shut in by streets and houses, and St. Austre-

ST. NECTAIRE, FROM THE NORTHEAST

moine in the plain, do not possess, for it crowns the hill on which it is built, realizing Ruskin's description of the church which is a joy and a blessing, bringing the light into the eyes when it is seen from afar.

And as you keep on in your journey across the plain or over the hills, which are "rust-red" in Swinburne's song, but in Nature sometimes radiantly green, the landmarks by the way will be a series of churches, unknown to fame, but as beautiful, and no less characteristic of Auvergne than the great chain of its Puys, now silent and still.

CHAPTER V

THE MOST PICTURESQUE PLACE IN THE WORLD

CHAPTER V

THE MOST PICTURESQUE PLACE IN THE WORLD

I

W E had always been hunting for it. We had always felt sure that somewhere, some day, we should find the perfect place which was to combine the charm of the Middle Ages with the comfort of the nineteenth century —the Albert Dürer town which could be reached in a railway-train, with medieval streets through which the dinner-bell would make a pleasant sound, where there would be plenty of picturesque dirt in other people's houses, plenty of fresh water and clean rooms in our own hotel. Perhaps this is a *bourgeois* idea. But, then, that is our affair.

There were times when we thought we had found it, but again and again we were disappointed. Rocamadour, Assisi, Fritzlar came very near satisfying us. But then, in Rocamadour our landlady forced us to fast on Fridays, which was much too middle-aged a custom to please us; in Assisi the discomfort, in a large measure, followed us into the hotel; in Fritzlar dinner was served at noon, a practice which savored of barbarism. Then there was far Segesvar, the German fortress-town in the heart of Transylvania; Elbogen, castle-crowned, among the Bohemian hills; Meissen, high above the Elbe where it flows through Saxony. But it was always the same: the medievalism might leave almost nothing to be desired; there was sure to be something wanting on the modern side.

Eight years of wandering had brought us no closer to our undiscovered country when, last summer, as we were traveling in the mountains of—but no! why should we tell the name? Why break the serenity of its hilly streets with the rush of personally conducted parties, or of easel-laden artists? Why turn it into another Barbizon or Grez, another Chester or Nuremberg? Besides, we have exploited so many

places in our day; we have, in our recklessness, presented the painter, the illustrator, the magazine-writer with more motives than they can exhaust in a generation; we have, by our enterprise, developed the cycling trade to an incalculable extent, and, by our praise, made the fortune of half the hotel-keepers of Provence. And the result for us? Not a cycle manufacturer would give us a machine if we asked for it, not a landlord would throw us a crust were we starving, not an art-student would find a spare moment to thank us. No; the name of the most Picturesque Place in the World we shall keep to ourselves. It is foolish deliberately to court the fate of Columbus or Stanley.

We were riding, then, among the hills of a land that shall be nameless, bound on a mission which, as yet, need be nobody's business but our own, when, one bright sunny afternoon, as we came over the top of the high pass, suddenly we looked down upon a landscape that might have been a picture by one of the Primitives—every feature in it sharply defined, the composition

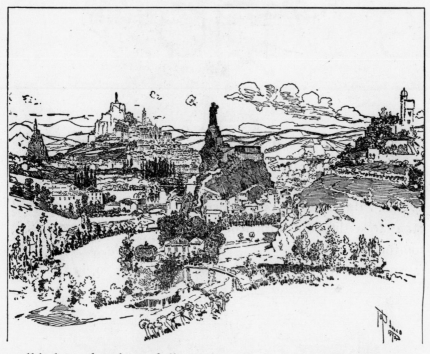

well balanced and carefully composed, the whole effect artificial, theatrical, impossible. The engineer and the capitalist had been there before us, and a railroad makes its way through the hills. From the train, as it rushes out of a long tunnel, the eyes of the traveler will rest upon another oddly composed view, no less Düreresque and incredible.

It was still more delightful to find, in this town that a middle-aged painter might have created, a hotel as perfect as only a sanitary engineer and an experienced *chef* could make it; spotless, airy bedchambers, with dressing-room and bath of the most improved pattern attached, exquisite little breakfasts, and no less excellent dinners served in the evening, at the one reasonable hour for dining. We can rough it if necessary. Many a day

have we eaten bread and cheese for our dinner, many a night slept in a peasants' inn and shared our room with other travelers, many a morning made our toilet at the pump or the nearest stream. But never by preference; we don't like it, and when it comes to settling down for work, why, then we insist upon being comfortable.

And we were comfortable, even luxuriously so, in the most

Picturesque Place in the World. "A deal of high living" we enjoyed there. And the charm of contrast was added when, fresh from the morning plunge in the cool spring-water of our

bath, we loitered upon picturesque bridges watching the washer-women at work in the rocky bed of the thin stream, or rambled into the narrow, smelly streets, where pictorial old ladies, practising an almost forgotten handicraft, were sitting at the doors of Rembrandt-like cellars, with their feet in undrained gutters.

To flee civilization for longer than from breakfast to dinner would have exceeded the limit of our ambition. We liked to know that our daily post would never fail us; that we were not cut off from the outer world; that we could read the latest news, if we chose, over our morning coffee. But, on the other hand, our pleasure in these things was doubled because of the certainty that, whenever we wished, we could leave the prosaic cares and interests of the present, and lose ourselves in these absurdly fantastic reminders of the past.

We did not have to go into church or museum, in the usual fashion, to hunt for our medievalism. It was everywhere about us. The landscape was as rich in strong contrasts as our daily life. It was always primitive, always like a background borrowed from an old woodcut or altar-piece; but it had its degrees of strangeness and beauty. Its effects were ever varying. There were hours when it was more fantastic, more dramatic, than others. At sunset the hillside, with its climbing houses and campanili, fairly shone.

We used to feel that, thus transfigured into a golden city, it was so great a marvel that, by comparison, all the other impressions it might have in store for us would seem commonplace. And then, not so much later, when the short twilight had faded and night had come, we were quite as ready to believe that nothing, absolutely nothing, could exceed the wonder of this deep, dark mass, with

> The mysterious distances, the glooms
> Romantic, the august and solemn shapes.

Indeed, we never came so near being romantic in our lives. There was, of course, less mystery in the clear, pure light of early morning, less fantasy in the bright afternoon sunshine. But these new differences, these new changes, lent added zest to our enjoyment. And, after all, the most matter-of-fact effects could never be ordinary in so extraordinary a land.

But the country did not depend upon the mere contrasts between day and night, between dawn and sunset, for its variety.

LOOKING WESTWARD FROM THE PORTALS

THE STAIRWAY UNDER THE NAVE

It had numberless resources of its own. We could not walk through the streets of the town, we could not venture beyond the houses, without its considerately arranging itself into a new and original composition for our benefit. At every turn peaks and plain, river and road, churches and houses, came together in a new way to make a new picture for us. And the best of it was that we never missed the harmonious proportions, the well-balanced arrangement, the conventional emphasizing of detail, which had so struck us in the first of the long series of designs our undiscovered country spread out before us. Now, we chanced upon so telling and impressive a subject as a lonely rocky peak with flying buttresses of natural rock, and surmounted by a colossal statue of the Virgin and Child. Again, when, in search of still another point of view, we went wandering into the hills, from the path winding upward we saw, like a map below, a most wonderful grouping of both natural and artificial elements. No matter whether we kept to the plain or to the mountains, no matter in which direction we followed, there was always new and irresistible material to be had. Nor did we begin to exhaust it, though we stayed in that enchanted world day after day, week after week, month after month. Mountains, plain, cliffs, towers, bridges, streams— the "motives" were without end.

Town and country, then, were perfection, and the hotel was no less irreproachable. And yet all these advantages cost us no more than life in exploited Barbizon or artist-ridden Concarneau. Within easy reach were two large busy towns; the capital was not much farther away, though to tell its name would be to put the envious on the trail. On each side of the hills two great railways connected important commercial centers. We were in the very heart of a prosperous country, but at the same time entirely out of the world, and in a town that seemed unknown to any one save the natives. Indeed, the chances are that we would run small risk of its discovery should the publisher see fit, as

we humbly suggest, to offer a prize—but not at our expense—
to the first reader of this chapter who could name the locality.

The place does exist, though we ourselves certainly would
never have believed in it without seeing. We have not between
us the imagination to invent a scene so unreal, so melodramatic,
so nearly grotesque. The drawings are the purest realism. We
will give no hints, geographical or geological, statistical or
social, historical or humanitarian, mechanical or moral, political
or intellectual, as to the site of the city forgotten by Cook, neglected by Murray. We will only ask triumphantly, tantalizingly,
"Do you not wish you knew where to find the most Picturesque
Place in the World?"

II

I NEED hardly say that the above description of Le Puy, rather
rapturous and with the twang of youth, is the article written
eighteen years ago for "The Century Magazine," to which I have
already referred. I republish it now in all its rapturous exaggeration, changing nothing, modifying nothing, omitting nothing, for two reasons. In the first place, it has for me an auto-
biographical value in my experiences among cathedral towns.
Not one I had hitherto seen, or was still to see, ever gave me so
wonderful a moment as when, that summer afternoon, I first
looked down on Le Puy, with its strange rocks and churches and
statues, set in the midst of the Düreresque landscape. Other
towns and other cathedrals interested me as much in other ways
and from other causes. But, for sheer picturesqueness, none
could rival it, and with my arrival there I reached the high-
water mark of the pleasure spread over so many years of my
cathedral journeying.

My second reason for republishing the article is less personal.
I think, immature and frankly ecstatic as it may be, it is a
genuine tribute to Le Puy, expressing in its own precipitate way

THE NAVE

the strength of the impression that town makes upon the traveler. In fact, I know it does from the number of letters and inquiries it has brought, year after year, even indeed until only yesterday. If it is a trifle breathless, breathlessness is the chief quality of one's amazement and joy in entering into actual possession of such an unbelievable place. It, of all the world's wonders, takes your breath away if there is meaning in the phrase, and anything short of breathlessness in writing of it would seem but a prosaic attempt to record its picturesqueness.

But, for all my enthusiasm, I had enough common sense left to look quietly and seriously at the details that go to build up the picturesqueness. Perhaps it is the most surprising thing about Le Puy that it is no less wonderful in those details than as a whole. Once it had arranged itself on its own peak in just the right relation to the neighboring peaks, to the streams running through the plain, to the hills on the horizon, it might have rested on its laurels and there would have been none to complain. It has not been content, however; it lavishes its attractions broadcast. It has crowned the nearest peak with the little Romanesque chapel of St. Michel, that repays the climb of the two hundred odd steps leading to it. It has buried a hero whose name stands for everything that was romantic in the past— Bertrand du Guesclin—in the old church of St. Laurent, that looks as if it might have been the background for everything medieval. It has filled itself with delightful old corners, with old turrets and towers, old convents and monasteries, old palaces almost Italian in stateliness. It has given its women lace-making as an industry because few occupations are so pictorial. It collects in its markets the most astonishing array of white caps, though I regretted to find on my last visit that the deliciously absurd little black hat like a muffin the women used to wear over these caps was to be seen only on a few of the older generation. It has provided enchanting views in every direction. And it has placed in the exact spot where the finest effect

THE WEST FRONT

THE WESTERN PORTALS

is assured, a cathedral that is the most wonderful thing in this wonderful town.

There is no anti-climax in the first view of the cathedral. It is as picturesque and unbelievable as the first view of the town. Wandering in search of it, for I always like to leave something to chance when I begin my acquaintance with a cathedral, I turned into a hilly street, and there, at the top, was the great Romanesque façade. On either side the street, in front of the houses, steps went upward, and I mounted. Presently the whole street became a huge stairway, and I mounted. And the stairway passed under the portals, and I mounted, and I saw before me steps still going upward under arch after arch, and when, resting a moment, I looked back again, it was to see the great black and white arches framing in, as in a picture, the steep street, the red roofs, and the distant hills. I know of no entrance to a cathedral that can rival this in solemnity and mystery. The shadowy stairs under the shadowy arches might lead to you hardly can imagine what strange and mystic sanctuary. It sets you to thinking of the secret offices of the Inquisition, of Oriental rock temples, of monasteries in the heart of the mountains, of all strange and holy houses of God where no profane foot is allowed to pass.

There is a simple matter-of-fact explanation. When the architect undertook to build the cathedral here on the rock called Mont Anis, he had to face a serious problem of space, and he was a genius. He took not an inch from the church, not a touch from the majesty of an entrance in dignified keeping with it, but he carried his great stairway under the church and brought it to the very center, before the sanctuary where, after the long climb, the faithful of old found themselves face to face with their God. Now, however, the stairway has been turned at the top, and you enter by the south aisle of the nave near the transept. The architect's idea was the best. Only the sanctuary, the holy of holies, should be the goal of that steep ascent out of the

THE DOMES OF THE NAVE

sunshine and through the shadows. It is said in the old days, before this change, that people in the *Grande Place,* or, at any rate, at the foot of the steps, could follow Mass as faithfully as if they knelt within nave or choir. Even now, on some great feasts, Mass is celebrated by the bishop at the top of the wide stairway which is filled, from top to bottom, with worshipers kneeling and standing in the sunshine—a sight to be seen in Le Puy alone of all the towns and cities of Europe.

I thought it the triumph of the cathedral that, after this imposing entrance, the interior should prove so impressive. It retains the religious atmosphere and the mystery of the cavernous portals and the shadowy stairs. In nave and choir you have again the effect of a succession of arches, the result of the arrangement of the domed vaults they support. The masonry is severe, the architecture simple and massive, with little decoration except the carving of the capitals: preëminently a reverent church, a church to pray in. It has been restored, more 's the pity, but not rebuilt in the reckless fashion of Périgueux, and the old feeling has not gone forever from it. I remember seeing it one Ascension Day, in its modern festal array. White and blue and yellow banners, flaringly new, hung on either side the choir, garlands of pink and white paper roses were looped above them, white and blue paper was festooned elaborately above the altar, and more inappropriate ornament in the somber interior there could not be. But not even this modern tawdriness could destroy altogether the serenity and severity of the effect at the hour of High Mass. It was irritating, an intrusion, as if a cheap glaring modern frame were made to inclose an Old Master, but the Old Master of art or architecture is not so easily killed.

III

THE church has traditions of such holiness that their influence must be felt, I used to think, had the architecture not har-

monized so completely with them. The whole conversion of
Velay brings us very close to Christ, for St. George, the first to
make it Christian, was sent there by St. Peter. The legend
pleases me, for it gives the homely touch of friendliness to the
relations of saintly men who have become to us so remote in
their sanctity that we forget they were ever human and capable
of friendship. The story shows St. George and St. Front, who
were bound for Périgueux, traveling together in sympathy and
good fellowship through Roman Gaul until, one day in Velay,
St. George died. St. Front made a grave for him by the road-
side and turned back at once for Rome, a journey of such length
in his day that it was not to be lightly undertaken. In Rome St.
Front told his story to St. Peter, whose staff accompanied him
when he started for the third time on the long journey in the
cause of Christ and friendship. When he reached the grave of
St. George he planted St. Peter's staff in the ground above it,
and the dead arose, and many years of life were granted to St.
George in which to begin the good work in Velay, a labor lightened, I hope, by frequent meetings of the two friends either
there or in Périgord.

It was not St. George, however, who founded the cathedral.
The site on Mont Anis was chosen by the Blessed Virgin, and
revealed by her with many miracles. Notre-Dame became her
church not only in name but in her tireless guard over it and
her love for the people of Le Puy. It was because the feast of
the Annunciation, her feast, once fell on Good Friday that the
Great Pardon was granted to all who came on pilgrimage to her
shrine, and granted whenever again the two holy days fell, or
ever will fall, that way together. Wonderful tales are told of
the people who have taken advantage of her favor, and of the
wealth they have brought. Such crowds still descend upon Le
Puy, it is said, that if you were there at the time of the Pardon,
and let anything drop upon the ground, you would not have
room from your place, among the other pilgrims, to stoop and

THE CHOIR

pick it up; which is hard to believe at ordinary times when space is at a discount. The Blessed Virgin showed further her favor by inspiring St. Louis to bestow upon Le Puy the Black Virgin, one of the most famous of her miraculous statues in France. It was offered by him in thanksgiving for his release when he returned from his captivity by the infidel in Egypt. The devout say that the statue was carved by the prophet Jeremiah, as a symbol of the truth he prophesied, and they add that this was done when he was in Egypt, for it seems that even to the devout there could be no question of its Egyptian origin. The skeptical say, on the other hand, that it was more essentially Egyptian than this, that it was simply the statue of the goddess Isis, who also was often represented with her son in her arms, or on her knee, and who once was worshiped on Mont Anis. I do not see that it makes much difference which of the two stories you accept. Whatever its origin, the Black Virgin was sanctified by ages of the people's trust in her of whom, to them, it was the portrait—a sign given to them of her love and of the power of her intercession with her Son, the Child on her knees, who was their God. To decide for yourself by examination of the statue, is now impossible. Le Puy is so out of the way, still so hard to get to, by rail or road, that you might think in the past it must have escaped even the rumor of any great agitation or crisis in France until happily too late. But as one reminder of how quickly not only rumor but the trouble itself could come to it, you will see, as you wander through choir and ambulatory, the tablet to a priest who perished in the Revolution, and he was far from being the only victim. Even at Le Puy there is no getting rid of the memory of the Revolution, and when in the Reign of Terror the miraculous statue was exposed to the same danger that threatened the Black Virgin at Clermont-Ferrand, no miracle was worked to save it, but, dragged from its shrine to the market-place, it was thrown into the fire which preachers of Freedom, the new superstition, believed would burn up all that they disowned as the superstition of their fathers. The statue was copied when the Terror had passed with its gospel of a day, and there is again a Black Virgin at Le Puy. But, no doubt because it is a copy, the fervor it excites is weaker, and Le Puy waits for the new sign, which will come with time, from the Mother of God, who still watches and directs its fortunes.

IV

You must be skeptical to doubt these miracles in a place that is a miracle in itself. The better I got to know it as the days passed, the more miraculous I found it, full of the beautiful and strange things of which time has robbed too many old churches, full of all sorts of corners and hidden rooms and secret passages that you could never have dreamed of, where a dozen Esmeraldas might live in peace, where a dozen Quasimodos could come and go unseen. There should have been a Victor Hugo in Auvergne to write the romance of Notre-Dame-du-Puy. George Sand did send one of her heroines there, and you may read her description in the "Marquis de Villemer." But Le Puy was a mere part of her background and not in any sense the inspiration of her story, which, anyway, is one of her dullest. The romance is not yet exploited. I felt it everywhere. Even in the old chapel entered from the north of the nave, once I believe the chapter-house and easy of access to any tourist, there is such an atmosphere, such a smell of the catacombs, that the sacristan's recital, long since got by heart, of the paintings on the walls discovered by Mérimée, cannot reduce it to the mere prose of a starred sight in Baedeker. But if you get beyond this, if your interest survives the first visit, if you show your pleasure plainly enough to be allowed liberty to ramble where you will, you penetrate into all sorts of unexpected places, up old winding stairways, into the amazing gallery with old pale frescoes where the organ is, into rooms used for what purpose you do not know, nor indeed care, eager not to dispel the mystery they suggest, though in one, where there is a rare old

THE SOUTH PORCH OF THE CHOIR

Romanesque chimneypiece, I stumbled upon, not mystery, but, of all unexpected things, a man quietly cooking potatoes in a

THE CLOISTERS, DOME, AND TOWER OF THE CATHEDRAL

saucepan and filling the place with savory odors entirely and encouragingly of to-day.

It is the same when you go exploring about the exterior, where, however, there is not much exploring, because the level of the plateau here is so well filled by the cathedral that space is limited for everything else; also because, I cannot say why,

locked doors and barriers keep you from exploring what there
is.   The cloisters form part of the regular tourist round on the
way to the Museum, and I would follow any number of tourists
rather than miss seeing them, for the cloisters of Le Puy have
none of the severity of the cathedral, but lightness and charm in
the graceful arcades of round Romanesque arches, in the richly
carved capitals, in the green of the sunlit square, though there
is massiveness in the effect of the cathedral walls towering

THE CLOISTERS AND ROCHER CORNEILLE

above them, unadorned, save for the black and white stone of
the window arches, and the patches of mosaic work of red,
white, and black peculiar to Auvergne, and well fortified as they
had need to be against the fierce lords of Polignac. Interest
undoes locks and removes barriers, and I saw a good deal besides the cloisters, wandering unreservedly in the little gray *place*
by the Bishop's Palace, where the history of Le Puy is written
plainly on the walls in the odd jumble of Roman and Romanesque and Renaissance broken ornament, and stone, and I know
not what, built into them, and where only you see as you should
the tower standing at the east end, a little apart from the church,
at its four corners the four ancient enigmatic figures that nobody was able to explain to me. Of all the impressions that
remain with me of this exploration, none is so ghostly and
so in character with the age and the interminable past of the
cathedral as my impression of the interior of this tower when I
wandered into it, and gradually, through the darkness, made
out the old tombs about me on the floor, and heard, like so many
voices from another world, the plaintive cooing of the pigeons
in the heights above.

For the ground plan of a cathedral with its surrounding
buildings, you have usually to rely on an architectural drawing
or dull description. But Le Puy, completing the miracle that
began with that first vision of it, has provided a high platform
on the rock above where you can study out for yourself the
ground plan of Notre-Dame, and all the town, and all the
country round it, without the help of an architectural draftsman or the possibility of a second's dullness. To the north of
the cathedral, curious tortuous passages, scarcely to be called
streets, and an easily ascending, zigzagging path lead to the
top of the Rocher Corneille, the highest point in Le Puy. Here,
from the tiny plateau, or platform, rises a huge statue of the
Virgin in bronze, made from the cannon captured at the Crimea,
an ugly modern statue, like the other statues on neighboring

THE CATHEDRAL OF LE PUY, FROM THE NORTH

peaks, and further vulgarized by the stairway it incloses, and by the traces on the walls left by the tourist who mounts up into the colossal head, is as proud of it as if he had mounted the Matterhorn, and would immortalize himself and his adventure. It must be said for the statue, however, that placed at this height its effect is delightfully medieval and its ugliness is not visible from below, and that the rock needs the figure to carry it still higher in lines that take away from the square top above the cathedral. Once on the platform, you can turn your back to the statue and look down at leisure over Le Puy. Just below, you see the great roof with the dome and tower, you look into the cloisters, your eye wanders from the Bishop's Palace close by the church to the east to the *Hôtel-Dieu* as near to the west, and you understand the way the buildings are grouped together, as you never did and never could while visiting one after the other. And then, having mastered this part of the picture, your eye wanders farther, and you see the near convents where, when I was last at Le Puy, gray Sisters and black walked peacefully up and down under the wide-spreading trees in their gardens, but where I fear they walk no longer, and will not until Our Lady of Le Puy again remembers her people. And then the eye wanders farther still, over the roofs sloping down to the green plain, to the windings of the poplared streams, to the other peaks left standing when fire from the bowels of the earth rent all that now peaceful countryside, and on to the hills at rest on the horizon. And the last time I stood there, with the wide medieval panorama outstretched before me, as the first, the wonder again swept over me that this beauty should exist, not in an old print or picture, but there in actual fact, for me to look at and rejoice.

CHAPTER VI

AT TOULOUSE AND ALBI

CHOIR, ST. SERNIN, TOULOUSE

CHAPTER VI

AT TOULOUSE AND ALBI

I

THERE are places, like people, you fall in love with at
first sight, without quite knowing why. Toulouse enchanted me from the beginning for no better reason,
as far as I could make out, than because it was Toulouse.
Something in the sound of the name perhaps, or the rich absurd
accent of the Languedoc, something in the outdoor life, the blue
sky, the fruit, the wine, the feeling of the South—how can I
tell just what?—appealed to me, and has kept on appealing ever
since, though I know as well as any one all that can be, and
usually is, said against it—that it is abominably hot, that its
winds are worse than the *mistral,* that it is as primitive as a
village, that its aspect does not justify its name and traditions.
But then, the Toulousain takes the heat with an irresistible light-
heartedness; any wind that breaks up a long hot spell is a blessing; I like the primitiveness of a big city that can go on holding
its daily market on its finest site, as if *Les Halles* were plumped
down in the *Place de la Concorde,* or Covent Garden in Trafal-
gar Square; and I think it is much to be thankful for that there
is any Toulouse at all on the banks of the Garonne. For when
I read the history of this part of the world, the problem to me
is how anything happens to be left of a town that for centuries
everybody seemed trying to get rid of in the struggle to possess

it. As it is, there has come out of this past, grim, blood-stained, worthy of an Italian hill town, not merely a Toulouse, but a very presentable Toulouse, far more pictorial than its reputation with the modern traveler. "If it were not for the superb church of St. Sernin, Toulouse would be quite destitute of monuments," Mr. James asserts, and we have got into the habit of accepting his opinions in France. But I notice there were many other things he managed to enjoy, even if not to the point of ranking them as monuments: the Capitol, the old hotels or mansions, the quays, the cloistered Museum, the venerable churches. Surely a town with these things in it has not got very far on the road to destitution.

II

To be honest, I enjoyed the less correct sights far more than St. Sernin, though all the authorities agree it is *the* monument of Toulouse, and though it was the special object of my visit. I remember my feeling, that I tried hard not to believe was dismay, when, sauntering down a narrow street from the Square of the Capitol, I had my first view of it, a huge brick pile displaying itself, alone and unencumbered, in the center of the space that has been cleared about it. I had expected a church that would look as old and romance-laden as its past, and St. Sernin has a past both ancient and vigorous. Sernin is the Toulousain's little name for Saturninus, and Saturninus was the saint who made Toulouse Christian in the third century, and, for his pains, was martyred there, dragged at the tail of a bull down the near street, as far as the near church, both called *du Taur* in commemoration of the event. And there was a church of St. Sernin from the earliest days, like all very early churches, pulled down and rebuilt, and rebuilt again many times, once by Charlemagne, who left in its care some of the holiest of the relics he was forever collecting and distributing in his travels. And in one form or another St. Sernin stood there through the long blood-stained history of the town, seeing such things done, such things of splendor and of horror, that you

THE WEST FRONT OF THE CATHEDRAL. TOULOUSE

feel every brick should shriek the tale as you pass, and, as the present building dates back to the eleventh century, shriek it with the beauty wrought by long years· of sun and wind and weather.

But what does it tell of its past as it stands there now, conscientiously restored to the modern idea of old Romanesque, the famous central tower, with its four stories of arcades narrowing in the ascent, without a flaw, and all rubbish swept away from the surrounding space, how well, you may know by a visit to the Museum, which is rich in spoils from the old cloisters? St. Sernin is the noblest example of the Romanesque of Languedoc, guide and other books of architecture assure you. But in this latest of its transformations it seemed to me little more than still another monument to the industry of Viollet-le-Duc, its new neat wall spaces as unlovely in color and quality as those of a factory. I do not doubt it had got into a shocking state before he was summoned. When Mérimée was at Toulouse, some years before, he regretted the coat of plaster that then covered the brick walls, and it fared badly enough with all old churches during the plaster period. But, as I have already said, William Morris was right in insisting that modern art never meddles with monuments of a bygone art without destroying them: it is not possible "to strip from a building this, that, and the other part of its history—of its life, that is—and then to stay the hand at some arbitrary point and leave it still historical, living, and even as it once was." Brick, more than most building materials, needs the touch of time to ripen into full beauty. Those old bare hulks of brick in many an Italian hill town often have the pathetic loveliness of abandonment and decay, and their walls have been stained and burned and faded by the sun of centuries into a greater tenderness and richness of color than their builders ever gave them. The wall spaces spared at St. Sernin —on the west front, and bits here and there where red blossoms in the springtime bloom between the broken bricks—show that the church might have had the same charm of color and the same pathos had Viollet-le-Duc's industry been less wholesale. Almost all that you can learn of the old architect's work in the new version is the tremendous scale upon which he designed and the difficult problems he was not afraid to set himself. Really, I never found anything interesting in the exterior of St. Sernin, except on Sunday mornings, when it is the background for the

THE INTERIOR OF THE CATHEDRAL, TOULOUSE

most colossal and astounding rag fair held from one end of Europe to the other.

What appealed to me more was the dramatic contrast between the noise and glare of this market and the dark, cool solemnity of the interior at the hour of Mass. Toulouse put off its gaiety and its sunshine at the threshold. The church, it is true, has been tidied inside as well as out. It is guilty, in the language of Ruskin, of "the moral delinquency" of hiding the stone of many of the piers under the painter's sham stone, glossy in surface and divided by lines of an accuracy never achieved by the mason unaided. But the decorator, even with the help of the restorer, has not been able to tidy away the solemnity that is the characteristic of a Romanesque interior. Its "extraordinary seriousness" is what must strike every one, as it struck Mr. Henry James, in the clear gray nave with the two low aisles on either side, in the spacious transepts, the deep, narrow choir, the radiating chapels of the apse: everywhere the mystery of dim vistas and vague distances. For me this atmosphere of seriousness thickened in the crypt, where Mr. James's impression was grotesque. I thought it still warmed by the piety that, in the old days, filled it with the treasure of relics only surpassed in St. Peter's at Rome, and made it one of the holiest places of pilgrimage in Europe. I was never in Toulouse for the feasts when these relics are brought into the nave and exposed to the faithful. But at all seasons and at all hours, without any such stimulus, the people prayed with an intensity equaled only in Spain. After all, Toulouse is on the border of Spain, and I suppose this is no stranger than the fact that never have I seen such picturesque Spanish costume as on the peasants within a few miles of the town. I should not care to visit the relics anywhere except in the crypt. For though the sacristan, who is your guide, may point with the gaiety of perfect belief to the head of St. Thomas Aquinas, swathed in linen cloths, and the bodies and bones of apostles and saints in their shrines;

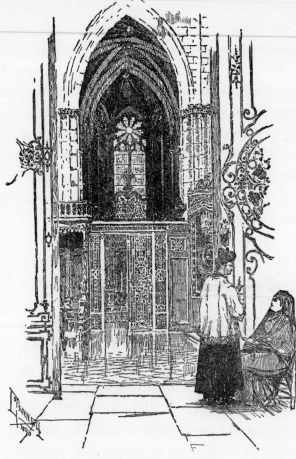

LOOKING INTO THE CHOIR

though the modern reliquary—the painted wooden bust with glass medallion in its breast—may inspire any emotion rather than awe, it is there that the memories of the past deepen and its shadows fall heaviest; there that, as the cheerful sacristan passes with his taper, the glow of gold from some rare old chest or casket reveals in a flash more of the spirit of St. Sernin than all the huge brick pile as you see it from the *Rue du Taur,* or towering above the booths of the Sunday market.

Now that I have given St. Sernin its due, I have the less hesitation in admitting my own preference for the cathedral of St. Etienne, dismissed in travel books as an "odd dislocated fragment" scarcely worth finding. As you walk toward it across the *Place St. Etienne,* you see a west front, shabby and weather-beaten, where nothing is straight or in balance. At the top, the façade slants up to the tall brick tower rising on the north, as if a great gable had been intended, but having reached the tower it stops abruptly. The rose window above the door is placed well to one side of it. In bewilderment, you start to walk round the cathedral. Here it loses itself in a mess of houses and roofs; here its gigantic buttresses mount abruptly,

TAPESTRIES WERE STRETCHED OUT ON THE SHABBY WEST FRONT

like cliffs, from the level of the pavement. As far as you can discover, it is without definite plan, a jumble of different styles, and as incoherent in line as Joanne's word for it. You go inside. The nave, without arches or columns or aisles, short, wide, like a big antechamber, is built on one axis; the choir, with elaborate ambulatory, on quite another. If St. Sernin is an architectural model, St. Etienne is an architectural puzzle.

But how much more expressive is the puzzle! Without opening guide or other book, you know that the church is old by the early thirteenth-century nave with its remnants of Romanesque. That it was rich, the tapestries on the walls and the splendors of the later Gothic of the choir are the proofs. That money was exhausted, or interest diverted, before the work was done, you cannot doubt, so unmistakable is it that the designers of the choir meant to rebuild the entire church on the same flamboyant scale. Of years of neglect and indifference, the empty niches

TAPESTRIES IN THE NAVE

and broken statues of the west door, the houses and roofs propped against the outer walls and between buttresses, are the record. In the Romanesque of St. Sernin the restorer had a native growth, useful, according to his useless theories, to preserve as an object-lesson; the Gothic of St. Etienne was a waif, a stray from the North, fit to teach only the advantage of adapting with discretion. This was its picturesque salvation. And so the nave has been left, dim and faded as I love an old church to be, its gray walls hung with pale tapestries and, above them, stained and somber canvases in their old frames; mystery is suggested with every glance beyond the western altar, which, like everything else, is set askew, and beyond the massive dividing pillar—*le pilier d'Orléans*—into the purple impenetrable depths of the choir. And when, on feast-days, more tapestries were stretched out on the crooked, weather-beaten, shabby west front, I would not have taken in exchange any one, or all, of the Viollet-le-Duc- or Abadie-made perfect churches for St. Etienne in its splendid shabbiness.

III

IF in the cathedral of St. Etienne at Toulouse I saw how fantastic Gothic, imported to the South, was at times, the cathedral of Ste. Cécile at Albi was soon to show me how independent it became at others—so independent that I do not know what the builders of the great Northern churches, who trusted to exuberance of detail for half their effect, would have said to the stern red fortress of a cathedral on the hill above the Tarn. They could hardly have believed it the outgrowth of the style they created, looking in vain, as they must, for the labyrinthine buttresses, the elaborate array of pinnacles, the luxuriance of ornament, that are the glory of the churches they built on the banks of the Seine and the Somme and the Eure. The Gothic of the South, when it is a mere reëcho as at Clermont, suffers from comparison with these masterpieces, but when it is independent with the character of Albi, it cannot be compared to anything save itself. Even if it could, I would still count my first vision of Ste. Cécile's huge mountain of brick as one of the most acute of the many pleasures I have had from the cathedrals of France.

To my regret, I did not come to it first by road, the real way to see cathedrals, but by the leisurely train that crawls through the garden of fruit and vines between Toulouse and Albi. I do not complain of the journey itself, since the fact that Albi is off the main lines of travel has been one of its chief safeguards from popularity. But I do not see how it can long evade the motor. Perhaps because I sat on the wrong side of the train, I had to wait for that first vision of Ste. Cécile until I was driving from the station. Nothing could be less associated than a hotel omnibus with a vision of any kind. But I use the word advisedly, for the solemn red pile, with its austere outline, as it first showed itself through the window, to disappear only too quickly, was so unlike anything I had ever seen that I could not believe it in the least real. And the same evening when, from across the river, I had another view of it, stretching its immense length high above the hillside of houses, I found it, in the unfamiliarity of its silhouette against the twilit sky, more unreal than ever.

It was only the next morning I understood why it is as different from other cathedrals as Albi's old quarter of narrow streets, winding between high brick houses with overhanging roofs, and *loggie,* and women making lace in the dark shadowy doorways, is from the newer quarter of broad boulevards, that are so out of place under the blinding sun of the *Midi,* with the *cafés* where Albi's entire population gathers under the gay awnings at the hour of the *apéritif.* Albi is small, but it has the ambition of every French town to make a little

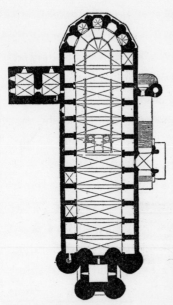

PLAN OF STE. CÉCILE AT ALBI

FROM VIOLLET-LE-DUC'S "DICTIONNAIRE DE L'ARCHITECTURE"

Paris of itself, though not as yet, I am glad to say, the means to sweep away the old houses climbing the hill from the river and huddled together about the cathedral and the Bishop's Palace. An Italian town, you might think, as you walk through the little maze of streets, cool and dark as Southern streets should be, and you pass the ancient houses in every stage of dilapidation, some timbered, some with Renaissance doors and windows, and you stop to look at the church of St. Salvi, its age chronicled in the patchwork of stone and brick of its walls, and its fate revealed in the warren for the poor made of the old abbey cloisters, until at last you reach the quiet *place,* from which the cathedral frowns down upon all the town, both new and old.

There was no suggestion of unreality about those massive red walls as I stood directly below them in the blazing light of the June morning—how could any one who has seen Albi think St. Sernin the finest brick building in the world? But there was still the unfamiliarity, for, as I quickly discovered, the cathedral is without aisles, without transepts, without chapels, without a west front blossoming unrestrainedly toward the sky. There

ALBI CATHEDRAL, FROM THE WEST, AND BRIDGES OVER THE RIVER TARN

is nothing to break its enormous length and height save a series of severe turret-like buttresses, a few ending in pinnacles; a row of long gargoyles projecting from under the eaves; the tall west tower, grim as a castle keep; and, to the southern door, the most elaborate porch Gothic in its most flamboyant flight ever inspired. The hill upon which the cathedral stands slopes downward from the tower, and, in sloping, leaves the level of the cathedral far above it, so that some fifty steps built against the red wall mount to this porch. As you look up to it, from

8

ALBI. WEST FRONT

the door at the foot of the steps, and you see nothing through the high open arch but blue sky, you might fancy it the gate into space, into eternity. And the grace, the delicacy of its detail is as unexpected a flowering from Ste. Cécile's stern heights as a rose-garden would be on the top of Mont Blanc.

I know it has been restored. The story told at Albi is that, at the time of the Revolution, it was sold to a man of the town for a hundred francs, and the broken pieces then left lying uncared for in his back garden, until the people, after their debauch of Free-

ALBI. ENTRANCE TO PORCH

dom, began to pray again, when he gave it back to the cathedral and it was rebuilt as well as possible. But even in rebuilding and restoration it has not lost its stateliness of design and gorgeous-

THE PORCH ON THE SOUTH SIDE OF THE ALBI CATHEDRAL

THE STEPS TO THE SOUTH PORCH OF THE ALBI CATHEDRAL

ness of ornament.   Just below the steps and without the lower
door, and round the fortress-like east end so terrible as you look
upward to it from here, peasants set up their stalls and big
umbrellas, spreading amazing collections of crockery on the
ground, on market-days, with the same familiar confidence in
this fortress of a church as other peasants show in Notre-Dame-
la-Grande at Poitiers and St. Trophime at Arles.

The choir screen is the flamboyant touch to an interior that
is as stern in its structural lines as the exterior, and that was
as unfamiliar the first time I entered from under the canopy
of the porch.   I missed the usual aisles in the nave and
the transepts which the builders in this part of the *Midi*
were glad to dispense with and so avoid the expense of
stone, and the difficulty of brick, columns.   It took me
a long time to understand buttresses that perform the
original feat of projecting inward.   Of only one fact I
was sure, that I had never imagined architectural decoration as amazingly, as incredibly beautiful as the screen
shutting in the choir.   "The most perfect Gothic screen
in France," Mr. Russell Sturgis pronounces it, and he does not
exaggerate.   But to say so with him, to add emphasis by ex-
plaining that this means it is more perfect than the screens of
Chartres and Amiens, gives no idea of the wonder of it, of the
bewildering richness of its carvings and traceries, its multitudinous pinnacles, its canopied niches, its array of statues—of
Christ and his Mother, disciples and apostles, saints and angels,
kings and queens.   These statues are tinted as the sculptors of
near Auvergne loved to tint their work.   But, for all that, to
look at them is to know that no Frenchman ever modeled and
carved and painted them.   They are German—German in sentiment and execution, German in their very excess of realism.
The young women are the same plain, buxom housewives you
see as Blessed Virgins in the Holy Families of the German
painter; the old women are the same amiable matrons, worn

ALBI. ENTRANCE TO CHOIR AISLE

and wrinkled not by prayer and fasting, but by the honest toil of their hands, who posed for St. Anne; the men are the same sturdy, honest, heavy laborers and tradesmen who were the models for St. Joseph. You do not need to see any records to be sure of the nationality of the sculptors, and, for my part, I would not believe the record I did see that pretended to prove them anything save German.

And why should n't they have been German? The southern

THE CHOIR OR EAST END OF THE ALBI CATHEDRAL

THE ENTRANCE FROM THE SOUTH PORCH OF THE ALBI CATHEDRAL

door is believed to be the work of masons who had strayed, nobody knows why, all the way from Strasburg to the town on the banks of the Tarn. And besides, if Dürer traveled here, there, and everywhere to sell his prints, if Holbein set up a

THE CHOIR-SCREEN OF THE ALBI CATHEDRAL

studio in London, why should not the German sculptor, or the German student in his *Wanderjahr,* have journeyed to more improbable places than Albi in search of commissions, and perhaps got stranded there? Nor did Albi ever show any objection to employing the foreigner. The blue, star-strewn ceiling of the cathedral was painted by Italians; so were the dreadful sham columns and cornices and balustrades, in dingy browns and grays, that divide up the buttresses into sham stories, when

all you want to see is the grandeur of their unbroken line from
the floor to the springing of the vaults; so, certainly, was the
more primitive and more decorative Last Judgment, or parable
of the Seven Deadly Sins, on the two huge pillars at the west
end, as certainly as the Last Judgment in the Campo Santo at
Pisa, though, happily, no Morellian has yet descended upon Albi
to present it to the Friend of Anybody by way of proving its
authorship. The painter remains unknown, though some of
those other Italians who came in later centuries were only too
ready to sign their names that we of to-day may know upon

ALBI. SOUTH AISLE—CHOIR

whom to lay the blame. The
bishop who undertook to make a
chapel nobody wanted under the
tower, and whoever erected the
organ—so irresistibly delightful
in its Rococo extravagance, between these two pillars—have
played havoc with the design;
and the gaudy parish altar, now
set up in front, breaks in upon
the somber color scheme. But,
all the same, this Last Judgment
is even now one of the most marvelous of all the marvelous things
in the cathedral, only out-mar-
veled by the screen with its German sculptures. I could never
stay very long from the choir
the screen incloses; but the hour
I felt its beauty most was when
the key was turned in the
wrought-iron gates, and the few
venerable canons, survivors of

the once powerful chapter, tottered into the stalls and sat chant-

END OF THE NAVE TOWARD THE MAIN, OR WEST, FRONT OF THE ALBI CATHEDRAL

ing office there in their weak, old, quavering voices, with the legion of saints and angels all around them.

To "a great rose flamingo soaring up into the blue of the sky," a local historian has likened the cathedral. He is right upon one point. All Albi, as you see it from the river, is rose-flushed. But you might as well compare the Bastille or New-gate Prison to a flamingo or anything that soars. Albi has none of the grace and lightness of the Gothic cathedral of the North. The regularity and simplicity of its lines contribute to the effect of strength and massiveness. Had Ruskin seen it before he wrote his chapter on the Lamp of Power, he might have taken it as the type of the strong old architecture that rose "out of the war of the *piazza* and above the fury of the popu-lace."

It is by its suggestion of power that it impresses, and you do not need Mérimée to tell you it resembles a fortress; you under-stand why it is supposed to recall the gigantic monuments of Egypt and the East. A church for defense, you would say, from every point of view, but above all when you look to its north wall, the grimness here unsoftened by any flamboyant touch, and, close by, the Bishop's Palace, another brick citadel, tall and grim and bare. Having brought with me to Albi, for all knowledge of the place, vague memories of the Albigenses, of the long struggle, bitter and cruel, as only wars in the name of religion ever are, I fancied that the cathedral had been built for the protection of the faithful against the heretic. I had to give up that theory with the first dip into the guide-book. The cathedral was not begun until the end of the thirteenth century, when the wars of the Albigenses were so well over that the price of lands forfeited by the heretics helped to pay for it. But the spirit of the men who had professed their faith on the battle-field must have passed into the builders, or it may be that Albi, having gone through with so much for religion, thought it wise to be prepared for anything it might have to go through

ALBI. ARCHBISHOP'S PALACE, FROM THE RIVER

with again. As it turned out, it had to go through with very little, except the Revolution, and to-day the cathedral holds itself, or is held, wholly apart from the affairs of the town, which, anyway, would be of the most comfortable tranquillity were it not for the daily raid of commercial travelers and the endless strikes in the glassworks.

Before I left Albi, I had explored the town until the cathedral in its every effect was, I hope, familiar to me. I had wandered through the old narrow streets and along the river-bank. I had crossed the bridges over the Tarn, for it is all bridges. I had mounted the winding stairs to the library attached to the

ALBI. FROM THE RIVER

Bishop's Palace, where there are so many rare manuscripts and *incunabula,* and I had looked from its high circular balcony down into the bishop's garden, a space of fruit and flowers and sunshine between the grim red citadel and the river, and beyond to the placid stream with the houses dipping into its waters, and, far away and dim on the horizon, the hills with the faint smoke from the mines hovering above: save for the growing town on the opposite banks and the curling smoke on the horizon, it was the same picture upon which Dominic of Florence and Louis of Amboise, each in his day, gazed as they sauntered along the high terraced walks of their garden, perhaps planning with their architect the porch and the screen that were to grace the cathedral and make their names ever memorable in the chronicles of Albi. But, wander where and as I might, the cathedral was never more imposing than as I saw it from the other side of the bridge that is the continuation of the main street of Albi. For from there it rises far above the river and the green shore, far above the turreted wall of the bishop's garden, far above the heights of the Bishop's Palace, far above the climbing red houses, always beautiful and strong, in the clear light of early morning as in the gathering shadows of night. Strange and lovely as are the scenes on its banks, the Tarn, in its flowing, passes nothing stranger and lovelier than Albi, rose-red, with the rose-red cathedral on its hill.

CHAPTER VII

AN ALBERT DÜRER TOWN: ROCAMADOUR

CHAPTER VII

AN ALBERT DÜRER TOWN: ROCAMADOUR

I

A PHOTOGRAPH which had often attracted us in M. Jusserand's book on "English Wayfaring Life" first made us want to go to Rocamadour, a little town only to be reached, we discovered, by taking the slowest of slow trains between Limoges and Toulouse.

When, after a long morning's journey one hot August day, we finally stopped at the Rocamadour station, we saw no sign of town or village, but a small crowd of French tourists, one carrying a camera, got out with us, and at once a fierce creature, with hoarse voice, big beard, blouse, and a brown *béret* that showed we were getting south, took possession of the entire party with an authority that no one ventured to dispute. "I am the correspondence of Rocamadour," he said, and as soon as the train had gone on, we meekly followed him across the track, through the station-house on the other side, and let him distribute us in three stages that were waiting. The road lay through slightly rolling country, strewn with bits of rock and boulders, and divided by low stone walls. We passed no houses or buildings of any kind until, after we had gone three kilometers or more, we came to a little church and a wayside cross. Here some giggling, chattering country girls waylaid the stage and scrambled up on top, and it was between their stout ankles, incased in bright red stockings and dangling before the front window, that we first looked upon Rocamadour. With a turn of the road we saw the hilly upland over which we had been driving suddenly fall away in steep cliffs to a tiny valley, and where the cliffs were most precipitous a cluster of brown houses and churches clung to them, half-way between the green pasture line far below and the fortified wall, topped by a belfry, which rose from the summit of the rocks. Seen from here, the town

seemed hanging in mid-air, or resting just for a moment on the cliff-side, where the first breath of wind must blow it away, or the first loose rocks dash it to the very bottom of the precipice.

In front of the high wall the driver drew up his horses, the girls sprang down, clambered on the steps and about the windows of the stage, and deluged us with cards, as if every house in Rocamadour were a hotel. I suppose we looked to our driver for help, for he took our bags, handed them to an angular, smiling, middle-aged woman in short skirts, and after her we started down, first, two or three steep and winding flights of stairs, and then a no less steep and winding path, Alpine-like in its many turns. The heavy baggage was left above to be lowered by a great crane set on an overhanging ledge of rock, by which a large portion of the provisions of Rocamadour are dropped into the town. Half-way down the hillside, the last zigzag ended in a little open space in front of a brand-new battlemented gateway. Under this our guide hurried us, and then, without giving us time to look at anything, on through a court shut in on one side by the cliffs, on the others by huge stone buildings, along a narrow tunneled passage, through a second quadrangle, surrounded by chapels, with a little booth to the right where nuns served behind the counter. Another flight of stairs went down to another gateway, which opened upon a small *place* and faced an inn with "Les Saintes Maries" in big letters on its white wall. Its front door led at once into the kitchen, bright with shining copper pots and pans; and Madame, a nice old lady in white cap, left her cooking to show us into a

FROM ACROSS THE VALLEY

room up-stairs, where a crucifix guarded each bed, a Virgin kept watch on the mantelpiece, and a holy-water font hung at the door; of its two windows, one commanded the valley below, the other looked out across the court, where oleanders blossomed in every corner, to the battlemented walls of the sanctuary.

Before the afternoon was over we had explored the hillside, descending by a long stone stairway of one hundred and forty steps from the narrow plateau of the sacred buildings to the village street, and from the village by a long rapidly sloping path to the valley, and we had even wandered up the opposite heights. We found that chance had brought us to a little Albert Dürer town set in an Albert Dürer landscape, as if for the benefit of the medieval draftsman. The tiny green valley, through which winds a stream, dry in midsummer, lies between two precipitous ranges of brown bare hills. The strata of the rock are as regularly and clearly marked as in a Dürer drawing. White roads, in long well-defined lines and zigzags, scale the cliff side; on the top of the hills trees rise singly or in stiff

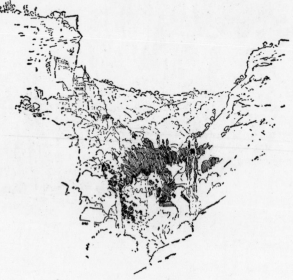

DOWN THE VALLEY

conventional grouping that might have been arranged by Dürer. But most Düreresque, most medieval, is the position of the town upon the cliffs. We saw this best when in the cool of the day we walked to the deserted pigeon-house, more like the ruins of a watch-tower, which stands alone above the valley and faces Rocamadour. Sitting under its shadow, we looked down to where, far below, a man in a white shirt was cutting grass in the low-lying narrow fields, and a few stray poplars were casting long slim shadows; and across to where, from the base of the hill, trees climbed thickly to the long street of white and brown houses, above whose roofs the rock reached upward

ANOTHER VIEW DOWN THE VALLEY

in great heavy cliffs. Out of these, as if part of the strange rock formation, sprang the wall of the sanctuary, with its towers and turrets and battlements grim as any fortress of old. Above, again, the cliffs still more abruptly ascended ever higher —in one place a long low house literally embedded in them; on their topmost ledge rose the fortified walls of the castle built for the defense of Our Lady and her shrine. We might have thought we were looking on an old picture enlarged and thrown by some wonderful new realistic process on a screen of rock, so impossible did it seem that anything as perfectly Middle-Aged should exist in this century of steam and electricity.

II

WE stayed not only that day, but many more in Rocamadour, and our first impression of its medievalism never grew less. That it has a history worthy of its position we learned from a guide-book written by a priest, and sold by the nuns at their little booth.

A DÜRERESQUE ARRANGEMENT

The remote ravine, which hardly a modern English-speaking tourist ever visits, was one of the most famous places of pilgrimage during the ages of faith. It dates back to the first century. When the blessed Saturninus was preaching in Toulouse, and Martial in Limoges, Amadour, their brother in Christ, hid himself from the world in a cave in these wild cliffs.

It was here revealed to him by the Virgin, whom he dearly loved, that henceforth the Shadowy Valley, as it has been called, would be the scene of her holiest miracles.   And Amadour the recluse made this known to the world, until from far and near,

THE TOWN AND THE VALLEY

from remote England and Italy as from the towns of the *Midi,* the faithful flocked, bringing gold and silver and precious stones to lay at the feet of her who had rescued them in the hour of need; and Amadour's name and fame spread as the renown of the Virgin's miracles went abroad, and to-day the tomb against the rock that marks the grave where his body once rested is among the very sacred spots in the sacred inclosure, and is always sprinkled with the *sous* of the devout, who, in their fervor, throw them there, upon the stone figure of the saint stretched behind the iron railing. Before long, in the place of Amadour's cave, there rose on the cliff side a fair shrine to the Virgin, and many chapels and houses where those who were her priests might dwell. All were well fortified, and a strong castle was set above, since in those days one never knew when the enemy might come, and the treasures of Our Lady of Rocamadour were soon great enough to tempt the greedy of gold, and as time went on they became ever greater. And, as about every castle and monastery in those times, a village sprang up close to the holy place, and it, too, had its gates and walls for defense. To the shrine the mightiest in the land journeyed on pilgrimage, sometimes to implore the Virgin's aid, at others to return thanks for her favors; for often the miraculous bell in her chapel rang when no human hands touched it, to announce the wonder worked on far seas where her faithful servant had called upon her name. In the church of St. Sauveur the frescoes on the walls bear witness to the greatness of the princes and nobles who, with the lowliest of their subjects, bowed before Our Lady in humble prayer. Here Louis XI—with how many medals in his hat, I wonder?—and Simon de Montfort, and one Count of Anjou after another

THE SANCTUARIES

came; here not only Henry II, but Englishmen of many ranks and many generations hastened in such numbers that Langland once protested,

> "Right so, if thou be Religious, renne thou never ferther,
> To Rome ne to Rochemadore";

and here Fénélon was brought, when an infant, by his mother, and restored to health by the Virgin so lavish with her tender mercies. But most famous of all the pilgrims was Roland, who, on his way to Roncesvalles, stopped at Rocamadour where he thrust his good sword Durandal into the wall opposite the Virgin's chapel in memory of his vows. Henry II, they say, drew it out in after ages, when before the holy altar he promised reconciliation with Becket; but another quickly replaced it in

THE UPPER CHURCH

honor of the legend, and there the rusted hilt and chain can still be seen.

And then evil days came. The Huguenots made desolate the lonely ravine, pillaged its shrines, and laid waste its sanctuary.

The destruction which they had so well begun the soldiers of the Revolution completed, and the old walls lay in ruins, and Our Lady was forgotten. The desolation might have lasted until now but for the pious zeal of Monseigneur the Bishop of Cahors, who, not many years ago, set about the work of restoration with an energy that would do credit to an English restoring dean or rector. It is he who renewed Rocamadour's old prestige as a center of miracles and a goal of pilgrims. Under his direction the walls, left in sad mutilation by religious and social vandals, have rearisen spick and span. Not from these cheerful windows, with the gay flowers on their ledges, which

THE HOSPICE FROM THE CASTLE

our bedroom faced, were arrows and darts cast upon the enemy; not under this spotless white gateway, with the arms of Monseigneur carved upon it, did the old pilgrims of fame pass. Staringly new are the buildings within the precincts. If once Rocamadour owed as much to its architects as to its cliffs, now little is left of architectural value save the beautiful portal with the faint fresco of the Dance of Death on the white wall close to it, and the graceful arches of Our Lady's chapel.

But there is much that is curious. Chapels of every degree of sanctity still surround the second court, or holy of holies, and open their doors upon it with a symmetry of arrangement which suggested to our profane minds a well-composed scene at a theater.   Besides the chapels, there are, as at Assisi, or San Clemente in Rome, an upper and a lower church.   St. Amadour's, where we discovered nothing of note but the old coffer containing the saint's bones, is the crypt of St. Sauveur's, a bare barn of a place, with rough stone floor, a huge crucifix in

THE MAIN STREET

the center of the nave, and atrocious decorations on the walls, but redeemed from utter commonplaceness by its western wall, formed of the bare cliffs against which the church rests. Where these rocks overhang the court most threateningly, they were turned by the old architects into the roof—a strange slanting roof it is—of a queer little shrine to the archangel Michael, which seems to have taken refuge in the cliffs.   And even in the Miraculous Chapel there has been no effort to conceal them.

THE PLACE OF RETREAT

Against their damp, harsh surface hang the crutches of cripples made whole, and the chains of prisoners set free, which, together with innumerable gold and silver hearts and marble tablets, bracelets, rings, and brooches, have been offered by many generations to the miraculous black statue of Virgin and Child, whose ebony faces peep out from the rich mass of gold-embroidered robes, enthroned above the tabernacle. Perhaps in all Rocamadour there is really nothing more medieval than this chapel. As you sit there you can still see pilgrims prostrate themselves before the altar as in the days of Roland; you can look up to the old bell in the roof, which the priests still believe may wake them some night from their slumbers in divine warning of the miracle worked on foreign seas or shores. There on its golden shrine is the very statue upon which Amadour's eyes rested during his devotions; there on the walls, on every pier and about the tabernacle, are votive offerings as in the centuries long past, when men fought for the Holy Sepulcher and poets sang the praises of Our Lady. The buildings may have been restored, but the faith which raised them, whatever it may be in the world without, has here endured, firm as the cliffs which gave Amadour shelter.

About a mile or less away, in a hamlet high on the hills, are the ruins of the hospice where pilgrims the last night of their pilgrimage rested before they came to pray at the miraculous shrine. Their way was down the road which now makes such a white line on the cañon's side, and through the delightful village street of Rocamadour, still spanned by its four old gateways, with here and there, breaking the pretty monotony of its white houses, an ancient palace showing a Gothic window or Renaissance portal, pink oleanders blossoming in August at almost every door. A shorter cut is by the rough foot-path above the road to the broad terraced walk, with marble benches under the trees, that overhangs the village street, and leads to the first gateway by which we had entered. But the route through the village was the holier because the harder, on account of the one hundred and forty steps up which the pilgrims climbed on their knees, singing hymns.

III

THEY were very quiet, the days we stayed in Rocamadour. Religion is the one occupation, the one trade, of the town, and we were there in an interval between the spring and autumn seasons of devotion. It is in the month of September that the important mission of the year is given, and then the strange house embedded in the rock, best seen from the opposite hillside, and approached only by a narrow balustraded ledge, is filled by the devout, who come to spend eight days in solitude and prayer, and even all the hotels are crowded. While we were at the Saintes Maries many people came and went, chiefly ladies with rosaries prominent, and priests in black gowns, who, except at breakfast and dinner hours, were always within the sacred precincts. Never, however, did we find the great multitude of pilgrims of whom our landlady liked to talk, and who, in a few more weeks, would descend upon Rocamadour. Then there would be bustle enough in the pretty street where, during the day, we saw nothing gayer than the old gray-haired women sitting with their distaffs under the oleander blossoms, or pigs and goats wandering amiably up and down, or a packhorse, home from weary travels over the neighboring hills; where, at night, the only lights were from the dying fire in a kitchen which a white-capped woman was putting to rights, or the single candle in a dark *café,* around which two or three men in blouses were playing cards.

There was, however, something in the daily life of the place, even in midsummer when comparatively deserted, that reminded me pleasantly of my convent days. I might have fancied myself back at Eden Hall, where all existence was regulated by church bells and rounded by a prayer. There was always on the steps and paths and in the precincts a flutter of nuns' robes and priests' cassocks, for a community of Sisters in charge of the holy shop live in a white house just beyond the hotel, and a dozen or more missionaries are established in the white château away at the top, reached either by the zigzags up the hillside, or by a mysterious steep dark stairway cut right through the rock from the loft of St. Sauveur's to the priests' bright flower garden. One of these missionaries, a friendly plump little

fatherly man, would, with the greatest pleasure, have baptized us both offhand; indeed, so determined was he that I don't
know what might have happened if at the week's end we had
not started suddenly for Toulouse. At all hours we used to
find people kneeling in the Miraculous Chapel, or making the
way of the cross under white umbrellas, starting from the gate
of the sanctuary, stopping to pray at every station, panting and

THE WAY OF THE CROSS

puffing on benches conveniently placed under the trees, finishing
at the sepulcher and great pilgrims' cross on the hilltop, and
then rushing frantically down for a last *sirop* or *absinthe* before
leaving, while the fiercely impatient "correspondence" of Rocamadour waited above under the cross, thundering his *"Sapr-r-r-
risti!* when are you coming to take the stage?" after them down
the ravine. At the inn of the Saintes Maries we were forced

to abstain whether we would or no, and were given no meat on Friday. On the hot breathless evenings, when in the twilight we wandered along the high mule track, from the valley below would come the voices of children singing *"C'est le mois de Marie"* and other convent hymns of my childhood. And day and night there hung over Rocamadour a monastic-like peace—the peace of a place which, to the people who live there, is, like the hospice of old, but one of many stations on the long pilgrimage to another and better life.

CHAPTER VIII

NOTRE-DAME AND OTHER CHURCHES IN PARIS

CHAPTER VIII

NOTRE-DAME AND OTHER CHURCHES IN PARIS

I

OFTEN as I have seen Notre-Dame, the marvel of it never grows less. I go to Paris with no thought or time for it, busy about many other things. And then, on my way perhaps over one of the bridges across the river, I see it again, there on its island, the beautiful towers high above the high house and palace roofs, and the view, now so familiar, strikes me afresh with all the wonder of my first impression.

The wonder only seems greater if I turn, as I am always tempted to, and walk down the *quais* on the left bank, the towers ever before me, and with every step coming more and more completely together; by the *Pont Neuf,* to the island; and, at last, to the great square where Notre-Dame fronts you in its superb calm. When you come close to it, so close as to take in the detail, there may be one moment of disappointment, for the restorer has not spared it. Nor has time been altogether kind, for the gradual leveling up of the *place* has dwarfed the great façade. But, from the other end of the wide, open square, the detail of restoration disappears, dignity has not entirely gone with the steps that once led up to the west doors, and you are conscious solely of the stateliness and splendor and harmony the old builders gave to their design. Notre-Dame is "the only

THE MAIN FAÇADE OF NOTRE-DAME FROM THE LEFT BANK OF THE
SOUTH BRANCH OF THE SEINE

un-Greek thing that unites neatness and majesty, elegance and awfulness," R. A. M. Stevenson, who knew and loved it, said. But, serene as it may be at most hours, in the evening light neatness is lost in the majesty of mass, during the storm or shower you are awed into forgetting the lighter quality of elegance, and you will form another idea of the vastness and

THE DOORS OF THE WEST, OR MAIN, FAÇADE OF NOTRE-DAME

height of Notre-Dame from the top of one of the lofty old houses on the near *quais,* with the extraordinary arrangement of bridges in the foreground.

There may also be moments of disappointment in the interior. I sometimes wish I had never seen it except during High Mass or some great ceremonial. They have fine music at Notre-Dame, and the right respect for ritual, and the stately architecture makes an appropriate background for the pageant of religion. But when the last priest in the procession has passed into the sacristy, when the last note of the organ has died away, when the last member of the congregation has dipped his, or more likely her, fingers in the holy water at the door, when you are alone in the silent aisles, then you cannot help feeling how barren this vast interior is of the color and warmth, the sentiment and atmosphere, of an old Catholic church. Once it must have been as perfect a background for prayer as for pageant. But, first Soufflot sweeping away stained glass, carved stalls, tombs, brasses, wholesale, in the name of Beauty, and then Republicans defiling what was left in the name of Reason, turned it into an abomination of desolation, stripping it bare, chilling it to the marrow; and the chill is still there. The dishonor they did to the architecture was long since repaired, and the architect may take his pleasure to-day in Viollet-le-Duc's version of what the old architectural plan ought to have been. But only the centuries can restore that which it took centuries to build up. There are no chapels laden and glowing with the spoils of

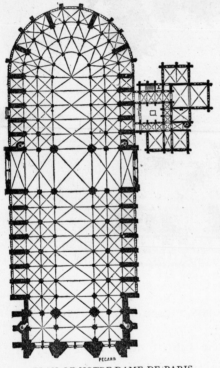

PLAN OF NOTRE-DAME DE PARIS

FROM VIOLLET-LE-DUC'S "DICTIONNAIRE DE L'ARCHITECTURE"

ages of devotion, no bewildering medley of old tombs mellowed and stained by time, no delicious little architectural inconsistencies born of the caprice of piety, no picturesque disorder or ornament on walls and columns. It may be that to come into Notre-Dame from the sunny square is to plunge into darkness, but dim as the light is, I have never

THE WEST, OR MAIN, FAÇADE OF NOTRE-DAME AFTER A SHOWER

found it religious. It needs no wild flight of imagination to discover why, to Huysmans' hero, Notre-Dame seemed a cathedral without a soul.

But there is another view that gives quite another impression —the view of the east end from the river. It is said that Notre-Dame is lost, hidden, ineffectual in the big modern town, which it does not dominate as it dominated the Paris of St. Louis. This is, in a measure, true. You never think of Paris as a cathedral city, as you do of Chartres, or Albi, or Laon. It is

A BIT OF THE NAVE AND TRANSEPT OF NOTRE-DAME

NAVE AND TRANSEPT. NOTRE-DAME

just a big city where there happens to be a cathedral because a cathedral, like museums and palaces, has come to be considered an indispensable ornament of a big city. In the life of the boulevards and the *Bois,* Notre-Dame may be, probably is, forgotten. Indeed, it would be easy to pass weeks and months in

Paris, and to be never as much as reminded of its existence except from the top of an omnibus on a hurried journey between the *Grands Magazins du Louvre* and the *Bon Marché,* or from the *quais* on a chance visit to the bookstalls there, or from the well-known little restaurant of the *Rive Gauche,* where a glimpse of the towers through an up-stairs window adds zest to the good dinner or breakfast.   But as you see it, if you go for the purpose to the *quais* on the left bank farther east, or if you come down the river from Charenton, Notre-Dame still

THE NAVE FROM THE CHOIR.   NOTRE-DAME

dominates the *Ile de la Cité,* which, with the nearer shores, is the Paris of St. Louis. As you approach in one of the little crowded boats, it appears to fill the island, as if the island had been designed to hold it from all eternity. The garden at this distance dwindles into a fringe of green to give value to the purple depths, a scale to the massive height, of that wonderful

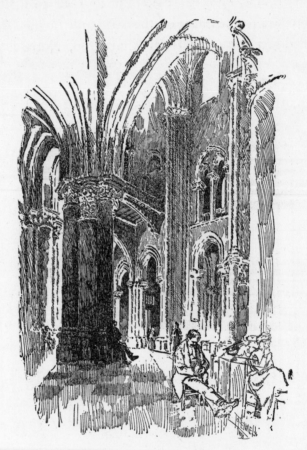

WEST END OF NAVE. NOTRE-DAME

apse with its labyrinth of flying buttresses and tall pinnacles. And the water between seems to isolate the cathedral, to remove it to a world apart, to some unexplored Garden of Armida where the church is the enchantress. Now it is all mystery, mystery above and beyond the melodrama of Victor Hugo;

THE NORTH SIDE OF NOTRE-DAME FROM THE NORTH BRANCH OF THE SEINE

mystery unrevealed to Méryon, though he etched very much the same view from the *Quai de la Tournelle* and fashion has made his mechanical plate famous; mystery that deepens when, at evening, detail is swallowed up in the gathering shadows, and Notre-Dame rises black and solemn against the sunset, now, in very truth, the "mountain of mystery" you hoped for.

But, wonderful as is the east end, Notre-Dame reserves its greatest wonder until you have gone in by that little door at the base of the northern tower, paid your half-franc to the man

sitting in the tiny office just inside, and climbed the narrow
stone stairway that goes winding up, and up, and forever up.
Now and then, through the darkness, glimmers a ray of light,
widening, as you draw nearer, into a slit of a window through
which you look out upon a bewildering mass of roofs, or, as you
climb higher, to clear sky.   Higher still, the ray becomes a

THE EAST END OF NOTRE-DAME FROM THE SOUTH BRANCH OF THE SEINE

space of light as if heaven were opening above you.   And you
climb, and you climb, and the space develops into a door, and
you go through it, and you are, not in heaven, but in the inner-
most circle of hell itself.   For it is up here, from their airy
platform, that the Devils of Notre-Dame watch over Paris.
Wherever you turn, there, perched on the dizzy parapet, are
monsters, demons, chimera straight from out the Middle Ages,

THE EAST END OF NOTRE-DAME FROM THE NORTH BRANCH OF THE SEINE

horrible, vile, revolting, even in restoration: the most Middle-Aged horrors that the medieval artist ever imagined. The *Stryge,* with elbows on the parapet for ease, face supported on long, slim, demon-like hands, tongue stuck out straight in a malicious sneer at that most splendid, most characteristic monument of modern Paris, the *Arc de Triomphe,* and all it represents; the leering ape and the nameless creature who both lean well over for a better view, their loathsome open-mouthed grin broadening as they lean; the obscene beast, half cow, half

THE GROTESQUE,
CALLED "LE STRYGE" (VAMPIRE),
ON THE MAIN FAÇADE

woman, lolling comfortably, with arms crossed, and evil eye wandering far away to the dainty little church of St. Etienne; the hungry ghouls; the insatiable vampires; the unclean flock of birds, one so grotesquely like Gladstone—there they all are, an infernal cohort of Devils, really looking, really laughing at the farce of civilization played for their benefit.

And the farce that makes them laugh, we glory in as art, we respect as history, we reverence as tradition. Think, for a minute, what the church is that serves as their pedestal: Notre-Dame, praised above all for its sanity, its virtues almost classic, ranked with Chartres and Bourges "among the most satisfactory Gothic cathedrals we possess," in Fergusson's guarded language; as the most perfect example of "the era of the great cathedrals," in the praise of more enthusiastic writers. In other churches devils almost as grotesque may be found, but they have their part, useful or decorative, in the general scheme. The most ingenious of those modern critics who know more about the motives of the medieval artist than he did himself could not assign to the Devils of Notre-Dame any function in the architectural design, any shadow of utility as a reason for their being there. They do not decorate the gallery; they cannot be seen from below; I doubt if, until Méryon's etching gave the *Stryge* its fame, the world in general had discovered their existence. They point no moral; they are not, like gargoyles, useful as drain-pipes; nor could the most obstinate seeker after symbols make them symbolize anything, except the caprice, or the cynicism, of the sculptor. They add nothing to the cathedral, they do nothing for it, they represent nothing. I can remember no collection like them except at Rheims, and there the grotesques perch on the balustrade above the apse, where they can be seen from below and where they have the decorative value of pinnacles. On Notre-Dame's airy platform they are as inconsequent as a howl of Eulenspiegel laughter would be at the end of the "Divine Comedy," or Satan, cloven-hoofed, horned, with barbed tail, enthroned among Fra

THE CREST OF THE NAVE. NOTRE-DAME

Angelico's saints and angels. In their hellish company the "Notre-Dame" of Victor Hugo, who, R. A. M. Stevenson says, "has treated it as the London atmosphere treats all things," becomes something more than a fabric of romantic rhetoric. Quasimodo swinging with the great bell, Claude Frollo hurled into space, are no longer mere marionettes of melodrama. If you stayed up there long

THE ROSE WINDOW IN THE NORTH END OF THE TRANSEPT OF NOTRE-DAME

enough, you too would yield to their uncanny spell. The very cat that lived with them a few years ago, as it went springing from precipice to precipice of stone wall, as it ran and leaped and crawled over pinnacles and along sharp ledges, seemed like one of the demons come to life, while the

THE FLÈCHE FROM THE TOP OF THE TOWERS. NOTRE-DAME

stories the *gardien* used to tell of mad leaps, of the sudden swift jump of the suicide to death, made the blood curdle as no tale of horror on the printed page ever could.

The traditions of Notre-Dame are as glorious as its architecture. Of the history of France, from the time of Philip-Augustus, it is the record, according to Viollet-le-Duc; from the beginning of time, he might have written. For the history of France centers around the island, and the history of the island centers around the spot where Notre-Dame replaced the earlier Christian churches of St. Etienne and Ste. Marie, and they had succeeded the Roman temple of Jupiter, and it, most likely, had been erected on the site of an older altar of the Gauls, which had sprung up from the primeval wilderness. All the characters in the obscure drama of events that made the old Lutetia—Julian's "little darling city"—into the Christian capital of Christian France, flit like phantoms, or strut like heroes, about the sacred place on the island: Clovis and Ste. Geneviève, Childebert and the complicated family of kings who lived and died, I used to fancy in my school-days, for my torment; St. Denis, St. Marcel, and a host of others as holy, but of reputation so local it had not reached my old convent home, though the hospitality extended there to saints of all nations was without limit. And no matter who reigned in later days, no matter what the form of government, you cannot get away from the island and its cathedral. To Notre-Dame the kings came from Rheims to offer thanks; in Notre-Dame they lay in state before they were carried to St. Denis. Sansculottism took possession of it. Napoleon looked to it for his most dramatic effects. The Commune would have done away with it forever. Under its shadow the laws of France have been administered, criminals punished—what associations from the *Conciergerie* alone!—the sick tended, gossip manufactured. You could not separate it, if you would, from the drama of France in the making. And, if you could, the Paris of to-day would still be the stage, the life of

11

Paris in its most intimate aspect the play for that audience of
mocking, gibing Devils.   There, immediately below, is the
heart of the island with the huge *Hôtel-Dieu* and the *Palais de
Justice,* the *Sainte-Chapelle* of St. Louis springing up like a
delicate flower in its midst.   On either side, far as the eye can
reach, is the town they have watched during centuries, as it

NORTH DOORWAY.   NOTRE-DAME

spread ever northward toward Montmartre, ever southward
toward the hill of Ste. Geneviève, and beyond, and still beyond.
Here and there a familiar landmark breaks the monotonous
vista of houses; on the one side, the graceful tower of St.
Jacques, the long line of the Louvre, the tall *Arc de Triomphe,*
in the late afternoon a gate to the flaming splendor of the sunset, and on the horizon, of a clear day, a cloud of smoke to
show where St. Denis stands, waiting for the kings who will
come there no more to sleep; on the other side, the *Institut,* the

Panthéon, St. Etienne with the near *Tour de Clovis* that, from here, seems but a part of it.   In front, the river flows seaward, tranquilly as when no bridges were thrown across its current, and the wilderness on its banks was one not of houses, but of forest and swamp.   Away in the distance, insolent symbols flaunting themselves against the sky, rise, to the left, the Eiffel Tower, that "gigantic specter of recent civilization"; to the right, Abadie's sham Byzantine Church, that lofty monument to the dead art of architecture.   And on the near bridges and streets and squares, the crowds come and go, little black pygmies to the watcher from the cathedral heights, and the roar of the great city fills the air.   All Paris is there, the Paris of a noble past, the Paris of an ambitious present.   And this, to the Devils of Notre-Dame, is, as it always has been, a farce for inextinguishable laughter.

II

THOUGH the Devils laugh, Notre-Dame is still the scene of church and civic ceremonial.   St. Denis, under that cloud of smoke you see on a clear day from the Devils' platform, is now but a sad derelict of the past to which both belong, the Historical Monument, forgotten by all save the tourist, and stranded in an ugly industrial quarter.

To get the full dramatic effect of the contrast, the way to go to St. Denis is by the electric tram that starts from just behind the Madeleine.   It takes you through a long unlovely workmen's quarter to the *Barrière;* through a dreary stretch of the kitchen gardens that encircle the city outside the walls as they once did within, and gaunt factories with tall chimneys belching smoke, and occasional barracks of houses; through a wide street of dull shops, crossed by other streets only a trifle less wide and a trifle more dull, all alike, except that one leads to the church where the Kings of France lie buried.   The only conspicuous feature in the journey is, when beyond the fortifications you look back, the domed *Sacré-Cœur* high on Montmartre, the Hill of the Martyrdom ever since St. Denis lost his head there for Christ. His miraculous walk, his head in his hand, as he appears in countless French pictures and sculptures, was over much the same route the tram follows, but "the faire crosses of stone carved with fleurs de lys," as Evelyn saw them, at the points where St. Denis laid down his head and rested, are gone. Industry takes no stock in sentiment or tradition.

When *place* and street in front are empty, St. Denis carries off its fallen fortunes with something of dignity. But as I last saw it, on a spring day, when the new conscripts of the year had gathered just outside, dancing, singing, buying big paper rosettes, not one with a thought or a glance to fling to it, the church struck me as being only in the way, useless, out of gear with the new life that had grown up about it, preserved entirely from a sense of duty. It looked to me forlorn with its one melancholy western tower; with the restorer's work half done on the exterior—not that I am not glad the work is only half done, but that it should be is exceptional in France, where restoration is so often overdone; with the long rank uncut grass in the inclosure to the north of the nave; with the mean houses shutting in the east end. And where care has been given, it is to mark it more unmistakably as the *Monument Historique,* the mere survival, its real life long since spent. The fine interior, so like and so unlike Westminster Abbey, has become a museum, practically; the royal tombs, reached by that picturesque wide stairway to the ambulatory, suggest in their neat rows so many specimens, labeled and catalogued. You cannot see without emotion tombs like that of the good King Dagobert—great, too, though best remembered for the affair of the breeches in the song—of Louis XII, Henri II, Francis I, with their beautiful sculptures, of the last of the Bourbons, with their bitter memories. But to follow the sacristan, as he drones out the story learned by heart and repeated until his very voice betrays his boredom with the whole business of royalty, alive or dead, is to see in St. Denis nothing save the show place for tourists. And this is the church that not even Notre-Dame can outrival in the sanctity or splendor of its past; its site chosen by

THE MAIN FAÇADE OF THE CATHEDRAL OF ST. DENIS

the holy man who was first bishop, first martyr, first saint of Paris; the building founded by Ste. Geneviève, whose first chapel over his grave grew eventually into the church in which the Abbé Suger made the first experiment with the pointed arch on so large a scale—the first great Gothic church: St. Denis, the shrine of the Oriflamme of France, the Louvre, or Versailles, of dead royalty.

And so it remains, but a Louvre, or Versailles, shaken by the storm of Liberty, Equality, and Fraternity. Patriots of 1793 had no more use for dead royalty in its tomb than living royalty in its palace. And, after "Patriotism has been down among the tombs rummaging," had played ball with the skeletons of kings —having to stop to hold its nose when that worst of old enemies

THE SOUTH AISLE OF THE CATHEDRAL OF ST. DENIS

Louis XV, appeared, suffering a relapse into loyalty before the embalmed body of that old favorite, Henri IV—after royal bones and royal ashes had been dumped into one unroyal common grave, after royal tombs had been broken and royal statues mutilated, there was not much left of St. Denis. But, defaced, roofless, a haunt of birds of prey, it was at least an eloquent monument to the hatred of the Third Estate for kings and priests. After the tombs, or so much of them as could be, were brought back by Louis XVIII, after new noses and hands and draperies were found for the poor dishonored effigies, after the building was roofed in, its walls mended, and everything generally put to rights by indefatigable Viollet-le-Duc, St. Denis was doomed to make its strongest appeal to the curiosity of the tourist. It is the irony of fate that royalty, dead forever in France, should rest, not in the capital, not in the cathedral, but in the parish church—to this rank has St. Denis been degraded —of a busy industrial center, the headquarters of Anarchists, where the people who killed it are too busy to remember, much less to resent, the presence of its tomb in their midst.

There may be other places of interest in the suburb of St. Denis. I never looked for them. I am content with my last impression of it, with wide street of dull shops and electric trams, with groups of conscripts, with gaunt factories, with chimneys belching smoke,—and with the old sad church, the last resting-place of the royalty France sacrificed a century ago, that just such a busy industrial town might live and prosper.

III

IT seems in keeping that the other saint whom Paris claims as its own—Ste. Geneviève—should also provide, in the church consecrated to her memory, a contrast as striking and as typical of the city which she loved. After the Patriotism that sacked St. Denis and worshiped Reason at Notre-Dame had scattered her ashes to the four winds of heaven, and burned the *Chasse,* emptied of them, in the *Place de Grève,* that place of cruel memories, St. Etienne-du-Mont, the little church on the high windy mountain under the shadow of the *Panthéon,* fell sole heir to her tomb and its associations. The virtue of Paris is said to be its faculty for remaining true to tradition on the traditional spot. The Romans would find the metropolitan church where they had their Temple of Jupiter; St. Louis would find justice administered where he held his open court; and so

THE AISLE OF ST. ETIENNE-DU-MONT, LOOKING EAST

Thomas Aquinas and Abelard would find the shrine of Ste. Geneviève still in the students' quarter, where they remembered it.

If at St. Denis you may study Gothic architecture at its dawn;
if at Notre-Dame you may enjoy it in its perfection; for its de-

THE CHOIR OF ST. ETIENNE-DU-MONT

cadence, its transition into Renaissance, you may go to St.
Etienne-du-Mont. Those who burn the Lamp of Obedience to

Ruskin will see in it nothing save the seven deadly sins of architecture. But I, burning no such lamp, think, with R. A. M. Stevenson, that it is a "charming church"—a church of great elegance and grace and holiness. Like Abbé Suger, its builders had the courage of experiment and their own individuality. They preserved all that pleased them in the old Gothic, they borrowed all that seemed best from the new school, and they made the adaptation with such independence and also such leisureliness, the building going on through a century, that there is not another church just like it. And St. Etienne, as one of its *abbés* says in a delightful little guide, knew how to be faithless to the traditions of art and follow its own caprice, without compromising its harmony. Certainly nothing is compromised in the west front, which is harmony itself. Nor in the interior, which is all lightness and airiness, an effect due chiefly to the open arcade replacing the usual triforium and clearstory; while caprice could not be more capricious than in the choir screen, with its stairs to the gallery, deliberately for ornament and careless of utility, winding about the piers on either side. Even the beautiful old windows contribute to the effect of airiness, for they date no further back than the sixteenth century, when the designers of stained glass were tired of the old somber schemes, but had not gone to the deplorable extreme of what has been called the Protestantism of *grisaille,* or no color at all. A worldly little church you would say, designed for feasting, not fasting, for the silks and satins of the courtier rather than the sackcloth and ashes of the penitent; as the church in which religious art died, Martin disposes of it in his history.

Religious art may have died, but not religion. For this "charming church," bright, gay, capricious, worldly, is the holiest place of pilgrimage in Paris. To pass from the nave and its aisles to the solemn chapel, where lights burn about the golden shrine of Ste. Geneviève, is to leave all suggestion of levity and worldliness behind you. People always kneel before the tomb, rapt in an ecstasy of prayer. A priest in surplice, his stole by his side, is always in attendance. Without being a Catholic, you can appreciate the beauty of fidelity in this homage paid, after fifteen hundred long years, to the little shepherdess by the people of the city she saved from the barbarians. God, it was said, meant her to do great things, and she did them.

And St. Etienne is filled to overflowing with other memories, inherited from the church of Ste. Geneviève, of which time has spared only the tower—the *Tour de Clovis*—you see rising from the *Lycée Henri IV* on the other side of the *Rue Clovis*. Of the basilica founded by Clovis it is the legitimate descendant, rather than that huge Temple built by Soufflot and now dedicated by a grateful country to its Great Men. A marble tablet at St. Etienne records many of these memories in a gold-lettered list of Merovingian kings, before which I find myself trembling as if it were the condensation of the awful school-book in which I was supposed to master early French history. And its memories are not exhausted by the tablet. The names of Racine and Pascal, among the dead it has honored, open literary vistas. To finish its story would mean to be confronted with ignoble crime there, in the sanctuary, where an unoffending archbishop fell before the assassin as late as 1857. But St. Etienne bears its associations as gaily as Paris, the city laden with a great, a stupendous past, chronicled in these three of its churches—St. Denis, Notre-Dame, St. Etienne—but on the surface light-hearted, with a charm irresistible to itself and to all the world besides.

CHAPTER IX

CHARTRES—THE HOUSE OF PRAYER

CHAPTER IX

CHARTRES—THE HOUSE OF PRAYER

I

I LIKE best to remember the cathedral of Chartres as I first saw it, on a wild, stormy evening in May. I had come late to the town, and when I went out to look about me, between showers, I hoped for little more than a glimpse of the exterior in the windy dusk. There was a flare of lamps, a screech of steam-organs in the long *Place des Epars,* which was filled with the booths and tents of the May fair. But it was dark and deserted in the little streets leading to the cathedral, a fearful wall of rock as it loomed up before me under the cloud-driven sky. A gale swept across the open square, but I faced it for the sake of those first impressions that count so much in getting to know cathedrals, like people, in the right way, and I was glad I did. For, in another minute, two or three women coming out of the door to the right showed that the cathedral was open, as it had not occurred to me it could be at so late an hour.

I hurried up the steps, passing under a high arched doorway where the pale, faint light from the nearest street lamp fell fitfully on rows of colossal forms, strange and awful as they towered above me in the mysterious gloom. Dusk dropped into night on the other side of the heavy curtain at the door, and I had to grope my way up the incense-laden nave. But, presently, I was conscious of a dim glow far in front and the sound of distant singing. The glow grew more golden as I went on, the singing louder. Huge columns came out of the darkness. I saw, deeper shadows in the shadow of the aisles, a vast multitude kneeling. I saw, of a sudden between the columns, an altar hung with lamps and ablaze with candles—the altar of the Blessed Virgin. Then I understood. It was the service for the month of May, which is the Month of Mary with Catholics everywhere, and the voices were those of children gathered about a nun at the organ, and their song was the old sweet canticle of my convent days, sung in the same sweet childish voices:

C'est le mois de Marie,
C'est le mois le plus beau.
A la Vierge chérie
Chantons un chant nouveau.

As my eyes grew accustomed to the place I could see that there were many men in the congregation and a large sprinkling

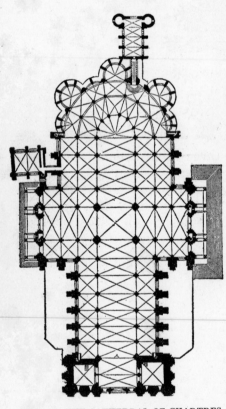

PLAN OF THE CATHEDRAL OF CHARTRES

FROM VIOLLET-LE-DUC'S "DICTIONNAIRE DE L'ARCHITECTURE"

of soldiers, and that the devotion was intense. A sermon was preached by the priest, who reminded the people of Chartres of the maternal love *Notre-Dame-du-Pilier* on the altar there had always shown them, and the miracles she had worked for them, and the special privileges she had accorded them, and he followed, stage by stage, her history through the centuries as they must so often have heard it before. Then came benediction, a moment's almost audible silence as the priest raised the ostensorium in blessing. And then, once more, the little nun struck the notes of the organ, and the children's voices rose in song.

CHARTRES. THE NAVE

When the last prayer was at an end, I followed the people through the transept door to another great porch, and again colossal forms, strange and awful, towered vaguely all about me. Had I never seen the cathedral a second time, that is how I should remember it: without, a fearful wall of rock under a cloud-driven sky, mystic figures on guard at its entrance; within, "dim, spacious, fragrant, and afloat with golden lights" as in the dreaming of Gaston de Latour.

II

As it happened, I had seen the cathedral at many hours and under many aspects before I was ready to leave Chartres. On the brilliant morning after the storm, the wall of rock rising from the wide *place* became a façade of noble design with two tall spires: arms upstretched, hands joined in supplication, lovers of Chartres have fancied them. The colossal forms at the entrance took more distinct shape as statues of kings and saints, the most splendid sculptures the artist ever set at a church door. There was still something rocklike, even in broad daylight, about the vast pile of the cathedral, with its titanic blocks of stone, its great cliffs of buttresses, its austere simplicity—the simplicity of the earlier Gothic builders. But as I drew near, I found that this exterior, as a whole so impressive in its austerity, was overflowing with ornament. It was extraordinary to me, the way the south tower, *le clocher vieux* they call it in Chartres, "the most beautiful medieval tower in Europe" the "Dictionary of Architecture" describes it, could interrupt the severity of its outlines to place an angel, with wings spread and a sun-dial for burden, at its southern angle, and use the stern sweep of its southern wall for a background to beasts monstrously evil and of close kinship to the Devils of Notre-Dame-de-Paris. It was extraordinary that the tower rising side by side with it, *le clocher neuf* (for it is as new as the sixteenth

12

CHARTRES CATHEDRAL. WEST FRONT

century), should be nothing but ornament, in deed and in truth, as in Mr. Henry James's phrase, a "sort of tapering bouquet of sculptured stone." Most extraordinary of all, however, was the elaborate loveliness of the doorways and transept porches.

CHARTRES. STATUES ON WEST SIDE

At Chartres, as elsewhere in France, after the destroyer of the eighteenth century came the restorer of the nineteenth. When I was there last, bald new patches on the south porch were witnesses of his recent industry, the north porch was hidden under the litter of his scaffolding, and his mark was visible on the Romanesque doors of the west front. But about

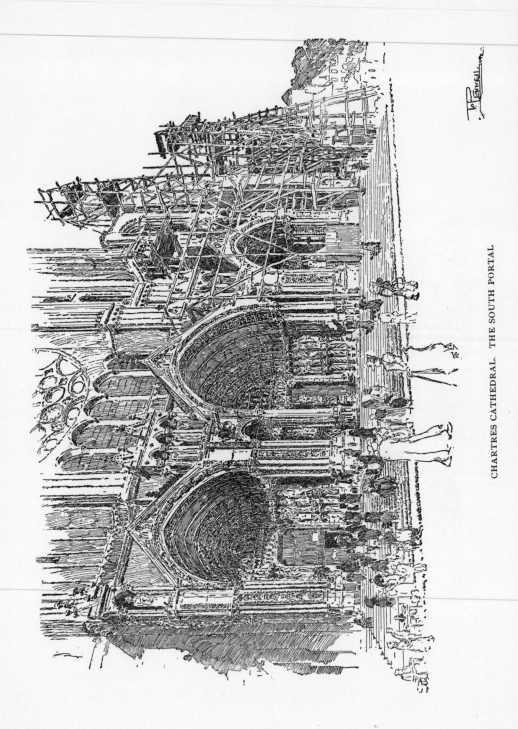

CHARTRES CATHEDRAL. THE SOUTH PORTAL

CHARTRES. THE SOUTH TRANSEPT

these doors the amazing statues of the twelfth century had not gone from the niches, and on their long, slim, attenuated figures the draperies still fell in the old rigid lines, on their inscrutable faces the smile still hovered. Who are they? The critics might

CHARTRES CATHEDRAL. THE NORTH PORCH

LOOKING INTO THE NORTH TRANSEPT FROM THE NAVE

be of as many minds about them as about any early Florentine or Sienese Madonna on her gold ground, and I would not care. I am content to know, and you cannot help knowing it if you look at them, that living, breathing, real flesh-and-blood men and women, if mere models at a bare pittance an hour, posed for them; that the sculptor was an artist, sometimes Gothic, sometimes Greek, who could see and feel and express character. His method of expressing it may be primitive according to modern notions, but many moderns aping the primitive have exhausted their meager originality in trying to imitate them.

And the stately transept porches are a mass of sculptures, of statues wherever statues can go, standing in lines on either side the six doors and on every column, climbing with the pointed arches, filling every niche and corner. Conscientious writers take it upon themselves to tell you of whom all are portraits or what they symbolize, but it cannot be done without degenerating frankly into a catalogue. Even Huysmans' descriptions of them read like an inventory. And, after all, they are there really to add to a building, structurally perfect, the beauty of detail that is a great part of the charm of Chartres.

The sunshine of La Beauce, transformed into angry imperious fire as it falls through the cathedral windows, could never make the interior less solemn than it had seemed in my first evening vision of it. I know no other church so entirely a House of Prayer. Everybody who goes to it will tell you the same thing. "Chartres has still the gift of a unique power of impressing," Pater says, stirred by the esthetic value of religion in such a setting; "nowhere does one pray so well as at Chartres," Huysmans says, feeling its power more intimately. It is not easy to explain just why this should be, any more than why out of an endless gallery of Madonnas a rare canvas by Piero della Francesca or Bellini will catch the eye and haunt the memory. Piety of itself alone would have been as poor an equipment for the builder of cathedrals as for the painter of

CHARTRES. FROM THE NORTH SIDE

Madonnas. Nor is the fact that the architecture of Chartres belongs to the period of Gothic masterpieces a sufficient explanation. Paris and Bourges and Laon and Amiens show the same architectural perfection, they belong to the same period, but from none of them do you get the same impression of mysterious majesty, the same urgent call to prayer. Other cathedrals are larger; some have the same five aisles and as spacious

CHARTRES. WESTERN DOOR, NORTH PORCH

an apse encircled by chapels; one at least, Le Mans, repeats the imposing arrangement of windows in the choir. And yet none can so awe you as Chartres does by the solemnity, the sublimity of size, by the height of nave and choir, by the endless vistas of aisles beyond aisles, chapels beyond chapels, columns beyond columns, by the dignity of an austere exterior, with spires pointing to heaven, and buttresses that not even the wheel-like supports to their bold flight over the aisles can make less severe, less vigorous in mass. There is no possible explanation except Pater's when he speaks of some secret touch of genius in the builders of Chartres.

The cathedral grows in solemnity and immensity the more you see it. Chance, it is true, has been more careful of Chartres than of most French cathedrals in sparing much of the detail without which the most perfect church seems bare and empty and cold. There never was a time when the interior, as in so many Italian churches, was rich in tombs where the dead, arms folded, kneel or lie on their delicately carven beds of stone and marble, or sit astride their horses, gallant and picturesque figures in death as in life. The faithful at Chartres saw in their church a bed for the Blessed Virgin, and could find no room in it for the tombs of men. If there was room once for innumerable altars, most of them, except the holiest, have disappeared. Lost too is a part of the old decoration, for, to our misfortune, it was offensive to the generation who believed with Racine that Chartres was barbarous in its grandeur, and who, to reduce it to their level of refinement, pulled down rare tapestries from the choir wall and exchanged them for cold, formal reliefs that, I venture to say, no one now ever troubles to look at, got rid of old carved stalls and the fourteenth-century *jubé,* employed Bridan to design his posturing, acrobatic group of the Assumption, which might be amusing in a palace but is disastrous as an altar-piece, and then, the better to flaunt their pedantic commonplace before the world, knocked out from the choir window some of the beautiful old stained glass that had been the gift of that barbarian in their eyes, St. Louis. Nor could the storm of the Revolution pass over Char-

CHARTRES. NORTH TRANSEPT WINDOW

tres without leaving desolation behind it, and it broke there with its maddest violence, for Paris, the storm-center, was not so many miles away.

But the beautiful old choir screen survived the century of desecration so well that, at least, restoration could not ruin it. There are people who, with Mérimée, object to a choir screen because it breaks up the constructional lines of the architecture and the effect of length and height. But at Chartres it gives back a hundredfold in mystery all it may take away in symmetry. Over and above this, it gives, with its elaborate sculptures and intricate canopies, a richly fretted surface where the colored radiance from the windows falls more softly and the shadows deepen into infinite depths. These sculptures, like everything else in the cathedral, are devoted to Our Lady of Chartres and tell the story of her life from the moment when, to St. Joachim, watching his sheep, the angel appeared to prepare him for the great honor that was to come to him and to Anna his wife in the birth of a daughter; up to the glorious sequel, the coronation of Mary as she kneels on the clouds of heaven before the Blessed Trinity. Some scenes in the drama abound in life and beauty; in others, some of the figures have been mutilated; but all, in their varying excellence and degree of preservation, are to the people of Chartres a book in which to read, as the sculptured façade of Notre-Dame-la-Grande is to the peasants and peddlers of Poitiers. The screen is not, as a whole, quite as rich and splendid as the screen of Albi, and I do not think any of the sculptures can equal in dramatic quality the story of Salome as it is presented on the screen of Amiens. But then, in the color of the stone perhaps, or in the lines of the design, neither of these might be in such perfect harmony with the interior of Chartres, and in none other does the play of light and shadow tell with such loveliness of effect.

The barbarism that laid waste the interior of Chartres and the care that put it right again might have been worse, and it

THE EAST END, SHOWING DETAIL OF THE SCREEN AND RADIATING CHAPELS

could be forgiven and forgotten in the miracle of light, burning and shimmering and drifting through the windows. Cleaning, restoring, patching has not destroyed the wonder of them, nor vulgarized the color. It may be that the same hues in the modern window would be crude and garish, as indeed they may have been, for all we can be sure, in the old glass when new. But time, with its dirt and corrosion, as the old twelfth- and thirteenth-century craftsmen probably knew perfectly well it would, has toned down whatever crudeness, if any, there was, and added richness to the harmony.

Around nave and transepts, around the chapels, around the choir save for those staring gaps, long lines of prophets and saints, in garments of flame, seem to set the cathedral all aglow with the fiery fervor of their love and praise. There are hours, toward evening, when you do not see those glorified figures, when you see nothing save spear-like rays of half lambent light, smoldering fires of blue and purple and scarlet burning through the shadowy gray walls, just as the splendors of the setting sun burn through the gray cloud-rift. There are other hours when the saints, each with the emblem by which you may know him, and the prophets of the Old Testament carrying the prophets of the New, but noble and dignified in their bearing for all the naïveté of their pose, and Our Lady herself with the Child at her knees, will not let you forget their presence up there, and you can imagine how, to the saint still of this earth praying below, they must often, in their shining rows, have been like a vision of the heavenly hosts ranged about the Throne. But, however seen, if only in the play of color reflected from them on wall or pier, the windows are the glory of the cathedral.

III

THE history of Chartres, when I came to read it, kept me in the same incense-laden air I had found in the cathedral, everything bringing me back, as the town was forever being brought back, to the shrine where I first saw Chartres at its prayers. The Virgin Mother had always been there. At the dawn of the town's existence, long before the birth of Christ, the Druids, with vague prophetic sense of what was to come, had worshiped her, and their altar, on the hill overlooking the broad plain of La Beauce, marked the site for the little Christian chapel that grew and grew into the cathedral of Notre-Dame as we know it to-day.

As time went on after the building of the first chapel; as Our Lady of Chartres survived the bitterest persecution—how bit-

CHARTRES. FROM THE PLAIN OF LA BEAUCE

ter, the deep well with its bones of martyrs behind her altar Under the Earth can tell you; as her church, burned down again and again, sprang ever up from its ashes more magnificent than before, it is not strange that the people should have fancied her re-creating herself in order to multiply her blessings to them. Notre-Dame at Clermont and Notre-Dame at Le Puy boast their one miraculous shrine of the Virgin. But at Chartres there were—there are—three: *Notre-Dame-sous-Terre,* in the perpetual dusk of Fulbert's crypt, the line of lamps always gleaming and glimmering like stars down its interminable length and fading into the far gloom, reached by strange dark underground passages and steps; *Notre-Dame-du-Pilier,* in the brilliant chapel above, always ablaze with candles, always surrounded by men and women in prayer, always attended by a priest in surplice and stole; *Notre-Dame-de-la-Belle-Verrière,* shining in a glory of color from up above in the old window opposite: the Virgin Mother, stiff, angular, Byzantine, once a favorite, now deserted save by the few peasants you at times find kneeling before her, or, it may be, a few mystics, like Durtal in M. Huysmans' book, whose special devotion was for the forgotten Madonna and the neglected shrine. And the people must often have seen in the whole cathedral one enormous shrine, one gorgeous reliquary for the holiest of its treasures, the Veil of the Blessed Virgin, or the Tunic as it was long described and as it appears on the seal of the cathedral chapter; a royal gift that kings and princes came to visit.

About the Veil and the three shrines the history of Chartres centers, and this not only when there is question of the cathedral. In the history of Notre-Dame naturally it is of paramount importance, the sacred treasure for which the church, its consecrated casket, was built and rebuilt, after the fires of the Middle Ages and after the passing of Christian soldiers who were as ready to loot a shrine as to pray before it; the holy relic that was a stimulus to fervor during the astonishing seasons when a passion of religion shook the land, and all the men, women, and children in it turned themselves into day-laborers and beasts of burden to help in the building on the hill, and the plain below became a vast camp for prayer. Something of the same kind happened in other parts of France. At Amiens, at Laon, at many a cathedral town besides, there was also a pious rivalry among the people, the desire to see who could do the most for the church inflaming each and every one to a frenzy of building. But nowhere was the rivalry so earnest, nowhere was the frenzy so exalted as at Chartres. All thought of self was lost in the eagerness to set up there on the hill a house worthy of Our Lady of Chartres. Incredible heroism is recorded of the citizens. The fires, which were the scourge of those early ages, broke out in the town, and they let their own houses burn to the ground rather than desert for a moment their sacred task. Peasants and townsmen gave all they had to give: their time and their unskilled labor. They quarried the stone, they dragged the huge blocks up the long hill, they held themselves at the bidding of the mason and the master of the work. Even the devout who came from afar on pilgrimage to the shrine of the Veil left everything to help, toiling in the quarry, on the hillside, in the mason's workshop, for days and weeks and months. The cathedral was indeed, as Lowell wrote, built "by universal suffrage," a miracle of faith and self-sacrifice for which the day is past and gone. Universal suffrage with us leads to "graft" and jobbery, not to the creation of the beauty which is the one solace and joy in a life of sorrow and struggle.

Though the season might be one of religious indifference, though the adventure might not savor of religion, Our Lady of Chartres and her Veil could not long be lost to sight. Close to the capital as Chartres was, on the highroad from Normandy, and therefore from England, to Aquitaine, it was caught by the high tide of almost every war that broke over northern France, at the time when the chief occupation of France, and all the world, was fighting. It resisted one enemy, only to fall before the next, passing from hand to hand with the rapid changes of fortune that reduce the record of most French towns during the Dark and Middle Ages to a hopeless blur of names and dates. When you consider all that the peasants of La Beauce have gone through, to them falling all the horrors and none of the glory, is it astonishing that they have become avaricious and sordid, *un peuple sombre,* as they say in Chartres? Always through the tangle of history, always above the struggle of French nobles with each other, above the endless feud between France and England, above the horror of wars fought in the name of religion, always, in clear relief, appears the serene figure of Our Lady of Chartres; now protecting the town she loved from the danger, now, from motives incomprehensible to mortals, deserting it to its fate, but always taking the active part expected by the people who loved her. She is the one unchangeable presence and hers is the one changeless rule through the chaotic years. From the crowded stage a few men and women emerge, standing out with the prominence a strong personality or a fine achievement or a royal name is sure to give: William the Conqueror, the Bastard, in his own country, and his queen; St. Bernard with his message from the East; the English Henry V in his sober manhood; the French Henri IV in his romantic splendor; the little Mary Stuart, the child betrothed—the list from beginning to end is long, for the heroes of Chartres are many. But, whoever they were, whatever their fame, however royal, they could never overshadow one whom all the town knew to be mightier still, and who, oftener than not, was the reason of the mighty and the lowly coming to Chartres, either that they might offer her their gifts, or that she might lavish hers upon them.

The enemy battered at the gates, a blight fell upon La Beauce, plague and famine swept the land, and Our Lady was still the first thought of the people, she still watched from her high cathedral. Not a battle, not a tragedy, that did not end in the triumphal procession of her Veil, or her Statue, through the town, or else the hasty concealment, no man could say where, of the sacred symbols. If you fix your eyes upon them, you may know, as though you watched from the battle-field or from behind the plow in the plain, how it has fared with Chartres since the first days of the Catholic church upon the hill down to those which men would have made the last, when the cathedral in Chartres, as in Paris, was turned into a Temple of Reason, and the sacred Veil was rent in twain, and the Black Virgin was burned in the public streets. The Revolution over, a piece of the Veil was restored, a new Black Virgin, as miraculous,

13

appeared in the place of the old, and once more about the sacred
symbols the life—the history—of the town centered.   The Bourbon, who bears its name, is powerless in this generation to do
anything for it save to lend his title to one of its hotels, but
Notre-Dame of Chartres remains supreme.   Without the cathedral you feel that the town would not exist.   And I thought it
further proof of the fidelity of Chartres to its traditions, that,
when I was there, the Veil once more had been hidden, no man,
not even the priest in charge of *Notre-Dame-du-Pilier,* could,
or would, tell where.   The thieves in the Department who
threatened it had not the romance of the soldiers of fortune
swaggering through the old chronicles, or even of the *sans-
culottes* drunk with liberty, but the sacrilege at their hands
would be no less, and, history repeating itself in the usual
fashion, the Veil was kindling new fires of devotion in its new
danger and the new necessity of protecting it.

IV

CHARTRES, as I found, has a busy life of its own.   It was difficult to believe it at first, for, swarming as it does with priests,
full of nuns long after the law was supposed to have suppressed
them, still drawing to it crowds of pilgrims every spring, the
impression I had in the beginning was that the whole place depended on the cathedral.   But it has also an equally important
military life.   Its barracks, swallowing up the remnants of the
old Abbey of St. Pierre, are enormous.   The bugle call is a
familiar sound in the streets, and the march of soldiers a frequent sight.   It has its cattle and horse markets, its May and
September fairs, which are moments and periods of animation,
and it does a very brisk trade in the big white horses, raised in
the neighborhood, with Americans, who, I was assured, were
much loved at Chartres for having given a new impetus to
its industries, and in the amiability shown me as one of them

THE SOUTH TOWER, AS SEEN FROM THE MARKET-PLACE

I profited by my countrymen's enterprise, of which I then heard for the first time.

But when the soldiers have passed, when the markets are over, when you are out of the reach of the steam-organs of the *Place des Epars* and the marionettes who dance the cake-walk at fair-time, Chartres relapses into monastic calm, as if it had nothing to do save to disclose new beauties in the cathedral by showing it from new points of view. Wherever you wander, you are sure to see it: now the gray towers above the market-place; now a portal or a space of gray wall, like a screen, at the end of a narrow gabled street. From the winding way to the *Porte Guillaume,* the only one of the old town gates that survives, from the steep steps past the Staircase of Queen Bertha, every time you look back, the cathedral will have arranged itself into some new composition, with the clustering roofs and the spaces of green in the bishop's garden. And if, turning to your left from the *Porte Guillaume,* you go farther along the banks of the little river Eure, where, at all hours, washerwomen kneel in a line in the washing-places along the yellow stream, you are amazed as if, instead of countless writers and artists having described and drawn that supreme view of all, you were the first to see how the buttressed east end rises high above the river, "with its old patched and interrupted wall, the ditch with its weedy edges, the spots of color, the white-capped laundresses in their little wooden cages," high above the tiers upon tiers of roofs, soaring high above the climbing town. You have only to keep on the walk called by Chartres the *Tour-de-Ville,* of which the road just here by the river is a part, to come at every step upon a new arrangement. From below, you can always look up to the cathedral on the crest of the hill and to the pathetic old churches of St. Aignan, with its Renaissance door and vilely painted interior, and St. Pierre, with its old glass and wide-flying buttresses, clinging to the slopes. From the high shady grove, where the well-dressed little children of

CHARTRES CATHEDRAL, FROM THE PORTE GUILLAUME

Chartres play decorously through the long summer afternoons, from the avenue of trees so majestic that you begin to wonder

CHARTRES. EAST END

if, as Châteaubriand thought, just such an avenue was not the model for the first architect who designed a cathedral nave, from below the massive wall built for the protection of the cathedral, here and there, the view may be shut out for a minute, but only that, the next, clustering roofs and gray walls and spires may come together more pictorially than ever.

And as in the town, so it is in all the country round. Above the wide plain of La Beauce, the cathedral of Our Lady is forever visible, "with the passing light or shadow upon its gray weather-beaten surface"—"like a ship forever a sail in the

CHARTRES. DISTANT VIEW FROM THE SOUTH

distance," the child Gaston de Latour thought. Above the old rolling Roman road leading to it straight from the South, it ever rises, the goal now of cyclist and motorist as it was of pilgrim and soldier in the past. There, out of the ancient city, "the gray cliffs of lonely stone" have for centuries been lifted "into the midst of sailing birds and silent air," a pledge of the sincerity of Chartres in the days of its faith, a reproach to the indifference that sees in it nothing holier than an Historical Monument, protected by the State.

CHAPTER X

ST. JULIEN OF LE MANS

CHAPTER X

ST. JULIEN OF LE MANS

I

AN enormous square full of a confusion of farmers and
peasants in blouses, cattle, carts, women in white caps;
on one side, a line of *cafés;* on the other, a line of trees;
at the far end, high above the busy market, the buttressed, pinnacled east end of a mighty church, silent and serene in the
bustle and stir and noise, gray with age, splendid in beauty—
this is the first picture that rises before me when I hear or read
the name of Le Mans, and it is the most beautiful of the many
pictures of the cathedral of St. Julien which Le Mans shows to
the rare traveler who comes to see them.

The town of Le Mans is only as far away from Chartres as
Chartres is from Paris. It is close to Brittany. It is the
ancient capital of the ancient province of Maine, that gave its
name to one of our oldest States and that was a convenient
battle-field for the long fight of France with England. But,
like so many other places, memorable, charming, and interesting, Le Mans still belongs as far as the tourist goes, or it did
when I was last there a year or so ago, to Undiscovered France.
However, if you should set out to discover it, if Chartres should
fire you with the desire to see more of the churches of northern
France, then my advice would be to take a late afternoon train
through the peaceful land between these two ancient cities, and,

arriving at Le Mans in the twilight, wait until the next morning, especially if it be the morning of market day, for the first view of the cathedral. Up till then, Le Mans, after Chartres, will no doubt have struck you as commonplace. On your drive from the station to the hotel, it will have shown itself to you as a big prosperous town, with modern boulevards and modern shops and modern trams, and with next to nothing on the way to remind you that it was not built yesterday, except the old church of Notre-Dame-de-la-Couture opening disconsolately on the sidewalk. Nor will it seem less modern when you are walking from the hotel toward the cathedral, along shop-lined streets, between windows hung in emulation of Paris. But presently a street, less Parisian, with fewer shops, ends abruptly in the great square, and of a sudden, above the market and the people and the cattle, you see the apse with its buttresses and pinnacles and curving chapels, one of the most beautiful east ends even in northern France, the country of beautiful cathedrals.

It is as lovely at all hours. Indeed, when I last went back to Le Mans and, after several years, saw the cathedral of St. Julien again, and then for the first time in the tranquil golden light of a May evening, the great apse circling upward from a delicate flowering of lilac and laburnum in the strip of bishop's garden at its base, and the wide market-place, deserted, I thought it had

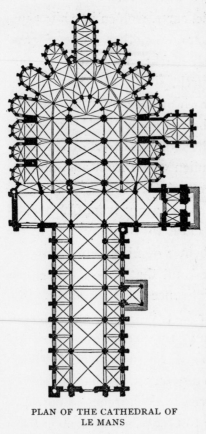

PLAN OF THE CATHEDRAL OF
LE MANS

FROM VIOLLET-LE-DUC'S "DICTIONNAIRE
DE L'ARCHITECTURE"

HIGH ABOVE THE BUSY MARKET . . . THE BUTTRESSED, PINNACLED EAST END OF A MIGHTY CHURCH

never been lovelier and more majestic. But the market gives scale to its age and its beauty, just as a figure will give scale in a drawing of architecture. Besides, the market is the most characteristic foreground to this most characteristic view of the cathedral. What the spires are to Chartres, the Devils to Notre-Dame in Paris, the cluster of towers to Laon, that the east end is to Le Mans. The apse, rising from the island in the

TOWER AT END OF TRANSEPT

Seine where it winds through Paris, shrinks when compared to St. Julien, and though in actual dimensions Beauvais is loftier, the position of Le Mans raised on a slight eminence above the market-place adds so immensely to the effect of height from this one point of view as to make it seem almost a rival. For here you can see no other part of the cathedral except a bit of the south transept and the one tower standing at the southern entrance, the last place you would expect to find it, so that in the

VIEW OF SOUTH TRANSEPT

square you might really think the cathedral began and ended
in this amazing apse.

To the south, from the market-place, a broad flight of curving steps goes up to the level of the cathedral. Mount it, and
you are in another town—the town to which the cathedral belongs: not Le Mans of to-day, with modern boulevards, modern

trams, modern shops, but Le Mans of the days when its lords and burghers were building their dark and narrow streets lined with sculptured and gabled houses. And the cathedral in this Le Mans is so ancient that the huge eastern end above the square seems young. For the apse and the transepts belong to the glorious period of Gothic. But the lower part of the tower flanking the southern transept, and the cathedral has no other; the door in the southern wall of the nave, with the statues so like those of Chartres, long slim figures, their drapery falling in rigid folds, their faces smiling inscrutably; the nave; the west front—all go back to earlier, sterner centuries, to the period of Romanesque which in the North is so much more austere than in the South. It makes no concession here to ornament except those statues at the southern door and a few sculptures on the severe west front. Something of the same contrast exists between nave and choir at Gloucester, but not as you see that cathedral from the exterior. At Le Mans the contrast between Romanesque simplicity and Gothic exuberance is more striking and bewildering without than within.

The nave is so much lower than the apse and so much more insignificant in size that it really looks, as it has sometimes been described, like the porch, the mere approach, to the body of the church. It seems impossible for a cathedral, ending at the east with such splendor, to face the west with a modesty many a parish church would disdain; three doors, low, heavy, round-arched, almost guiltless of decoration, in the place of the lofty portals, charged with sculpture, kings and saints in their well-ordered rows, everywhere the gray stone breaking into a rhythmical tangle of flowers and foliage and figures and interwoven tracery: the portals by which the great Gothic cathedral is usually entered.

The nave, still old in effect without, is now distressingly new within. I found, to my regret, that, since my first visit to Le Mans, it had been done up until to-day it might pass for the

THE NAVE OR WEST FRONT OF LE MANS, FROM THE NORTHWEST

newest instead of the most ancient part of the building. It has that look peculiar to the recently restored church of having just recovered from a fearful attack of spring cleaning. Walls and columns are as clean and white as if the stone had only just been brought from the quarries. Even the glass, which is the oldest in St. Julien, or in any other church in France, has been patched and repaired until only here and there, by a deeper tone in a passage of blue, by the richness, the fullness of color the modern craftsman has never rivaled, can you make sure which are the twelfth-century windows, the pride of Le Mans. No one could any longer feel quite as Mérimée did when his tour of inspection brought him to Le Mans and he wrote to his Ministers at Paris that to step from the nave to the choir was like leaving the old religion of barbarism for the new creed of tenderness and benevolence; though, he added in one of those passages that make his official reports good reading, he could see no difference between Christianity in the twelfth and Christianity in the thirteenth century, if it were not that in the thirteenth bishop and chapter had greater power and made greater abuse of it. To the architect the nave of Le Mans has still much to say, much to tell of the way cathedrals were built and decorated in the ages of the barbarism we try so hard, and in vain, to equal in beauty. But now that its history in the interval has been wiped out, it is to me a sadder ruin than if the blue sky shone through its broken roof, and the grass grew between its shattered columns.

It is not so, however, in the choir, which is as supremely beautiful, as dramatically pictorial as you knew it must be when you looked up to the buttresses that support its walls and the chapels that curve round with its curving line. More marvelous it was, no doubt, before the usual fate of the French cathedral befell it, before the Huguenots sacked it; before the eighteenth century tried first to reduce it to eighteenth-century standards and then to get rid of it altogether; before the nineteenth century

WEST FRONT OF THE CATHEDRAL

began by turning it into a Historical Monument and finished with the endeavor to make it look like one. It may seem cold and empty while Chartres is fresh in your memory—Chartres

THE CROSSING SHOWING ROMANESQUE NAVE AND GOTHIC CHOIR

with its screen of carven stone inclosing the choir, and its holy shrine afloat with golden lights. But you feel this only for a moment. The two aisles still encircle the choir at Le Mans, the chapels still open from the outer aisle, the old thirteenth-century glass still fills many of the windows, the ceremonies of the cathedral church still have something of the old gorgeousness. Even Chartres could never be more impressive than Le Mans as I have seen it at solemn High Mass—the *Messe Capitulaire.* The services are conducted with great ceremony and dignity, it seems to me with even more to-day than before the recent troubles between Church and State, and the choir is a marvelous setting for ceremonial. No spectacle of medievalism could have exceeded the 'reverent splendors of this Mass, when the bishop, in his gold and purple robes, was seated on his throne in the choir, with behind him the glorious succession of arches, one opening beyond the other as if into infinity, and over his head the wonderful windows rising in tier over tier, somber with deep glowing blues and purples below, kindling above into smoldering fires of gold and scarlet, as if the artist who placed them there, like the artist who designed the ascending lines of pillars and arches, had sought ever to lead the eye higher and higher heavenward. As at Chartres, so at Le Mans, in the light of those fervent windows, of those rows upon rows of saints and prophets, bishops and donors, in shining garments, the choir, had the Vandal stripped it bare, would be transfigured.

II

IN the south transept is a tomb you could not overlook even in a cathedral less empty than St. Julien. It is not as beautiful as its date—it belongs to the thirteenth century—should make it. Indeed, in the chapel opening into the north transept, are two others much later, but far lovelier, especially the monument to Langey du Bellay, with the bas-reliefs that ought to be by Germain Pilon if they are not, and the epitaph that, for the sake of association, it is pleasant to attribute to Clément Marot. The name of Berengaria, however, gives a special interest to the earlier monument, laden with the romance of Walter Scott as it is, and you wonder idly, as you stop before it, why this Queen of England should be buried in a French cathedral, or why at least it was not to an English town she was carried when, not a hundred years ago, her tomb was brought away from the abbey of L'Epau, where it had stood through the ages. Leaving the cathedral by the transept door just beyond, you are almost at once in the *Grand' Rue* of the old town, where a Renaissance house, that restoration cannot make altogether unlovely nor the narrow darkness of the street altogether hide from you, also bears the name of Berengaria. She could never have lived in it; she had been in her grave many a long day before it was built. But house and tomb together show there must be some reason why her memory is held dear in Le Mans.

And there is a reason—the best. The cathedral had been founded, and had grown greater and greater, in the fashion of all old cathedrals, centuries before she was born. In the very first of the Christian era, they say, a Christian altar had been raised there, on the highest ground in Le Mans. And it had developed into a chapel, the chapel into a church thought worthy to receive the body of St. Julien, and the church into an important cathedral. And the cathedral had survived fire and the carelessness of builders who were not always so holy in their work as in the books now written about them; it had survived the endless wars and raids of Normans and Bretons, the endless interference of Kings of England who saw a menace to themselves in the House of God when it occupied so commanding a position in a town that, like Chartres, was on the highroad between Normandy and Aquitaine. But though, by much rebuilding and repairing, the cathedral had survived, it bore the marks of the trials through which it had come. Besides, it had grown old-fashioned or whatever was the medieval word for out-of-date. Artists then were not given to going back to earlier ages in search of models; they relied upon themselves. By the end of the twelfth and the beginning of the thirteenth century, there were springing up in the *Ile de France* and all the near provinces the churches of the new school of builders, of the young men, the independents of the day, with

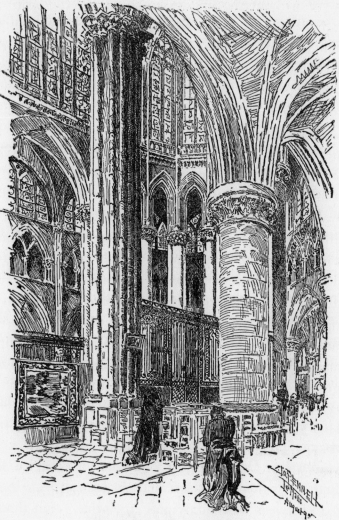

WITHIN THE APSE OR EAST END

wonderful new ideas and genius soaring to masterpieces hitherto undreamed of. And in Maine were ambitious bishops and pious people who did not wish to be outdone by their neighbors in Chartres or Amiens, in Rouen or even Paris. The young

men of the thirteenth century never had to wait long for a
chance or a patron. The clergy and the faithful in Le Mans
were eager to set up on their hill one of the new great churches,
but if they had the will, if they knew they could get the money,
they were without the first essential of all, the space for it.
The cathedral of St. Julien stood close to the city walls, where
no room was left for the simple Romanesque apse to expand
into a Gothic array of buttresses and pinnacles, nor were the
times yet so peaceful that even a lord bishop could tamper with
the fortifications. It was at this crisis Berengaria made her
name forever beloved in Le Mans. For the tradition is that
she interested herself, and put the case before Philip-Augustus
with reason and eloquence until he, being something of an
enthusiast in these matters, also interested himself and gave
the royal order to carry out the new design, though, in so doing,
the cathedral must extend beyond the ramparts. Berengaria
might be a more shadowy figure in history than she is for me,
she might be more overshadowed by her Lion-Hearted husband
in Walter Scott, and I would think no honor too great to pay to
one to whom the world owes the apse which is the glory of
Le Mans to this day, and a marvel to all who come to visit it.

Some say that the architect got his idea for the apse from
Bourges, so like is it to the east end there, though with a difference. For all the detail, to the arrangement of the chapels,
is lovelier at Le Mans, especially on the exterior, where the buttresses are magnificent in themselves and something more than
the bare supports essential to the structural scheme which they
so obviously are at Bourges. But if the architect borrowed
his model from Bourges and improved upon it, if, as it is also
said, he borrowed too from Chartres and Paris, from churches,
here, there, and everywhere, in Normandy and Picardy, taking
his good where he found it, he only showed his intelligence in
understanding that half of genius is the knowing how to be
original by carrying on great traditions. The choir was fin-

ished, spreading in its bold loveliness beyond the old city walls, to the very edge of the hill. The transepts dragged on to later centuries, to the time of Adam Chastelain, Bishop of Le

FROM THE CHOIR LOOKING WEST

Mans, who shines in splendor from the great rose of the northern transept. The nave never got rebuilt at all. This is why in few places, as in Le Mans, can you see how cathedrals grew and developed architecturally through the ages before their degeneration into show places. Almost every architectural step from the beginning of the big church that replaced the first timid crypt can be traced, though largely through the restorer's version, and not always with the certainty that he respected this historic growth as he found it. For if Le Mans succeeded in escaping Viollet-le-Duc, it was only to fall into the hands of an industrious rival. From the day Mérimée came to it as Inspector of National Monuments, the history of the cathedral is the record of its restoration, except for the one bitter season of new trial, when French soldiers were quartered in aisles that had seen the passing of so many armies, and, worse sacrilege, Prussian soldiers held their Lutheran rites in the choir as Huguenots had done three hundred years before. All traces of their passage have been effaced from the cathedral, but the monument to General Chanzy in the *Place de la République* is the witness of the new enemy Le Mans had to face so recently as 1870.

What the next stage will be, what new history secularized France will make for Le Mans and all French cathedrals, only the generations who come after us can know. But religious France is preparing for the future. I have a vivid memory of the groups of children who were gathered in the north transept of the cathedral one May afternoon, for religious instruction from an ardent young priest, and also of a First Communion day there and the hundreds of little girls veiled in white, and little boys with the white badge on their arms, marshaled by nuns and priests, who marched up and down the aisles in solemn procession, filling the old building with the religious *Marseillaise, "Je suis Chrétien."* It seemed to me as if Le Mans, anyway, were arming itself to meet the new dangers, as it had so often to face the old foe.

III

It was by some rare stroke of good fortune that, while all the rest of Le Mans was prospering and developing into a modern town, the little old quarter on the crest of the hill, close to the cathedral, was left in its medievalism to decay picturesquely. It is only a few steps from the southern transept and the beautiful door with its group of statues to the dark streets, one of them dignified as *Grand' Rue,* though the modern Haussmann would think alley too fine a description for it. In places the houses almost meet overhead. Some are carved with fantastic figures after which they are called—*Aux Bons Amis, Maison Adam et Eve;* others have names recalling the associations clinging to them for centuries. There is not only the House of Berengaria, but the House of Scarron, where Scarron, who was, though Heaven knows why, a dignitary of the chapter, lived during his residence at Le Mans, and spent some of those cruel wakeful hours that made him, in the epitaph he wrote for himself, pray all those who passed by his tomb to step lightly and not wake him from his first night of sleep. But the pleasure in these old houses is, above all, because of the way they complete the medievalism of the cathedral. Very much as it is now must this quarter have been when the work of building the new east end began. It is all in character, and you know that for centuries the people have seen the cathedral exactly as you see it, when, from the end of a narrow street or with its turning, you look up to the gray walls and the great apse. And if a funeral passes— and funerals were forever passing during the hot summer of my first visit to Le Mans—the last touch of medievalism will be added, for the horses in their funereal trappings, were it not for the somber scheme of black and silver, might have walked out of the tournament in some old print or faded tapestry, and the sad procession, winding from out the narrow streets, sometimes seemed but a solemn pageant for my pleasure.

You do not have to go far in this little quarter before you find yourself on a railed roadway above a deep tunnel leading to the river, and for the first time you realize that it is no mean hill upon which the cathedral stands. The ascent, slight and gradual from the railroad station, is much more abrupt from the banks of the Sarthe, and as you wander on you have glimpses of the town spreading on the opposite shores, of the river winding between pleasant green banks, and of the stretch

LE MANS FROM THE RIVER

of fair country beyond. Long flights of steps lead to the quays, though you can go down more gradually by the wide streets that Le Mans, apparently as indifferent now to the past as Mérimée found it, prefers to gabled narrow alleys and has opened from the center of the town to the Sarthe.

Once at the foot of the hill, it is worth while crossing to the other side of the river, if only to see the old Romanesque church which is older than the cathedral in the suburb there, or to saunter along the poplar-lined road to the graveyard of the town. I remember this graveyard as a fitting sequel to the endless passing of horses in medieval trappings up on the hill.

For there was a never-to-be-forgotten August afternoon, when I walked to it, hunting for a view, and found rows upon rows of freshly dug graves ready for the morrow, as grisly a spectacle as ever it presented in the days of pest and plague, and all the grislier to me when I discovered later on that cholera was raging in Le Mans that summer. But something else I saw on my walk. There, opposite, crowning the hill above the river, was the cathedral commanding the town so well that it is no wonder Kings of England feared to see strong towers rising from a building already made so formidable by its position. You will not know the cathedral, you cannot follow its history, unless, from down here, you have looked up to it on the hill where it keeps watch over the valley. But after you have seen it from this, and from every other, point of view, after you begin to understand what it has meant to the generations who have come and gone along the Sarthe; even then, if you climb back to the square at its east end, you will say that never is it mightier and more dramatic than when, beyond the crowd of farmers and peasants and cattle and carts, the buttressed, pinnacled apse rises, gray with age, splendid in beauty, silent and serene, above the noise and bustle and stir of the market-place.

CHAPTER XI

"IN THE PERIL OF THE SEA": MONT ST. MICHEL

CHAPTER XI

"IN THE PERIL OF THE SEA": MONT ST. MICHEL

I

WHEN I first attempted to describe "The Most Picturesque Place in the World," I knew that to almost everybody it would seem as mythical as Camelot or the Isle of Avalon; but it is another matter with Mont St. Michel, which, of all picturesque places, is, as Mr. Henry James once said of Venice, the easiest to visit without going there. It has been painted and drawn and photographed and written about again and again—the most exploited place in the world, one might almost call it.

And yet, when one sees it for the first time it is as unreal as the little hill town of the primitives. It is unexpectedly, preposterously, fantastically, magnificently medieval.

On the first glimpse, when it is only a bewildering shadow on the horizon, one's impression is of a stupendous inconsistency, of an impossible meeting of irreconcilable extremes. Viewed from the point where the road to it leaves the orchards and pastures for a wide causeway across the sands, the vision becomes a solid fact: a lonely rock, walled, battlemented, towered, springing up from the sea, and in its picturesque medievalism more perfect, more complete than anything any medieval painter or engraver ever saw or imagined.

My stay in Mont St. Michel extended long beyond the usual

day's outing, but I never got over my first impression. From my balcony, and from the pretty arbor in the garden where I ate my first breakfast, I looked down upon a wonderful collection of old houses, all turrets and tumbled roofs, and then out

MONT ST. MICHEL, FROM THE CAUSEWAY ACROSS THE SANDS

upon an endless stretch of sands, crossed and recrossed by innumerable streams running in long, flowing lines and beautiful curves, the color changing with the flight of the clouds and the journeying of the sun across the heavens.

I could sit there for hours, watching the light wander over the gray level, or waiting for the tide to come in and widen the Couesnon—the river that separates Normandy from Brittany— into an enormous bay, and never was there a moment of monotony. Of the abbey, higher on the hill behind me, nothing was to be seen, except in the late afternoon, when it threw a gigantic shadow across the sands.

Mont St. Michel is isolated, detached; it stands alone; it is complete in itself. And it is comparatively small, with its whole life and architecture centering about the abbey. There is room for nothing else but the handful of houses clinging to the southern slope.

From the first gate up the one village street a ten minutes' walk brings you to the abbey; you need be no longer on the way if you follow the walls; while in half an hour or so of plodding through wet sand and scrambling over rocks you can make the entire round of the Mount.

If I left my high perch to wander up and down the endless steps or along the narrow paths on the hillside between abbey and village, it was to come at every turn upon some new arrangement, some fresh outlook, more picturesque than the last. And on stairs, or foot-paths, or street, or walls, or sands, I could seldom forget the isolated position of Mont St. Michel, which is at once its charm and its distinction.

II

Mont St. Michel has the romantic air. It suggests Dumas and Scott. Its history is a romance, but it was curious to learn that the first monks did not settle there because of a position I thought too obviously, even ostentatiously made for monks. When they came, Mont St. Michel was not an island "in the peril of the sea," but rose in the midst of a great forest, with a Roman road leading through it to the hill where the Romans had long before worshiped Jupiter, and the Druids had long before that set up their mystic stones. It was after the Christian hermits had been there a couple of hundred years, and Aubert, Bishop of Avranches—the white city you see with its towers glistening in afternoon sunlight, on the hills across the sands—was busy building the shrine to St. Michael, that one day (it was early in the eighth century) there was a terrific trembling of the earth, and out at sea the tide rose, as never before in the memory of man. It swept in over woodland and village, and when it swept out again there was no forest; Mont St. Michel and Tombelaine near by were the only dry spots of land in a vast bay; the hills of the Cotentin were far to the east, those of Brittany as far to the west. Northward was the open sea, never before seen by the monks from their hilltop. Southward the sands stretched toward Pontorson.

Had there been no earthquake and rising of the waters, the story of Mont St. Michel would be very like that of any other medieval abbey in France: the story of saintly monks and miracles, of shrines and pilgrimages, of piety expressed in noble architecture, of love of art and learning, of increasing wealth and power and abuse of it, of reform and revived ardor and fresh relapse, and finally the Revolution. Only Mont St. Michel answered too well as a prison to be destroyed. And when jailers and prisoners had got done with it, enough was left to be turned into a national monument.

But if the monks were like all other monks, their abbey was by no means like all other abbeys, either in its architecture or as a fortress. When the other abbeys increased in importance, and the monks in number, new courts and cloisters were added, more ground covered. But at Mont St. Michel, after burrowing down into the heart of the rock, there was nothing to do but to build upward and ever upward, to pile story upon story, until the abbey, springing higher and higher heavenward, became everywhere visible to the people on the mainland.

If you walk to it now by the climbing village street, or, better still, by the walls, where you mount flight after flight of steep stairs, you come at last to that grimmest of all grim abbey gates,

THE ABBEY FROM WITHIN THE WALLS

Le Châtelet, with its battlements, its high, frowning wall and cannon-shaped turrets; and there you look up a long vista of stairs, and you mount into the *Salle des Gardes,* and there you look up another long vista of stairs, and you mount and mount, under bridges thrown from building to building, high above your head, and you mount to airy platforms, where—if the wind does not absorb you in your effort to keep on your hat—you see the houses of the village like little specks on the hillside beneath. And then you go down again to floor below floor, down into the *Crypte de l'Aquilon,* with its suggestion of terrible tragedies.

I kept thinking of cloisters in England, with the square of green in the middle, and the old yew-trees, and the friendly rooks cawing overhead, and of those others in Italy, sunlit, fragrant with roses, full of orange- and lemon-trees, when I dived down into the underground, dimly lighted *promenoir,* where the monks of Mont St. Michel first took their daily walk, and even when I mounted to the later thirteenth-century cloister that seems to hang in mid-air, and overlooks miles and miles of lonely sands and sea, the wind always—to my knowledge— blowing a hurricane from the cold North, with the sea-gulls flying before it.

You cannot look at the sands from the abbey without remembering the difficulties of the builders, and yet they made it the stateliest and most perfect example of ecclesiastical architecture in France, and so it remains, for all the fires that have defaced it, and the insignificant west front of the last century, and the modern restorer's scaffolding inside, his trolleys and cranes outside, and the brand-new belfry and *flèche,* topped by Frémiet's absurd little St. Michael, so tiny, so out of scale, that from below it is more like a golden insect than a glorious winged archangel as beautiful as the morning. Once inside the *Châtelet,* as you fall in with other tourists behind a guide, it degenerates into a national monument, an authorized "sight," a specimen duly labeled and catalogued. The restorer has already accomplished much, and is preparing to accomplish still more. The upper hall in *La Merveille* is spick and span, and soon the lovely *Salle des Chevaliers,* where Louis XI's Knights of St.

Michael met, which Madame de Créquy described brilliant with their banners and coats of arms, gleaming with their shields and swords, will be as neat and clean. But below, on the

THE WOOD ON THE SIDE OF MONT ST. MICHEL

sands, you see nothing of this; you see only how the little wood, all that is left of the Forest of Scissy, and the village climb to the abbey, and how nobly it towers above them.

And there is something else best seen from the sands, the wall

THE WALLS OF MONT ST. MICHEL FROM THE SIDE OF THE WOOD

that runs round the little village, from the succession of gates I entered first one brilliant September morning, to the northeast side of the hill, where, with an abrupt turning, it ascends to the abbey. I should have to know a great deal more about the doings of Bretons and Normans, Angevins and English, to tell the history of that wall, which played a leading part in preserving the abbey for the modern pilgrim. During the long hundred years when English and French were fighting virtually for the possession of France, when in Normandy castles were tumbling like houses of cards, Mont St. Michel never once fell before the enemy. Not that the enemy did not want it and try hard enough for it. Year after year there were days when the monks, looking down to the sands—now empty save for a chance fisherman or tourist, now silent save for the screech of the sea-gulls—saw the gleam of armor and the rich color of many banners, heard the trumpet call and the harsh war-cry. But many as were the sallies of the English from Tombelaine, they could not conquer the Mount.

III

FOR thirteen centuries the monks prayed, great buildings rose upon their hill, miracles were performed, prisoners tortured, battles fought, the walls stood firm, solely that Mont St. Michel might provide a pleasant playground for tourists: fifty thousand in a year, according to the generous calculations of the authorities. A few, a very few, are pious pilgrims to the shrine of St. Michael; to the rest the visit is a picnic pure and simple. And it is the French, who travel less perhaps than any other people even in their own land, who have appropriated Mont St. Michel. Americans and English do visit it, but they are the exception. The crowd is essentially a French crowd.

The first arrivals came with my morning coffee, if it were low tide, in a train of carts across the sands from Genets:

mostly peasants these, in blouses and extraordinary caps, and priests who disappeared into the smaller inns. After that the diligences from Pontorson followed at stated intervals and in between a ceaseless stream of bicycles, motor-cars, carriages, carts. And the minute one was seen, a black speck in the distance, the hotel touts, men and women, rushed down the road to fight for the unfortunate passengers.

Most of them stayed only the day. There was just time for the famous omelet at Madame Poulard's, the visit to the abbey, the walk back by the walls, and to shoot off their kodaks at anything and everything they saw.

I remember the pathetic disappointment of an Englishwoman whose husband did like a good band after dinner, and of an American who, as he sat in the *café* staring dismally into the kitchen, declared Atlantic City to be lively enough for him, for there was really nothing to do. A tramp over the wet sands, barefoot for comfort, with a guide for adventure, as if you believed in the quicksands that no one ever stumbled into, could fill up the afternoon, and the correct *apéritif,* the last hour before dinner, when Mont St. Michel, like every other French town and village, reeked with absinthe. But, after dinner, coffee and even a *petit verre* could not be prolonged indefinitely and the one excitement was to fetch a Chinese lantern, "Poulard Aîné" in big blue letters on the white paper shade, and go out to walk with it. There were no street-lamps, and every one who went anywhere carried a lantern. The effect was charming as the lights wound through the narrow hilly street between the shadowy figures at every door, or, as you saw them from the *digue,* like huge fireflies fluttering along the walls and up the hillside, or, from the window of the *Maison Verte,* flickering here and there on the stairs and higher terraces, while, in the deep blue of the summer sky, the harvest moon hung over the clustered chimneys.

I found endless occupation in looking at the place. It was

never the same two days or two hours in succession. There
were days when, in the sunshine, sands and sea were hot and
blinding as the South; days when the storm broke, and sands
and sea were swallowed in gray mists. There were hours
when the tide came in, the winding streams meeting in raging
whirlpools or overflowing into one great sheet of water; hours
when the tide went out, leaving the sands wet and shining; and,

THE MOUNT FROM THE ROAD ACROSS THE SANDS

at the end, there came the equinoctial tide, when, scarcely had
you noted a white quivering line far to the north than, with a
roaring and rushing, Mont St. Michel was completely surrounded by water (except for that modern causeway), as you
see it in old prints where the ships sail up close to the walls.
There were flaming sunsets, beautiful starlit nights, and wonderful nights of moonlight, when it was more impossibly fantastic than ever. Its most memorable effect it amiably reserved

for the last evening of all, when the moon was high in the heavens, and the abbey rose upon its rock, white and ghostly against the luminous white clouds that piled themselves up in great masses on a sky as blue and splendid as in a romantic landscape. Then Mont St. Michel was as dreamlike as Milton's "great vision of the guarded mount" on the Cornish coast.

In another generation the rock, like the hill at Dol, may

OUTSIDE THE WALLS OF MONT ST. MICHEL

spring tamely from fields where sheep are browsing, and a building as new as the newest hotel on the new boulevards of Paris may crown its heights. Before long a railway will bring visitors almost to the door where Madame Poulard makes her famous omelet and smiles her famous smile; and why not next, as some one has suggested, a funicular road up to the abbey? The church is to be rebuilt, *La Merveille* to be restored, that is to exchange the tone and color of time for a clean wall neatly ruled by lines of mortar. If I mention this fact, it is not to grumble. I do not see the need of breaking one's heart over the misfortunes of posterity. The picturesqueness is as yet only threatened. Were it to remain as it is now, there would not be much reason to complain. But I want to remind those who have not been there that before they are twenty years older there may be no Mont St. Michel to see.

And it would be a pity not to see it. We are continually regretting the past, and yet here is one of the most picturesque bits of it safely brought down into the present for our special benefit.

CHAPTER XII

NOTRE-DAME OF LAON

CHAPTER XII

NOTRE-DAME OF LAON

I

IF, when you travel from Calais to Bâle, your one idea is to hurry through France, convinced that it is a dull, flat country, with nothing in it to break the monotony of hedgeless fields and poplared roads, you need go no farther than Laon to find your mistake. For here, from the window of the train—if you are not at lunch, or it is not night, and you take the trouble to look—you will see a hill rising abruptly out of the plain, and on this hill a tree-girt town, and in the midst of the town a cathedral, with gray walls and more towers than you can count, standing head and shoulders above the house-tops: a place that, as has been said, "as you approach it, reminds you of a quaint woodcut in an ancient folio." If you have already been in Italy, it will remind you even more of the towns there that sit upon the hills and look across the valleys. And should you leave the train to mount into it from the station, it is again of Italy you will think. For, unless you climb the precipitous flight of stairs called *casse-cou municipal* by the natives who know it to their cost, or take the trolley I regretted to see on my last visit, you must drive up a road that lies in easy zigzags along the hillside, like the white road winding up to Perugia or Cortona.

16

Except for the group of new houses about the station in the plain, Laon keeps to the top of its hill, covering the long narrow plateau there, and, with it, following the almost right-angled turn made at one point by the hill itself. There is space only for a long main street, throwing off a few short streets to right and to left, for the citadel and the cathedral at one end, the old church of St. Martin and the barracks at the other, and for the

A DISTANT VIEW OF LAON CATHEDRAL FROM THE SOUTHWEST

well-shaded walk that encircles the town. And just as Laon is now, so I have seen it in an old sixteenth-century print that shows the curiously shaped hill standing solitary in the plain, and the town on its top stretched along the narrow ridge and widening where it widens at either end, with no difference save that, in those days, two tall spires went springing upward from two of the cathedral towers. And as the town was then, so it must always have been, changing only when its destruction dur-

ing the battles it was forever
fighting, or by the fires that were
forever breaking out, gave the
new generation of builders their
chance. It could never have
been bigger; there is not room
for it to be bigger in. I do not
see how it could have been
smaller, for, as it is, nothing in
Laon amazes me more than the
magnitude of its history in proportion to its size.

The historians say, and I have
not the learning to dispute them,
that it saw the passing of Gauls,
Romans, and Franks, and was
already old when Brunhild died
under the shadow of its hill;
that it was for long the capital

PLAN OF LAON CATHEDRAL

FROM VIOLLET-LE-DUC'S "DICTIONNAIRE
DE L'ARCHITECTURE"

of the kingdom; that, in the Middle Ages, it fought with
whatever enemy came along, from the bishops who were
its lawful tyrants, to the English, for whom it always
cherished the Frenchman's healthy hatred, which I do
not believe all England's most diplomatic talk of an *Entente
Cordiale* will ever break down; that it struggled even
harder than most of the old French communes for its rights;
that, in brief, it is Laon you would choose for a type, as Thierry
chose it, if you were making a study of the French town in its
growth and development. And yet, I doubt if it ever took me
more than ten minutes for my most leisurely stroll from end to
end of this history-laden place. The walk round the ramparts
was, of course, another matter. And Laon, so far from thinking as I did about its size, was, in its prime, ambitious enough
to divide the hilltop into three sections, or *arrondissements,* and

each of these into several parishes, and to build sixty-two churches and chapels, though there could not possibly have been the people to fill them; no wonder the pious called the town *ville sainte* in an ecstasy of admiration. I should have put this number down to sheer bragging, had I not come across a plan of the cathedral, dated 1718, in which the small *place* in front is shut in on one side by the church of St. Remi-à-la-Porte, and on the other by the church of St. Martin-au-Parvis. Never were names more honestly come by. If the churches of Laon were built at this rate, the real puzzle is how and where the people squeezed in their houses.

These are mysteries of history. What I found at Laon—and I have spent many weeks and days there at various times—was a sleepy, idle town, comfortable and well-to-do, fairly ancient in appearance, but with no life in it apart from the cathedral and the soldiers, who, as they walked or slouched through the streets, were, all unknown to themselves, keeping up its traditions, for there must always have been soldiers in a place so given to fighting. I could not believe in the pretense Laon made on market days of being a busy, bustling market town, though the farmers in blouses, who descended upon the hotel at midday, thrust their prosperity in our faces by paying for champagne, while the rest of us did not run beyond the ordinary wine included in the dinner. But even if they were only trying each other's brands, Laon being almost where the champagne comes from, they would scarcely have made the trial there, had the town been without barracks and cathedral to fill it with a population calling for food and for drink. In the barracks I was not interested, but had there been no cathedral, what would I have been doing at Laon?

II

THE cathedral alone would be reason enough for the existence of the town.   If it would set off any church to stand on such a hill crest, it would still more set off any hill crest to have such a church stand upon it.   Laon belongs to the age of the great Gothic cathedrals, the age of Paris and Chartres and Amiens and Bourges, and its architect was not the least among the great artists who built them.   But if not one of the others seen from a distance, not even Chartres, has such dignity of position, such a cluster of gray, weather-beaten towers with the sky shining through their open windows and arches, not one, not even Notre-Dame at Paris, is so apt to disappoint at a first view near at hand.   Every one who loves cathedrals has felt the thrill of wonder this first view can give, and the excitement of the first walk in search of it.   But there is a moment of disillusion when, with a turn or a bend in the narrow street leading from the center of the town, you first come upon the west front of Laon.   It could never have had the elaborate splendor of Rouen, of Rheims or Amiens, of Bourges or Chartres, for the men of Laon who built it were rude and strong, a race of giants is Viollet-le-Duc's description.   But seldom anywhere has the restorer been so pitiless, and now, as you first stand before the façade, instead of being awed by its rudeness and strength, you are impressed chiefly with the excessive care the State has taken of it.

The cathedral would seem to you the well-preserved Historical Monument, rather than an old church with years of change and weather behind it, were you to come to it first from the north, from under the trees of the walk on the ramparts and up the wide stairs that make such a noble approach.   Nor would you get rid of the impression were you to linger, as I once loved to linger, in the sunny garden, with its bit of cloister,

THE WEST FRONT OF LAON CATHEDRAL

belonging to the *Palais de Justice,* that was the Bishop's Palace when Laon had a bishop. It is there you see, above the green, the square east end, one of the characteristics of Laon, and an unexpected contrast to find in France to the usual rounded apse with wide-flying buttresses. My heart fell when I went back to the garden and the cloister last spring, all this end of the

cathedral had been so terribly done up since my long summer in
Laon ten years earlier, so many changes had been made for no

TRANSEPT TOWER AND CLOISTER

better reason, as far as I could see, than for the mere sake of
change. Even in the Palace the big crucifix had been taken
down from above the judge's seat, where it had hung for so
long. A woman in Laon, telling me about it, cried, and, really,
I could have cried with her. It was bad enough to convert the
Romanesque chapel of the bishops into a museum, but to take

THE NORTH APPROACH TO THE TRANSEPT

down the sacred symbol from walls where it could hurt no one, is the sort of wanton act that would enter into the mind of no one save M. Combes to commit. You are always rubbing up against political crimes or mistakes of the kind in the State-

LAON. EAST END

protected cathedrals of France and their precincts. But, on the whole, I am not sure that this is not less irritating than to rub up against the vandalism of dean and chapter in the cathedrals of England, for there the Church and not the State is to blame.

It was only in the southern walls, against which the low, long building, with waving roof and tumbling chimneys, was still propped as I remembered, that I found some semblance of age. But I had to try and forget what they too may be when next I see them, for already last spring the scaffolding of the restorer concealed the south transept. The worst of it is, when your eyes, wandering upward, at last rest in peace on the dulled gold-gray of the towers with the patient oxen looking down as they have for centuries from the open arches and windows, you know what loveliness and tenderness of color all the cathedral might have, had it never been patched and pieced and refaced, especially as the chalky-white stone with which the work has been done is so hard and unlovely in its freshness. The architect will object that, without the patching and piecing and refacing, not only the color but the beauty of the beautiful architecture would have vanished. Perhaps, but when a cathedral has lived through seven centuries, I want it to give me something besides beautiful architecture. Who would care for the portrait of the old Rembrandt had he painted himself with the smooth skin, the jeweled splendor, the feathered hat, the studio trappings of the young Rembrandt staring placidly out of the canvas, life all before him? The old cathedral should wear on its face the wrinkles and creases and marks of its seven hundred years; it should stir you to the soul with the tragedy of its time-stained, crumbling stones.

The beautiful interior of Laon has fared no better. It was already barren when I first saw it; it is a barren place still, though an old fifteenth-century inventory of its treasure of gold and silver and precious stones shows it must once have been as rich and glowing as St. Mark's in Venice. But from its seasons of desecration and restoration it emerged cold and frigid, more like an English cathedral no longer warmed by the faith that built it than a French church still used by the people for prayer. I always fancied that the frigidity of its atmo-

LAON. TOWERS

sphere had got into the congregation, and that their devotion was frozen in the clear cold light. I have been in the cathedral on feast-days and great occasions. I have seen it crowded, every labeled, padded *prie-Dieu* round the choir occupied, the nave filled with nuns and orphans, priests and school-boys. But never have I felt anything like the wave of emotion that, in the

THE CHOIR FROM THE NAVE

May evenings at Chartres, swept over the people before the altar of *Notre-Dame-du-Pilier,* never anything like the ardent surrender to faith that sets the tapers alight in the crypt of *Notre-Dame-du-Port* at Clermont or before the shrine of Ste. Geneviève at Paris.

I may ask too much of Laon. Probably one should be grateful that it has emerged in any state, fervent or frigid, after the fires that did their best to burn it down, and the earthquakes that threatened to throw it down, and the enterprising jerry-builder who, during .the Revolution, with a zeal worthy of the London County Councilor, offered to pull it down and turn its site into eligible building-lots.   Instead of grumbling, I ought

LAON. NAVE, TRANSEPT FROM TRIFORIUM

to see the romance of fidelity to tradition no less in the secular bareness of the interior and the attitude of the congregation than in the soldiers marching and sauntering about the town. For it is useful to remember at Laon that the great Gothic cathedrals of France were built for the people not only to pray in but to meet in, to use as halls for social and civil as well as religious ends; that they belong to the period when the citizen of every town was beginning to remember that he had rights,

and to claim them; and that to this claim they were the concession then, very much as the *Bourse de Travail* should be
to-day. Laon was, of all towns, the one whose citizens were
most persistent and stubborn in their demand, stopping at nothing, not even the murder of their lawful tyrant, the bishop, and
the burning of his palace, to get it. When they wanted a thing,

LAON. WEST DOOR AND INNER PORCH

they did not, in modern fashion, think their work done when
they had met in the public square, murmured, and passed a few
resolutions; they fought for it hard like the giants they were.
And as what they wanted in such dead earnest was democracy,
it is natural that in no cathedral should the architecture be so
democratic in character as in theirs. At least, as well as I can
follow it, this is the theory of Viollet-le-Duc to account for the
fact that Laon, which he admired, had not the religious aspect

of Chartres or Amiens, that it struck him as brutal and savage, more like a castle than a church. It may be the reason of Laon's striking individuality, for it is curious how every one of the great French Gothic churches has a distinct character of its own, though all were built almost at the same time and according to the same general principles. Describe Laon constructively, and you would say it might be Paris, or Chartres, or

LAON. SIDE CHAPELS, WEST END OF NAVE

Amiens. Describe its detail, and you would say it can be no other French cathedral but Laon. None other has that high inner porch, none has the same row of chapels down either side of the nave, inclosed with beautiful screens—you must go to Spain to see anything like them—none has the same great gates to the choir, none has the same graceful triforium, none has the same glorious cluster of towers with the mild, patient oxen in stone looking down to the hillside, up which they toiled in the flesh, weary and goaded.　The personal touch to the architecture is in the detail.

Like the architecture, the history of Laon, in its main outlines, resembles that of every other cathedral in the land.

THE CHAPELS IN THE TRANSEPT

There was first the little chapel or crypt, when, in the third century, St. Béat came all the way from Italy to make Laon Catholic, and, shortly after, St. Preuve journeyed all the way from Scotland to keep it so.　It is astonishing how the old

saints traveled; they were always on the road, like Gypsies.
And after the little chapel, there was the church getting bigger
with each rebuilding, there were the miracles, the saintly
bishops—St. Remi the saintliest—the fires, the wars. But turn
to the detail that makes the difference. The cathedral was
begun at the very end of the twelfth century, when the people
had not time to think about anything save the rights they had
just secured. They never turned themselves into beasts of
burden like the pious at Chartres, they never dragged the stone
up the long weary zigzags; they sensibly left that to the oxen
whose portraits they afterward stuck up on high in the towers
by way of thanks, just as in other cathedrals donations of money
were rewarded by the statue of the donor or the stained-glass
window commemorating his virtues. At Laon the people were
far too busy keeping their bishops straight and themselves free,
they were far too eager to get on in this world, to let cathedral-
building absorb them. And the result, for all who care to
reason these things out logically with Viollet-le-Duc, is the
secular feeling in their cathedral, the frigidity apparent in its
atmosphere.

As a rule, in an old church I can dispense with the history
that it does not tell itself. I do not ask for facts at Chartres,
the House of Prayer, nor at Albi, the citadel of orthodoxy, nor
at St. Etienne of Toulouse, the marvel of picturesqueness. But
at Laon history lends color to the bare walls and warmth to the
empty aisles. It helps to fill the church with the life cleaned
and scraped out of it by the restorer. The cathedral, though
from the "nakedness and vacancy" of the deserted aisles you
might not think so, did, after its building, have a life, and one
not altogether so secular as Viollet-le-Duc makes it out. That
old fifteenth-century inventory to which I have referred proves
the people to have been pious enough to lavish wealth and treasure upon it. But treasure, wherever found, was irresistibly
tempting to royalty hard up, as royalty mostly was, and after

17

LAON.   THREE GREAT DOORWAYS.

Francis I had helped himself liberally, and plenty more had gone to fill the penniless treasury of Louis XIV, there was not so very much left for the Revolution to scatter. There are records too of sinners, white-shifted, barefooted, doing penance at the cathedral door, of men and women possessed by the devil coming in crowds to be exorcised; records these that suggest intervals when temporal matters were set aside. The thoroughness with which the people of Laon celebrated their Feasts of the Innocents and Feasts of Fools also points to the perfect faith that alone can afford to play with religion and its rites. And if the bishops of Laon were the real fighting bishops of old days, never happier than when brawling and squabbling with somebody, with their rival brigands in the near castles of the plain, or the flock under their pastoral care, or the chapter, when no better enemy turned up, the cathedral, anyway, was not always the background of the battle, and there were years when the only drama in order was *Les Jeux de la Vie de Monseigneur Saint Denys,* or other innocent mysteries, in which the canons played their peaceful part. And Laon was staunch during the Revolution, and the people who turned their cathedral into a Temple of Reason still loved it so well that they let no company promoter or jerry-builder of the town destroy it. Altogether, if the cathedral no longer produces a religious sentiment, the democratic tastes of the people in the twelfth and thirteenth centuries were not so entirely responsible for it that something was not left for the destructive genius of the restorer in the nineteenth.

III

IT was the fashion at one time to write of cathedrals as if their beauty grew miraculously out of the holiness and happiness of the builders. But from the little we know of these builders, it looks as if they were very much the same in the thirteenth as in any other century, depending on sound technical knowledge and going about acquiring it in much the same way as now. That the medieval architects journeyed where there were fine things to see, just as the student with a traveling scholarship does to-day, that they used their sketch-books assiduously, that they were not above appropriating the ideas of others, is known for a fact, one of the sketch-books having remained to prove it. The architect was Villard de Honnecourt, who came from a village near Cambrai, and whose work for the cathedral of that town brought him fame and commissions from as far away as Hungary. Wherever he went, he noted down designs and details, never hesitating to adapt those that pleased him to his own needs, as he showed by the use of the hints he gathered at Rheims. The men who built cathedrals, like the men who painted Madonnas, had a more robust standard than ours. "Raffaelle," Ruskin says, "carries off a whole figure from Masaccio, or borrows an entire composition from Perugino, with as much tranquillity and simplicity of innocence as a young Spartan pickpocket." That was the method of the architect of the Middle Ages, and a highly successful method it was.

Among the places de Honnecourt visited was Laon. Nothing there appears to have interested him as much as the towers. Of one he made a drawing, a memorandum for reference of the tall open arch, the oxen looking down from above, and a suggestion of the spire springing upward as it did then, as it has long ceased to do. By the side of this sketch he wrote: "I have been in many countries, as you see by this book, but in no place have I seen a tower equal to that of Laon." The traveling student or architect of to-day will—or should—agree with him. If Laon is, as some say the name means, the "glory of the mountain," the tower, or rather the towers, are the glory of its cathedral. The architect planned a great cluster of them, two at the west front, two at each transept, the lantern in the center. The entire group was never completed, and not one of the spires designed to crown them all remains. But the towers that were built did not lose their nobility of design with their spires. I can recall others of more delicate elaboration, of more graceful outline, but none of such stateliness, in their simplicity, none that, for all the rude-ness and strength they share with the rest of the cathedral, have such an effect of lightness and airiness as you look up to the long, nar-row, open arches and windows with the blue heavens shining through. If they have been restored, the restoration does not show, ag-gressively white, on the surface of dull gold-gray with which centuries of wind and rain and sun, on their exposed hilltop, have cov-ered them. They are as beautiful when you

LAON.
TRANSEPT TOWER

stand immediately below as when you catch a sudden glimpse of them at the end of one of Laon's narrow streets, or when, from the ramparts, you watch them, as you walk, grouping themselves into new beauty against the sky.

Most of my memories of Laon bring me back, sooner or later, to that high well-shaded walk about the town. It was there I used to take my book in the summer morning, there I went for a stroll in the long summer afternoon, there I sat or saun-tered in the cool of the summer night when the plain looked like the sea it once was, with the lights shining here and there as of ships at anchor, as it stretched away for miles and miles to meet the sky on the low horizon. It was there all Laon found its amusement, having no place else to seek it without going down the hill, which was not to be thought of, since going down meant the bore of coming up again. But this restriction never struck me as a very serious hardship. Every other French town has its green alleys and gardens; some, like Chartres and Angou-

LAON. BISHOP'S PALACE

lême, are encircled by wide boulevards and avenues under
pleasant shade.   But not one I know has a walk as lovely from
end to end, as complete, as full of variety, as Laon.   Now this
walk is terraced and now it opens into a formal grove where, on
feast-days and at fair-time, the people dance in the starlight; now
it passes by an old town gate or under the old town wall where
the crumbling stones meet the solid rock, and grass and bushes
grow tall and thick to hide the meeting, and now it becomes a
rough way through a wood with trees, unclipped and untrained,
meeting overhead.   Always it overlooks the plain, and constantly it discloses a new view of the town or the cathedral or
the palace: the town old and gray, save for the new red brick
houses I saw to my sorrow last spring on the slopes near the barracks; the cathedral brooding over it, gray and solemn, and

never more imposing than from across that harbor-like valley made by the acute curve of the hill on its southern side. From here you look to the widening of the plateau where Laon tries to justify its pretense of being a big city and where, at the foot of the gray walls and towers, is a space of climbing roofs.

Sometimes I had the courage to face the boredom of coming up the hill, for the sake of going down and out into the near country, so rich in the beauty France is seldom given the credit for. Not very far away is the Château de Coucy, and all around are towns and villages each with a church. But no matter what interest or beauty I discovered by the way, there was nothing more wonderful in my eyes than Laon as I saw it on my home-coming, with the cathedral and its towers black against the sunset or paling in the twilight, just as the bishops of Laon, riding back from raid or mission, must often have seen it in their day. They were strong enough to hold their own against the brigands who were their neighbors, even against the terrible Sire de Coucy. It was only before what we like to call modern progress that they weakened. But if Laon now is bishopless, the symbol of episcopal might still stands—the cathedral on the hill, as much more beautiful than the near castles as its lords were once more powerful than theirs.

LAON. GENERAL VIEW

CHAPTER XIII

ST. ETIENNE OF BOURGES

CHAPTER XIII

ST. ETIENNE OF BOURGES

I

EVERY building of the Gothic period, it is said, differs in some respect from every other. St. Etienne at Bourges differs in having a façade built on so grand, so titanic a scale that it is without a rival even in France, the land of great cathedrals. And yet, while the spires that make the difference at Chartres are ever before you in the plain of La Beauce as in Chartres itself; while the east end of Le Mans is set upon its hill, as upon a stage, above the market square; while Laon's clustered towers, clear against the sky, are a joy to all the country round, the west front of St. Etienne, from near as from far, seems to baffle you, to refuse to let you see it in its imposing immensity. I cannot say why this is. Bourges climbs, if gently, a little hill, not very high, but high enough to lift the cathedral well above the flat pasture-lands of Berry. "Seen from a distance"—I quote Mr. Arthur Symons—"it is formidable and seems to brood over the town as if weighing upon it, like an oddly shaped rock or mountain. Seen from near, it imposes by its immense breadth, raised higher than the ground before it by a broad flight of low steps." The neighboring houses are of modest height, what great buildings there are stand on a lower level. But though I have come to the town by road and by rail, I have never yet found the point of

THE WEST FRONT

view from which the façade makes quite the effect which you would expect of its majestic beauty, its monstrous strength. A small *place* opens immediately in front of the cathedral, and the lofty flight of steps mounting to the lofty portals adds to the height already so tremendous without it. But from this *place* you seem to look at the façade only in bits, wonderful bits it is true, but never the wonderful whole. You are too close. It is like looking up to the Matterhorn from the Schwarz-See or the Gorner-Grat. You lose the scale. Stand where you will, the perspective is too violent. You might almost fancy that the architect, who, in those amazing days, planned deliberately, or so it seemed, his pictorial and picturesque as well as his architectural effects, had intended this, designing his work so that there before it you must wonder the more at a façade too colossal in proportions ever to be seen as one immense whole.

It is more likely a mere accident that the hotels in a French cathedral town are so often just where the most direct walk from them will bring you to the point for the right first view and therefore the right first impression, of the cathedral. As at Le Mans the way from every hotel where you are apt to put up leads to the east end, the glory of St. Julien's, so at Bourges it leads as surely to the west front, the triumph of St. Etienne's. And you know which way this is, for since, in any town where there is a suggestion of a hill, the cathedral is almost sure to be on its top, you have only to follow a street slop-

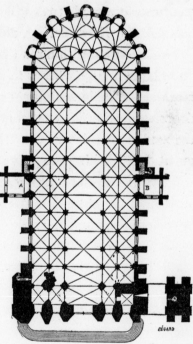

PLAN OF THE CATHEDRAL OF BOURGES

FROM VIOLLET-LE-DUC'S "DICTIONNAIRE DE L'ARCHITECTURE"

ing upward to come sooner or later into sight of it. The first time I followed that sloping street in Bourges was on a cloudless July afternoon, and I had come to the end of its cool shadow too soon for my comfort when the rugged mass of the northern tower loomed up before me in the clear sunlight. I had already seen several of the greatest cathedrals in France, but they had not prepared me for the breathless moment of astonishment when I turned out in front of the façade of which this rugged mass was only a part. From the *place* I looked up the wide flight of steps to five cavernous portals where even Rouen and Rheims and Paris and Amiens are content with three; I looked to their rich setting of sculpture, to a row of gables above them, and, still higher, to windows with bold and delicate traceries, to galleries and arcades, to mountainous buttresses, and, at last, to where the gray stone, worn by wind and storm and sun into new loveliness, rose into the highest gable of all, pointing skyward between the two towers. The hugeness of it was dazzling, bewildering, almost oppressive.

The astounding thing is that the artist, who could see beauty on so large a scale, was as mindful of it in detail. There are no more remarkable sculptures anywhere than those on the west doors. Nowhere is the story of the Last Judgment, the story the medieval sculptor never tired of telling, told with more eloquent detail, with more naïve skill, than above the central doorway, with the stern Judge on his throne, his awful arm outstretched, the angels in attendance, the horned, hoofed, tailed devils, leering and horrible, the good rising impetuously, the wicked as reluctantly, from their graves. There can be no smile here for the fantastic ignorance of the early sculptor. And nowhere is any other Scriptural drama recorded in stone with such scrupulous fidelity, scene after scene, incident after incident, carved so simply that any child could understand and so well that any artist would rejoice.

Mr. Arthur Symons found in these sculptures less fine

THE GREAT PORTALS OF THE WEST FRONT

homely feeling for character in faces than at Amiens; for "the body counts for more, and the body is ashamed of nakedness and uncomely without a covering." And this means, if anything, that there is more of the true medieval feeling in the sculptor's work at Bourges. It was because the body counted for so much in sin that its nakedness was its undoing, that hell was opened in such grotesque frankness on the portal of the temple. You can see how uncomfortable it makes the men and women, the saved and the damned alike, as they start up out of their graves when summoned to the last tribunal of all; you can see how large a part it is of the evil in the grinning, lascivious, horrible demons; you can see how it aggravates the tortures of the lost as they are plunged by their tormentors into boiling caldrons, or bitten on the legs, or pushed and bullied and baited. Mr. Symons discovers a kind of cheerful horror in all this. But I confess that I was too conscious of the horrid cruelty in the medieval conception of the final act in the tragedy of life to see much else. I think it must have been because I had been first to Bourges and familiarized myself with the sculptures there, in the course of many days of going to and fro between my hotel and the cathedral, that I was so grateful, as I have said, to the sculptors of St. Pierre at Poitiers for having spared the damned some of the cruelty that pursues them at St. Etienne. I may be wrong, however, for Mr. Henry James who took in Bourges on his "Little Tour" agrees rather with Mr. Symons, and was struck more by the gaiety of the good than the fear or shyness of the wicked as they obviously hang back, as well they may, from their fate, and he remembers best of all "a charming detail," the angel who saves a little child from the leering devil on the point of appropriating her. There are innumerable scenes to the drama. Days can be spent in studying it before the figures and their meaning are exhausted. But when you come to study and look again at the great façade and the five portals as one splendid whole, the sculptures never obtrude themselves upon the general design. The sculptors appear to have gloated over the story they had to tell, dwelling upon the anecdote as anecdote should never be gloated upon by the artist according to our modern canons of art. But all the

THE TOUR DE BEURRE

time they never lost sight of the space they had to decorate, the harmony with which it was their business to fill it, the unity of effect it was their supreme end to attain. It is astonishing how well they succeeded. Anecdote is a trap to the latter-day

18

artist; to them it was a stimulus, an inspiration to the accomplishment of which the secret has been lost.   The sculpture at Bourges satisfies both the artist who asks for beauty and the public who ask for a moral tale.   It keeps in its place perfectly—a Bible if you care to come close and read, a lovely decoration, a mere carven pattern, if you care too much for its beauty to search for a meaning.

I know that much can be and has been said in objection to the façade: that it gains its great width by disregard of the actual proportions of the building behind it; that it was designed on so prodigious a scale, it could not possibly be completed within the perfect period of the thirteenth century when it was begun, and, indeed, it is not entirely completed yet; that it is, in consequence, a jumble of styles; that the two towers are too low for it, the southern reaching scarcely above the central gable, the northern, the *Tour de Beurre,* erected in the sixteenth century, though taller,. needing the spire each was planned to carry; that the building to the south, a house in itself, but, practically, an additional support to the already well-buttressed tower, increases the width inordinately.   But grant that all these objections are just, grant that as many more might be made.   What does it matter when the mistakes and the delays, the want of balance and the exaggerations, have not taken away from the impressiveness and hugeness of this most impressively huge of all Gothic façades?

II

THE rest of the exterior scarcely equals the astonishing west front.   It would be miraculous if it did, if architect and sculptor had kept throughout to so extraordinary a standard.   Were the façade simpler, the great long stretch of the nave as you see it from the little streets to the north, or from the archbishop's

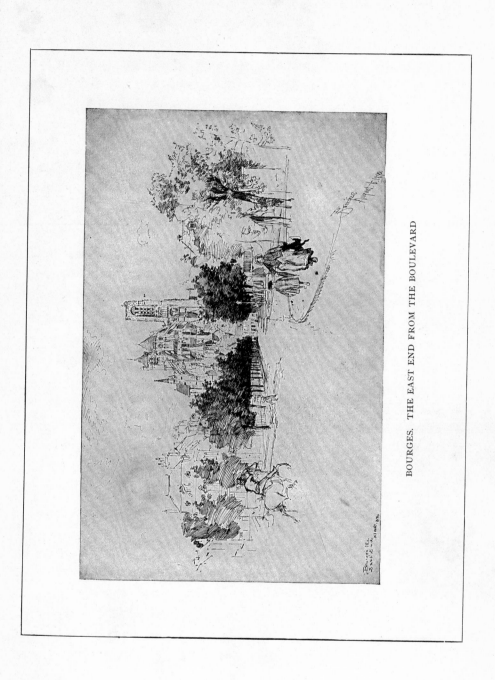

BOURGES. THE EAST END FROM THE BOULEVARD

garden to the south, might seem less plain. That garden is one of the most charming things in Bourges. You expect a charming garden of every French town, but it is not often laid out for you, as here, with the cathedral overhanging it, so that from the clipped alleys and formal walks, from between the prim flower beds and well-placed statues, you can, at your leisure, watch the passing of the light and shadow over the gray, weather-beaten walls. I spent a long succession of hot mornings there, the summer I was in Bourges, and I came to know this view of St. Etienne intimately, as one knows the view out of one's own window.

Chance, sometimes, had as much to do with the design of an old cathedral as the architect. At Bourges, the want of money was the chance that went far to modify and alter his plans. For one thing, it made him dispense with transepts altogether, and their absence, though an advantage to the interior, gives to the exterior, as you see it from the garden, too rigid and severe a sky-line. And the same want of money first, and then want of the old enthusiasm that had filled France with its fair flowering of churches, left the towers unfinished and spireless. Before the west front, I might feel that to have finished them, to have set upon their summit tall tapering spires, would have made the façade too incredible—as above and beyond human power as the precipices on the Splügen or the peaks of the Velay. But in the garden I had to admit the cathedral's sore need of something to break with more force and emphasis its long line from west to east. Think of the difference made by the one tall tower to Ste. Cécile at Albi! Only when you approach the east end of Bourges from the wide boulevard leading to it from a lower level, do the towers tell in the composition. There was little of the critic in me as I sat, morning after morning, in my cool corner; you do not criticize a thing that gives you so strong an emotion of wonder. But I knew the wonder would have been greater far had the

THE CATHEDRAL FROM THE GARDEN

buttresses of nave and choir been carried out on the same lavish scale as the west front. As it is, they never build up into solemn cliffs as at Chartres, they never multiply into labyrinthine intricacy as at Le Mans, they never overflow with ornament as at Rheims. In them you seem to see the skeleton, not the gorgeous covering of Gothic. Again, of course, want of money was the reason. But it looks as if the builders, having proved by the west front what inexhaustible beauty of decoration they could create, chose in the wide spaces of buttressed wall to show only the beauty of their theory, their method of building. Really, I know of no place, especially if you go to it with Professor Charles H. Moore's book in your hand, where you can, in cold blood, reduce Gothic architecture to a "system of balanced thrusts" better than in the garden at Bourges.

If you walk round the cathedral, you will find that it breaks, if not its sky-line, at least the length of its walls and the succession of its buttresses, and that it does so with anything but reserve or bareness.   For the north and south porches, though not quite so wonderful as those of Chartres—no cathedral porches could be so wonderful—are among the very loveliest

THE SOUTH DOOR

in France.   Thirteenth-century architects, in their pride, never hesitated to pull down earlier buildings to make way for their own, but they were artists enough to preserve what they thought best in the old work, if they could without injury to the new design. Statues—long, slim, and strange, the draperies falling in stiff archaic folds, the faces smiling inscrutably— like the statues of Chartres and Le Mans, stand in their niches at the entrance to the Gothic cathedral, as they stood at the entrance to the Romanesque cathedral it had replaced. Nor did the thirteenth-century builders shrink from drawbacks that might appear insurmountable to the academic architect of to-day, who prizes absolute regularity above all other virtues. When they found the site for their cathedral not squarely on the top but on the slope of the little hill, it only presented another excuse for the variety they loved. And so it happens that, while you enter the south door, with its ancient statues, with Christ and the Apocalyptic beasts above, from the level, you must go up a flight of steps to enter from the north.

But, whichever way you enter, whether from one of these porches, or from the great western portals, the interior, like the exterior, will impress you above all with a sense of its immensity. Uninterrupted by transepts, the long line of the nave, with its two aisles on either side, seems the more inter- minable, though it is really shorter than in many French cathe- drals. There is no choir screen to break up the spaces, only an iron grille that does not interfere with the great sweep of the vista from the west end to the beautiful curve of the apse. And the height is the more striking partly because the outer aisles, like the nave, have their triforium and clearstory. There were times when I thought Bourges too big, so titanic that prayer cannot warm it. The atmosphere is secular, frigid, as at Laon. It can delight you with the most dignified archi- tectural compositions, with the noblest arrangements of pillars and arches, ever varying as you follow the inner aisle up the nave and round the choir. But it rarely awes you with the darkness and mystery of churches where faith is most fervent.

It amuses me to compare my own impressions in the nave, as before the western portals, with the impressions it made upon

IN THE INTERIOR

both Mr. Arthur Symons and Mr. Henry James. It is often
said that if three painters sit down before the same landscape,
each will bring away a different picture, and this is usually
what happens in the case of three travelers. Mr. Symons saw
in the interior "weight, solemnity, with something incalculable
in its separate effects, though with none of the daintiness of

Amiens. . . . Unity, ease, sequence, elegance are the qualities.
. . . The aisles surround the church like arcades; the low
inner one, which remains always dim, while the nave and the
outer aisles are open to traveling rays of light, has a touch of
mystery." Mr. Henry James was struck with the simplicity,
the majesty, and above all the tremendous height: "there is a
tranquil largeness, a kind of infinitude, about such an edifice;
it soothes and purifies the spirit, it illuminates the mind." Both
were moved by the beauty of the glass where it still fills some
of the windows in the choir. I am the readier to quote them
both because I differ from them as to the touch of mystery, the
solemnity, and the effect upon spirit and mind, though the vast
interior filled me with awe and admiration no less than theirs,
but, on the contrary, so profound that I can think it an advantage to allow their warmth to make up for any shortcomings
in the degree of my appreciation.

As to the windows, there can be no two opinions. They burn
as if with a light from heaven, and yet the church, cold in my
eyes, scarcely thaws in the flaming fires of the beautiful old
glass, of which there is much. Of all the restorer has done at
Bourges, and even Viollet-le-Duc thought the restoration overdone, I can least forgive his tampering with this glass. The
worst is, I do not know how serious the injury to it will be, or
is now. For only a year or two ago the west wall was all bricked
up, and the great rose window—when seen from the east "pale,
like a star appearing at the end of an alley of trees," Mr.
Symons writes—had been taken down to be cleaned and
repaired, I was told, the work was finished, but there was not
enough money to put it up again. Of this I am sure: when
the money is found and the window put back, it can never be
the same for our generation, or for many generations to come.
Only time can mellow the old glass, like the old walls, into a
fuller, richer beauty.

The very crypt at Bourges, one of its wonders, immense like

everything else, is cold. It contains no Black Virgin with lights gleaming from shadowy aisles, no golden caskets of relics flashing out upon you as you pass and sinking again into the gloom. It had, when I was last there, the undevout and practical look of a stone-mason's workshop, for which, indeed, it was being used. In the litter of broken sculptures, and of old stone coffins made before Bourges was French but dug up only when modern furnaces and pipes for heating the cathedral were being laid, I saw the Duc de Berri—John the Magnificent—on his monumental slab, waiting patiently for a new nose, but even in his pathetic mutilation looking not only the great person he was, but affable and gay, a good fellow, so that I should wonder why he struck Stendhal so disagreeably, if Stendhal at Bourges had not been in a humor to see the disagreeable. Before the cathedral itself, however, his mood had to give way: it awed him by its noble vastness, from façade to crypt, as it must every one who comes to it.

III

WHEN I could bring myself to leave the cool of the cathedral and of the garden it overhangs, I did a great deal of wandering along Bourges in the long summer days, for you have not got to the end of the beauty of a great Gothic church until you have got to the end of its every possible view under every possible aspect. Incidentally, I saw much of the town, and there is much in it to see. Bourges reeks with history, and many monuments remain that this history colors more vividly than St. Etienne, the greatest of them all. You do not always think of the *Roi de Bourges,* the hero of the town's chief drama, up at the cathedral, but you cannot forget him at the house of Jacques Cœur, without whom Charles never would have had the money to be king of anything else. And if you remember Charles at the palace of this Rothschild or Vanderbilt of the fifteenth century, you must also remember Joan of Arc, and Agnés Sorel, and a host of smaller figures who follow in his train. But in the quiet of the garden on the hill they fade out of the picture. Even Jacques Cœur, though he has his chapel in the cathedral, and though his son was once its lord, seems a less important person there than many a now unknown archbishop: for instance, that tender-hearted Berruyer, who added nothing to the history of the world, and has no more substantial claim to fame than his love for the poor, for whom he turned his own bedchamber into a dormitory and his palace into a sort of soup-kitchen and shelter. There are other old houses with other memories—of Cujas, of Calvin, of many famous men. And there are old churches, and old corners and little houses with no memories at all, but with gables and carvings and projecting upper stories. And there are shady avenues and sloping roads, with bits of red wall showing here and there. I am sure I do not understand why Bourges seemed to Stendhal so mean a place, and to other travelers so filled with ugliness and dullness. But I admit I never found anything in it, however historical and memorable otherwise, that could surpass the cathedral in beauty. If I wandered farther, and left the streets and houses for the rich green meadows, and the rows of poplars, and the straight banks of the Canal de Berri or the windings of the two little rivers that meet it here, always the colossal church was the most splendid feature in the landscape as in the town.

And this is what the cathedral has ever been, since the days when, in the new dawn of the thirteenth century, it rose, magnificently huge as we know it, in the place of the older, smaller church on the little hill. One of the most vivid chapters of the history of France was made in the town, the chapter was closed, and the cathedral still stood there in its beauty, splendid and strong. A wave of Protestantism swept over Bourges, the town where Calvin studied, it rolled away again, and Mass was

still said as of old in the cathedral, where only the broken statues
on the façade and the broken tombs in the chapels bore witness
to its fury. The whirlpool of the Revolution would have swallowed the cathedral forever, leaving in its stead a Temple of
Reason, the Revolution passed as the Huguenots had passed,
and St. Etienne survived in its immensity, unchanged save for
more broken statues and tombs, scattered treasure, and, perhaps

FROM THE RIVER

as a last cynical sign of revolt, the name of Etienne Dolet given,
I am not quite certain when, to the *place* opened about it.
Bourges relapsed into calm, the peaceful town of little houses
shut in by high garden walls that it still is in the quarter near
the cathedral. It made the most of literary names and associations, and, as you wander, you come to the Rue Victor Hugo
and the Rue Georges Sand, the Rue Michelet and the Rue
Mirabeau. It developed into an industrial center and though it
is, on the face of it, so obviously what the French call the *ville
bourgeoise,* in opposition to the *ville ouvrière,* I have not for-

gotten, during the year of the King of Spain's visit to France, the violent posters pasted all over the walls of Bourges in strong protest against the reception prepared for him, because Spain is the country where the rights of the workman receive least recognition, and the language in which the protest was written was seditious really, quite revolutionary. And Bourges has become a military stronghold, and it has made the usual concessions to modern progress in the shape of boulevards and electric trams and a big Potin store in the central square. And the cathedral, unmoved by fashions that pass, wears serenely as ever the beauty with which men clothed it seven hundred years ago, and within its walls prayers continue to be said that Bourges learned before France was. It broods above the history, as above the housetops of the town, beautiful, immense, serene, like some giant Alp at peace above the restless labors of the valley.

CHAPTER XIV

AMIENS: "THE PARTHENON OF GOTHIC ARCHITECTURE"

THE CATHEDRAL OF AMIENS FROM THE WEST

CHAPTER XIV

AMIENS: "THE PARTHENON OF GOTHIC ARCHITECTURE"

I

WHEN I go to Amiens now, I take with me the memory not only of Ruskin's eloquence, as everybody must, but of my own impressions on my first visit of all.   For I had seen no other French cathedral then, had seen hardly anything of France, and the beauty of town and church was the more astonishing to me because I did know many of the English cathedrals and did not imagine that any others in this world could be more beautiful.   I was almost afraid afterward that, to return to Amiens, would be to risk disappointment.   I have been there many times in the many years since then, again only the other day, and it has lost nothing when thus put to the test of my enthusiasm and Ruskin's approval.   It was as astonishing on my last visit as on my first, its beauty equal to the demands of my old memories and associations.

The cathedral could be put to a still more severe test and lose nothing.   It is, in some ways, the most beautiful, the most perfect of the French Gothic cathedrals.   It belongs to the finest period of Gothic in France, the thirteenth century, and was almost all built within that period.   It has greater symmetry, less chance picturesqueness than almost any one of its rival churches, and few have preserved so much of the original detail

both of exterior and interior. It is well placed, for, if the immediate surroundings are swept a little too bare and clean, it is on
high enough ground for the old town below to provide a more
appropriate setting. In the streets about the principal hotels,
you cannot forget that Amiens is a big, busy, modern city. But
to the south of the cathedral there are picturesque old streets
of gabled houses almost untouched, the more medieval in effect

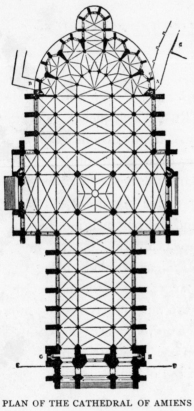

PLAN OF THE CATHEDRAL OF AMIENS

FROM VIOLLET-LE-DUC'S "DICTIONNAIRE
DE L'ARCHITECTURE"

because of the squalor of the
life lived in them and the primitiveness of the people: a quarter
made to the hand of Zola, I
often thought. Through several streets the Somme and its
branches, or canals, go winding,
giving Amiens the name of
"the Venice of France" and
bringing to it on market days a
large fleet of the peasants' curious low, flat-bottomed boats with
high prows. When the boats
are unloading and unloaded, they
are moored in long lines along
the riverside, the market is on
the quay close by, there is the
green of many trees, and
high over all looms the cathedral, in its immense buttressed
length from apse to western
towers.

If, before you explore the old town, you obey Ruskin and
walk to the top of the near hills for your first point of view,
there, looking back "to the cathedral and ascending slopes of
the city," you may get at the very beginning the right understanding of the "real height and relation of tower and town."

STATUES ON THE WEST FRONT OF AMIENS CATHEDRAL

But for pure beauty, for Amiens at its loveliest, I should say, follow the Somme or one of its branches or canals, until it brings you beyond the ugly suburbs into the country where you see the cathedral set in the midst of the lagoons and poplared glades, and under the pale skies, of Picardy. Laon and Chartres have greater majesty of position, Rheims broods more sphinx-like over the plain, Notre-Dame-de-Paris stands in the midst of a more animated city life. But for loveliness of form and line, for delicacy and elegance in harmony with the French landscape of which it is the commanding feature, Amiens has no rival throughout the length and breadth of France.

The visit to the town should be in the springtime, because when the poplars are first powdered with green, and the fruit-trees blossom in the gardens of the lagoons, and the lilac is all abloom, Picardy has more of this elegance and delicacy to offer than any other part of France. I am never carried through the tunnels and railroad station of Amiens, on the way to the Paris Salon in early May, without a regret that I cannot break the journey, as I did when I cycled there for the first time so long ago, and again see Amiens from the flowering banks of the Somme and its canals.

II

Fortune seems to have seized upon Amiens for her own, lavishing upon the church of Our Lady all the great gifts more sparingly distributed among most of the other cathedrals. Everything about it is interesting. The town cannot be left out of any history of France, whose first capital it was; and to Clovis as a leading hero, Peter the Hermit, who was born and has a statue there, plays a good second. The saints of Amiens appeal to me with more than the usual human note and intimacy: Firmin, who converted it, appearing "out of space," preaching in the public places like any modern reformer and

19

proving as much of a nuisance to the authorities no doubt, for the Romans, who had a more effectual way of getting rid of nuisances than we, beheaded him at the end of forty days; and Honoré, the patron of bakers, and so of course of the "charming *patissiers*" Ruskin has not been alone in discovering at Amiens; and Martin, who divided his cloak with the beggar on a near windy hilltop, and who has been painted almost as many times and represented as almost as beautiful as Sebastian stuck full of arrows, but who never makes so gallant and gay an appearance as in that early picture of him by Van Dyck. Ruskin refers to St. Martin as "the patron of honest drinking," and you may take that, if you will, as a more picturesque reason than because you are so far North to account for the drunkenness you see in Amiens and so seldom in the more southern towns of France. And Amiens has inspired people to write about it with more than common eloquence. Viollet-le-Duc described the cathedral as the "Parthenon of Gothic architecture," and almost every authority after him has had to quote the phrase. Even Arthur Young, chary in praise of most cathedrals, thought Amiens "very large and beautifully light and decorated," but that may have been because he generously gave his countrymen the credit for having built it. When Ruskin set to work to record What Our Fathers Have Told Us, it was with Amiens he began. And it was Amiens that William Morris chose, when he wanted to make people know how he loved the grand churches of northern France—"for I think these same churches of North France the grandest, the most beautiful, the kindest and most loving of all the buildings that the earth has ever borne." "The crowning glory of Gothic art," Professor Charles H. Moore says of Amiens, looking at it with the eyes of an architect. "The greatest house made with hands, . . . like a precious casket adorned for some priceless jewel," Mr. Arthur Symons writes, seeing it with the eyes of the poet. Pater, the man of letters, found the architecture "full of excite-

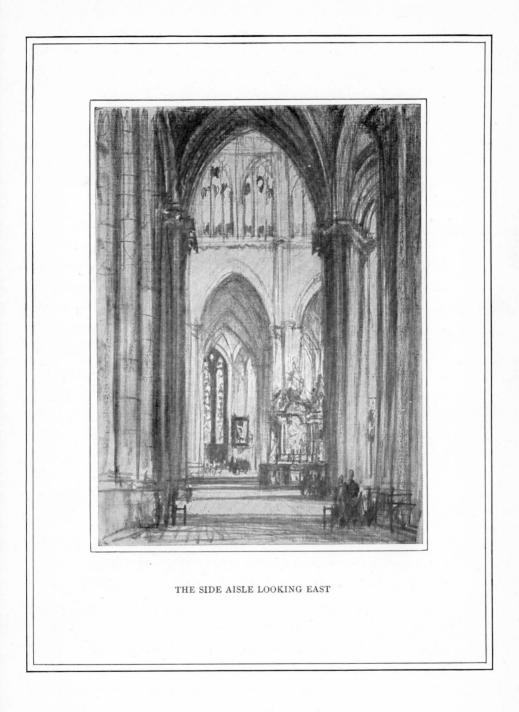

THE SIDE AISLE LOOKING EAST

ment"; to L'Abbé Roze, the priest, the church was the "Queen of Cathedrals." Few have written quite calmly who have written of Amiens at all, and enthusiasm is roused in the reader long before the cathedral is known.

History and praise would count for less if the cathedral had not been still more fortunate in its architects and the conditions under which they worked. No great Gothic church of France was entirely completed within one architectural period, Viollet-le-Duc says, but Amiens came nearer it than any other, and the period was splendid. Paris, Chartres, Rheims, and Amiens are the four greatest of the great French Gothic churches, and Amiens was the last of the four in the order of their building. The architect therefore had the experience of the builders of the other three to profit by. Moreover, he could come to the work with a free hand. Fire after fire had raged in Amiens since the erection of the first little chapel over St. Firmin's grave, and the last, in 1218, did what it had to do with all its might so successfully that when the foundations of the new church were laid, two years later (1220), there was no older building or any part of one to be incorporated into it. The architect, Robert de Luzarches, knew how to make the most of this opportunity, and one feels that it is only right he should be remembered by name, as medieval architects so seldom were, and that this name should be constantly recalled to the native and the foreigner by the street upon which it has been bestowed. At the end of some sixty years (1288), the cathedral was finished almost exactly as we see it now. Little was left for later generations and masters of new styles to add, except the western towers, the *flèche,* and details of decoration. And not only was the cathedral quickly built, it was staunchly built. It never met the fate of Beauvais, it was spared the tumbling in of roof, or tower, or too high-soaring spire. Some weak parts had to be strengthened, some bracing and girdling had to be done here and there, and the restorer has been too often let loose upon it.　But the wear and tear of time has called for comparatively few changes, and there is not in France so complete an example on so large a scale of thirteenth-century work.　This is why it is so universally praised by architects who prize unity of style above chance picturesqueness and historical records.

I do not think anybody can look at the cathedral without being impressed by this unity.　It has the harmony and the repose of all perfect works of art.　Technical faults can be pointed out, I believe.　Fergusson regrets that the west towers are too low and that the façade is a sham, since it gives no true idea of the size and height of the huge church behind it; others criticize the façade as a mere screen for the display of sculpture.　Ruskin objects to the *flèche* as the pretty caprice of a village carpenter.　Nor is modern meddling beyond reproach. Every one must deplore the tampering with the old steps that led up to the western portals, and the new painting of the chapels, and the tidying up in places of the stonework.　But these are minor blemishes and they cannot destroy the perfection of the cathedral.　Indeed, sometimes I could almost wish the nave less perfect.　The exquisite formality, unrelieved in the clear light of the many and spacious windows, is more in character with its lay purpose as the House of Justice it once was, than the religious ends to which it has since been adapted. I should like to give it the color of a warmer devotion and to set burning in its windows the "imperious angry fire" that, at Chartres, awes you into prayer.　As it is, it has never made me feel with Mr. Symons "an immense cheerfulness in .this daylight church," and, anyway, cheerfulness would be the last thing I should want to feel.　One of the missions of Gothic architecture is said to be to lift the eyes of the faithful heavenward, but another is to suggest mystery, and there is no mystery in a nave so perfect.　It has a serenity more in keeping with the spirit of Greek, than of Gothic, beauty, and it fully justifies Viollet-le-Duc's description.

Transepts and choir, however, are full of the color, the chance picturesqueness, the magnificence, the richness, the variety, that I expect Gothic to supply for my pleasure. Ruskin, bullying his reader in his usual fashion, insists that the cathedral must be entered for the first time by the south transept door— the door of the *Vierge Dorée,* that "soubrette of a Madonna." This is a case when I do not mind being bullied. For once you pass through the door, and the passing through is in itself a reward for obedience, you are in a world of golden shrines and splendid tombs and elaborate carvings. And the transepts are like a beautiful antechamber to the beautiful choir, which is the richest and most magnificently adorned part of the cathedral, as the holy of holies in the Temple ought to be. It is true that I would like to set alight in the choir, as in the nave, the solemn fires of the windows of Chartres, but there would be no need to borrow the choir screen, another of the wonders of Chartres, for Amiens has one still more wonderful. It is not as complete as the screen at Albi, but the series of sculptured stone panels surpass in detail even the carvings of the southern cathedral.

St. John the Baptist is specially honored at Amiens, where his head, after many adventures, was brought to rest in peace and has been ever since the cathedral's most precious possession. The panels on the north side of the choir wall, facing his chapel, are the chronicle of his career. The story is told with the respect for subject that the faithful expected of the sixteenth-century sculptor and the fine sense of decoration that was instinctive with him. Realism could scarcely go further than in the rendering of the castled, turreted background, and the people who look from the windows or sit at table or crowd the foreground, and the costumes which are those of the sculptor's own day, the artist then being happily free from archæological responsibility. He could reserve his energy and imagination for the treatment of his subject, and the incidents in the saint's life were never made to follow each other with such dramatic movement. They begin with his sermon in the wilderness, and lead on, one by one, to the last acts in the tragedy when Salome dances before Herod—the dance that has become an esthetic motive for poet, dancer, and musician to-day, but that was then only too real a part of the tragedy of the New Testament,—and when, as the price of her dance, the Baptist's head is presented to Herod, Herodias pierces it, and Salome faints in horror. The story of Firmin, carved a century earlier, fills the panels on the south wall of the screen and moves with the same simple realism and dramatic force. You see the saint entering Amiens, you see him preaching, you see him meekly bowing his head to the executioner who wears red tights, and whose little dog follows close at his heels. And then, you assist at the discovery of the saintly relics, and watch them as they are borne triumphantly into Amiens. Each panel is "packed" with detail, and each figure was assuredly studied from life and was a faithful portrait. It is only because we know the story of Salome so much better that we are apt to linger before it and to pass by the legend of Firmin more quickly. In realistic truth and force there is little to choose between them, and, indeed, Firmin's executioner in his red tights stands out as one of the most vigorous figures of them all.

The realism in the panels of the screen never takes away from the quality of the design, and time and the Revolution have dealt gently with the detail. As at Albi, the sculptures are painted. The colors may have been, most likely were, strong and crude when fresh, but they have faded into pale tender tones, and the spaces of tinted stone break in softly upon the grayness, the richly fretted surface seems placed there for the more brilliant and subtle play of light and shadow. On the wall behind the choir, perched on a big pompous tomb, a little seventeenth-century cherub—the *petit pleureur* who reappears in every material in every shop-window of Amiens—weeps ostentatiously, and you might fancy that his tears flow less over

WEST FRONT OF AMIENS CATHEDRAL

the emblems of death at his side, than over the degeneracy of a public who for long preferred him to the unconscious actors in the tragedies of Firmin and John, and has now at last been taught better.

The choir walls, with their sculptures, inclose a greater marvel of carving. I must quote Ruskin, for I know I could not, and I do not think any one could, describe the choir stalls more graphically and with more charm: "Aisles and porches, lancet windows and roses, you can see elsewhere as well as here— but such carpenter's work you cannot. It is late—fully developed flamboyant, just past the fifteenth century—and has some Flemish stolidity mixed with the playing French fire of it; but wood-carving was the Picard's joy from his youth up, and, so far as I know, there is nothing else so beautiful cut out of the goodly trees of the world. Sweet and young—grained wood it is: oak *trained* and chosen for such work, sound now as four hundred years since. Under the carver's hand it seems to cut like clay, to fold like silk, to grow like living flame. Canopy crowning canopy, pinnacle piercing pinnacle—it shoots and wreathes itself into an enchanted glade, inextricable, imperishable, fuller of leafage than any forest, and fuller of story than any book."

There is not a square inch of it all uncarved, and there is not a square inch of carving that does not relate or make beautiful the history of events without which the cathedral, and therefore the different parts of it, could never have been: the history of prophets and patriarchs, saints and prodigals. There is not an inch that is not lovely both in itself and as a subordinate part of a regal whole. Kings or emperors, on their thrones, may well envy these stalls where twice a day, at the hours of office, a few old and feeble canons meet to chant Matins and Vespers.

Outside, the cathedral has the same variety and magnificence. The buttresses seem less cliff-like, more delicate and daintily decorated than in most churches as large. Ornament is everywhere; buttresses and walls and transept doors are laden with it; but nowhere does it blossom and flower with such profusion and loveliness as on the west front. Here the sculptor used the same realism in the choice and treatment of subject as in the choir screen and choir stalls. It was his edition of the Holy Scriptures, the "Bible of Amiens" Ruskin called it, for the people to read in those days when they could read no other. Old and New Testament were translated into stone, plainly that the people might understand, beautifully that God might be glorified. Chapter by chapter, almost verse by verse, the old, well-known Bible stories were told; incident by incident, the lives of those saints to whom Amiens looks as its special patrons were faithfully put down. In the center of the central porch stands the *Beau Christ d'Amiens,* as the Amienois name him, appropriating him with familiar reverence. Prophets, apostles, and saints, each in his canopied niche, are in attendance. Below, carved in relief, stories from the Bible and stories of saints fill a double row of quatrefoils. There you will find Adam and Eve, Noah and the Ark, Abraham and Isaac, Moses and the Burning Bush, Jonah stepping in imperturbable placidity out of the whale's mouth; there too are the Wise Men coming out of the East, adoring at Bethlehem, and the Innocents being massacred; there the Blessed Mother of God lies on her deathbed, ascends into heaven, is crowned by her Son. Above the central door is a Last Judgment, only less naïve and grotesque and terrible in its realism than the Last Judgment at Bourges. Wherever the sculptor could, he added symbolic and allegoric figures: the Wise and Foolish Virgins, the Signs of the Zodiac, strange beasts and monsters. And this mass of detail was copied by him accurately and vividly from the life he knew. The people of the Scriptures go about their daily affairs as he saw the people of Amiens go about theirs, allegory is expressed in the terms of every-day life, the monsters are the bogies of a child's imagination. Reality is aimed at and achieved, with no concession to convention, except that demanded by limitation of space and of the sculptor's medium. As far as the eye reaches upward, the ornament is carried. I have spent days, as the Amienois I hope spend them, studying it out and reading its meaning. And yet it never monopolized the beauty, was never disturbing, when I turned from it to look at the beauty of the façade as a beautiful whole. Then, at åll hours, the multitudinous detail would lose itself in the surface, giving a new quality to the texture of the stone. But the west front, extraordinarily rich always, was never so resplendent as when it glowed and shone in the evening light more radiantly than any mountain slope, and held the shadows with a deeper mystery.

Walks through the old streets, walks to the one or two old churches, walks through the country so green in its fertility and so brown with the upturned peat, were sure to bring me back to close the labor and the pleasure of the day before the west front that seemed like one great carven prayer, more solemn than the spoken or chanted *Nunc dimittis,* more soothing than the ringing of the *Angelus* at dusk.

III

I DO not know whether to account it another piece of good fortune that Amiens is so easy of access. Cathedrals like Le Puy and Albi, to which a special journey must be made, are visited only by the few with a genuine love for cathedrals. But Amiens, on the main line between London and Paris, attracts the many, to whom I do not grudge whatever pleasure in it they may get, but in whose trail the disaster of commonplace is too apt to follow. The crowd of tourists bring after them guides, who do not let you stray comfortably where you will, and beggars, who do not let you stray anywhere alone and unattended. The beggars at the cathedral doors in the South have their picturesque value, no less than the statues in their niches. But the beggars of Amiens, who overflow into the interior, have not even picturesqueness to recommend them, and the very babes in arms pursue you as persistently as if they had read Ruskin and knew his advice to give them a *sou* prettily and without question. Tourists also bring money, and money may mean restoration, and the restorer, so far, has been Amiens' worst enemy.

An interval of neglect, if not too prolonged, would do the cathedral no harm. Old buildings have been cleared from its immediate neighborhood. The *Parvis* is as neat as a newly paved square can be. The little house for the Suisse at the foot of the north tower, with curtains at the windows and red geraniums on the sills, has the look of a lodge at the park gates of some pretentious modern mansion, though, at least, it helps to give the scale and that touch of domesticity to the House of God which, to me, is one of the charms of every Catholic church. Inside the cathedral, when I remember the fate of Angoulême, and Périgueux, and many another national monument, at the learned hands of Viollet-le-Duc or Abadie, I tremble before the evidence of official interference. Time, in its indifference, can be more merciful than the government, in its paternal care. However, the church of Our Lady may be strong enough to outlive popularity and prosperity as it has outlived wars and revolutions, heresies and persecutions, and many generations to come should still be able to read What Our Fathers Have Told Us in the carven stones of Amiens. For their sake I trust that the old streets will never be swept clean and the lagoons never be made into dry land, that the poplars will remain as slim and graceful and the lilac bloom with the same fresh fragrance. Lovely as the cathedral of Amiens is, it is the lovelier for the town and landscape over which it watches to-day as it has during seven long centuries.

THE CATHEDRAL AS SEEN OVER THE MARKET-PLACE

CHAPTER XV

NOTRE-DAME OF ROUEN

CHAPTER XV

NOTRE-DAME OF ROUEN

I

FOR the first view of most great cathedrals, the approach should be by road. But there are a few to which you can come by train without fear of loss, and Rouen is one of them. I know that William Morris, the true lover of France and its churches, thought differently and said so in a letter written many years ago and since published: "All the roads (or nearly all) that come into Rouen dip down into the valley, where it lies, from gorgeous hills which command the most splendid views, but we, coming by railway, crept into it in the most seedy way, seeing actually nothing at all of it till we were driving through the town in an omnibus." If the journey is made from Paris, however, the railroad also dips down into the valley. The country through which you have passed hardly prepares you for the moment when, from your carriage window, you look to the Seine far below, long narrow islands dividing it into two streams, bridges spanning it from shore to shore, a big modern town spreading from it to the low hills on the horizon, and, out of the midst of houses and factories and chimneys, the cathedral towers rising in their beauty. Before you have time for any impressions save one of the grandeur of it, or for any criticism of the cast-iron central spire that adds so immeasurably to the effect of height, the train plunges into a tunnel, and you do not see the cathedral again until you are almost at the door. Nothing could be more dramatically planned.

Rouen is the most dramatic of cathedrals, not only from the near hills, but when its door finally is reached. "Many times I think of the first time I ever went abroad and to Rouen," William Morris wrote years later in a letter to a friend, "and what a wonder of glory that was to me when I first came upon the cathedral rising above the flower market"—a wonder that made up for the disappointment of his arrival. It is a beautiful way to come upon the cathedral at all hours, and the beauty puts one in good humor at the start. But if the hour and the way could be deliberately chosen, I should prefer to see it first toward dusk on a May evening, and from the *Rue de la Grosse-Horloge,* one of the most historic of Rouen's historic streets, with the old tower of St. Romain, ghostly white in the blue twilight, at the far end. Because the month is May, the cathedral doors will be open, and candles burning on the altar of the Blessed Virgin. On my last visit at this season, the nave too was ablaze with light, and it was crowded from end to end, for, as it ever has been and ever will be, to persecute the Church is to stir the faithful to new ardors. Rouen is a big manufacturing town and, as a rule, piety languishes in the modern industrial atmosphere; the Month of Mary is not a service of

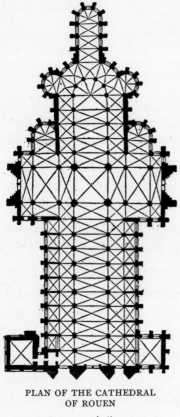

PLAN OF THE CATHEDRAL
OF ROUEN

FROM VIOLLET-LE-DUC'S "DICTIONNAIRE
DE L'ARCHITECTURE"

PORTAIL DE LA CALENDE. ROUEN

obligation; but never of old, at the most important ceremony, have I found people assembled in such numbers and so fervent in prayer. To surprise the cathedral thus in its most intimate devotions, is to see in it something more than a monument existing by the care of the State and for the curiosity of the tourist. It helps you then to understand, better than when you study it guide-book in hand, why its builders made it beautiful, and why its history is one of all the tears and laughter of Rouen since the town became Christian until now when statesmen would have it cease to be Catholic. The interior is never so solemn as at this hour, the great piers and arches in shining light leading the eye straight to the fires of the altar, while choir and chapels are lost in the shadowy space beyond, where the white columns loom dimly, and the priest, bearing the Blessed Sacrament, passes and disappears as the acolyte's little bell tinkles faintly and ever more faintly into silence. The mystery of the sanctuary colors and deepens the beauty of the vast church.

Daylight gives less mystery, but intensifies the drama of the architecture, which in no cathedral is so overwhelming. Even Fergusson, chary with his enthusiasm, describes the west front as "a romance in stone." Even Ruskin, quick to detect uselessness in ornament, describes the central door as "the most exquisite piece of pure flamboyant work existing." The whole façade is an incredibly flamboyant array of sculpture and statues tier above tier, of niches and canopies, gables and pinnacles, arcades and traceries open to the sky, and it is unlike all other west fronts, with its turrets and spires, and with its two towers, set beyond the aisles and the doors, adding to the effect of width and size, the difference in their design increasing the magnificence of the architectural confusion. You cannot go further back in the architectural records of the cathedral than the base of the Norman tower of St. Romain to the north; you come to the end of fine Gothic in the *Tour de Beurre*—the Butter Tower—to the south. Some think it brings you also to

THE WEST FRONT. ROUEN

the end of the people's piety, because it was paid for from the dispensations granted to the weak who could not do without butter in Lent, the reason for the name. But the Church, that insisted upon sacrifice of some kind in the season of penance, was merely exchanging a lighter for a heavier one, and again

THE SPIRE FROM THE OLD STREETS

proving its wisdom by the alternative.   All Rouen might have gone butterless, and there would be nothing to show for its abstinence; but the sacrifice of its purse raised, as monument, one of the loveliest towers in the world.

The transept doors blossom as luxuriantly into decoration. The apostles are grouped about the southern portal, *Portail de la Calende,* as if summoned to bear witness to the truth of the story of Christ told in the tympanum above.   At the northern portal, the *Portail des Libraires,* St. Romain, with Gargouille, who is own sister to Tarasque of the *Midi,* and who reappears on two of the cathedral windows, presides over nothing more serious than the capricious fancies of the most capricious genius who ever carved in stone.   On a series of little panels about the door, acrobats tumble, strange monsters play on violin and lute, mermaids balance on their curling tails, dogs gnaw and worry their bits of bone, grotesques upon grotesques reach up as far as the eye can follow; while, from near niches, Mary and Martha, Geneviève, Apolline and Mary of the Desert look on, as they have for centuries, and smile the pleasantest, gayest smile ever copied by the medieval sculptor from the smiling models who posed to him as saints.   High steps descend from the *Portail de la Calende* to the *place* where the flower market is held to this day; the long narrow court leading to the *Portail des Libraires* was once filled with the shops of the booksellers who gave it the name and whose tradition still lingers, if feebly, in the little shop where you can buy holy pictures and picture post-cards.   In no French town do you realize better than at Rouen that the French cathedral was not, like the English, shut off from the life of the people, but belonged to them, theirs to use as they would.   They made their home, they did their work, under its shadow.   It was a national edifice before it became a Historical Monument.   It should be respected as the symbol of democracy, and the endeavor is to destroy all traces of association between cathedral and people.   There is rejoicing when

20

the old houses and hovels that propped themselves up against
its walls, or shoved themselves in between its buttresses, are
cleared away, and yet they did honor to the Church which could
gather to itself all who were weary and heavy-laden with
poverty. Besides, their picturesque value more than counter-
balances the architectural loss. I do not suppose anybody,
except the restorer, would be eager to reduce to neatness and
order the one old corner that remains in the *Place d'Albane* to
the north of the nave, as it is sure to be in the course of time.
Now, when you enter, through an archway by the tower of St.
Romain, you see a little timbered, gabled house comfortably
attached to, and protected by, the old eleventh-century stonework, and, opposite, the remnant of the old cloisters, with,
above, an amazing medley of stone wall, timbers, dormer windows, and waving tiled roof, with, here and there, flowers
blooming gaily on a window-sill. When I last saw the *place*,
it was inclosed by a wooden fence, and was used as a workshop
for the masons who were restoring the west front behind a huge
screen of scaffolding, which I should rather keep there forever
than exchange for the old stone done up to meet the restorer's
ideal of finish.

The interior, in its architecture, is simpler than the exterior,
for it was built mainly in the more austere thirteenth century.
But the piety of the people kindled it into warmth, and, though
time, with its changes, and revolution, with its brutalities, have
stripped it barer than it should be, it is still rich in the incident
that fills a great church with color and life and variety: the
incident of chapels and shrines and tombs, of stained glass and
sculptured stones and carven stalls. I cannot remember, even
in Italy, statelier and more noble tombs than those in the Lady
Chapel of Rouen, where, on the one side, in a sculptured recess,
the two cardinals of Amboise kneel with priestly dignity, their
hands clasped in prayer, their robes spread out behind them in
official splendor; and, on the other, the Duke of Brézé is seen

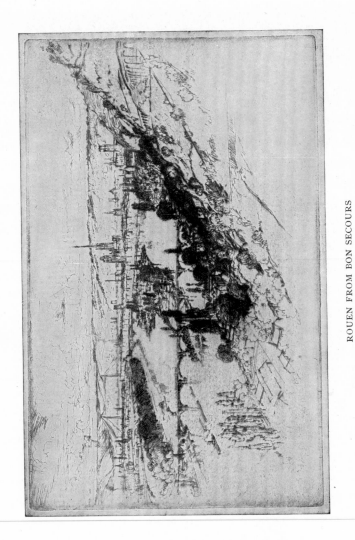

ROUEN FROM BON SECOURS

above in armor, sitting gallantly astride his horse, while below, between his wife, Diane of Poitiers, bent in the grief royalty was to comfort, and the Madonna with the Child in her arms, he reappears, lying on his shroud, naked, shorn of all earthly goods, in the poverty that Death, whose supreme gift is equality, brings alike to the rich and to the poor. The figure at all hours is as irresistibly human and touching as it seemed to Mr. Henry James standing before it in the fading light, when he felt "a sort of impulse to smooth out the shroud and straighten the helpless hands." The monument is said to be the work of Jean Goujon, and it most likely is. There are other tombs, some older, all of interest, but none quite so fine as these two.

If usually a cathedral has some one point which distinguishes it from all others—the choir heights at Beauvais, the windows at Chartres, the nave at Amiens, the clustered towers at Laon, the façade at Bourges—at Rouen the distinction is, if anything, its many-sidedness. It has everything a cathedral should have: beauty of architecture, beauty of incident, beauty of history, beauty of sanctity, beauty of picturesqueness. Within and without, Notre-Dame of Rouen is as inexhaustible in interest as the west front is in ornament.

II

The cathedral does not put its surroundings to shame. Rouen is a town of much history, and also, as Mr. Henry James has said, of "much expression." To Ruskin, it was one of the three centers of his life's thought; to William Morris, one of the greatest pleasures he ever had, such a hold did it take upon him with its mingled history, beauty, and romance, which it still keeps in evidence for a later generation.

It does not let you forget, if you would, the Norman pirates who stormed its gates, or the French and English kings who reduced it to a battle-ground, or, above all, the Maid who saved

France and who found her reward in the flames kindled by Rouen. You are reminded of its great and stirring past, not only by the statues set up in public places and the names given to streets and squares, but by the ancient and picturesque aspect of the town. In spite of Haussmann, it has not entirely wiped out the signs and marks of age. It is astonishing that a big, busy manufacturing center should have preserved so many relics of its less practical days. Narrow streets, shut in by tall houses, gabled and timbered, are by no means the exception. You cannot escape them for long in your walks through the town. Even in my hotel, I could not go up or down stairs without looking from the windows on a confused pile of ancient battered time-stained masonry, almost within reach. Everywhere you come upon old buildings that, each in itself, might make the fame of a bigger place: the *Palais de Justice,* flamboyantly imposing; the *Hôtel Bourgtheroulde,* with the sculptured story of the Golden Fleece told upon its wall; the donjon of Philip-Augustus, the oldest in France, with tragic memories of Joan of Arc, whose name it now bears; the *Aître Saint-Maclou,* where grass grows peacefully over those who perished of the pest centuries ago, and where, on the inclosing gallery, the wood-carver leads Death through the awful measures of his medieval dance—the *Danse Macabre;* the square of the *Haute Vieille Tour,* with the chapel where every year the canons of the cathedral set one criminal free in the name of St. Romain; the *Grosse-Horloge,* the town's timekeeper for ages—a step from the boulevards with their trams, from the *quais* with their *cafés,* from the new markets and latest shops, and you are in the heart of medievalism.

Old customs also linger. The first evening I came back to my hotel from the Month of Mary, a bell from the belfry of the *Grosse-Horloge* began to ring, and rang for fifteen minutes. I asked the *patron* what it was. "The belfry bell," he said. "Yes, but why is it ringing?" He looked surprised. "It 's

THE LANTERNS, ST. OUEN

nine o'clock," was his only answer.   It was quite natural to him
that, when the clock struck nine, the belfry bell should ring,
for no better reason than because it always has rung at that
hour during a thousand years and more.

   To me, it is more astonishing that so much of the religious
past should survive, not in tradition alone, but in solid stone.
Rouen is a city of churches.   You stumble upon them at every
turn.   The abbey church of St. Ouen is only second to the
cathedral, though, when you recover from your disappointment
before the rigid and mechanical west front of the nineteenth-
century vandal, and step inside, you would hesitate to call it
second.   It is unusually empty of incident.   It may be that the
monks were the careful guardians the present sacristan would
make them out, and that they allowed nothing to take away
from the simplicity of the architecture; it is quite certain that
a church could hardly be anything but empty after the Protestants of the sixteenth century had swept through it like a
cyclone, and the Republicans of the eighteenth had made of it
a smithy.   But a church never stood less in need of incident.
The slender shafts of its columns rise straight from floor to
roof, unbroken by capital or ornament, with a simplicity that
is the charm throughout.   A tremendous effect of height is
thus obtained.   You are not overwhelmed by it as in the choir
at Beauvais, you feel only the great grace, the perfect balance
of a well-proportioned design.   "Its proportions bring tears to
the eyes," Mr. James has written of St. Ouen, and after
this Fergusson's praise of it as "the most beautiful thing of its
kind in Europe" seems lukewarm.   The exterior has a loveliness we associate with English rather than French churches,
for the transepts and apse are surrounded by a garden of shady
walks and many flowers.   It is a place to idle away a spring
morning in, looking to the walls that seem built of glass, to
the bewildering arrangement of buttresses and pinnacles, and,
higher, to the lantern that Ruskin's abuse cannot make any-

thing but beautiful in its lightness and delicate elaboration. While you look at the beauty created by the monks of Rouen, children are playing round the statue of Rollo who ruled Rouen's fortunes, the air is filled with the fragrance of wall-flowers and lilacs, and the stately avenue is all abloom with the horse-chestnuts, that, in their sweetness and beauty, are neither of heathendom nor of Christianity, but of all time.

St. Maclou is third in size, but in no other respect, for it has an individuality that puts it in a place apart. It is original in its name, which is that of a Scotch saint, though no authority I have consulted seems to know just who he was or what he is doing as patron of a French parish. Better still, it is original in its architecture, for though it may be classified as Flamboyant, neither its architect nor any other of the fifteenth century ever again built a church quite like it. He rounded the west end so that it looks almost like another apse; he squandered the wealth of his, and his sculptor's, imagination, grave and gay, on the three great portals and their wooden doors; he filled the interior with the same flamboyant exuberance, adding a spiral stairway to the organ loft which could not be excelled for grace and lightness; he made it, within and without, so beautiful and so complete that the central spire of the modern restorer cannot ruin it, nor the high winds of Rouen, sweeping traceries and pinnacles to the ground, altogether deface it.

Rouen's old churches do not end with St. Maclou. St. Godard, St. Eloi, St. Vincent, St. Patrice, all have some rare beauty of architecture or painted windows, of tapestry or carving. You may find bits of the most primitive churches of all if you go far enough; you cannot miss the beautiful remains of the old abbey of St. Amand, nor the tower of St. André and the walls of the closed, dishonored St. Laurent, where, just outside, in a little green space, the statue of Flaubert helps you to remember that the associations of Rouen do not end with Norman barons and Gothic architecture.

ST. MACLOU. ROUEN

III

FROM these many churches, from Rouen's other famous monuments, you come back to the cathedral to find that it loses nothing by the comparison, that it unites in itself the beauty scattered among them, that it is ever the center of interest, as of the town. There is nothing they give that it does not offer in double measure.

From the second century, when St. Nicaise converted Rouen, all Rouen's history revolves around the cathedral. The history of Rouen's saints is carved on its stones and painted on its windows; the history of Rouen's makers is recorded in its tombs, for Rollo and his son lie here, and the ashes of the Lion-Hearted were its treasure until the Revolution scattered them; associations with Rouen's past gather thick about you with every step you take. From the time there were great architects in Rouen, they worked for the adornment of the cathedral, and though fire and restorers have destroyed some of the intermediate stages, you can still follow its growth beginning with the eleventh century in the base of the Tower of St. Romain, to the sixteenth in the *Tour de Beurre* and the western façade, where the splendor of flamboyancy reached a height beyond which it has never gone—beyond which it could never go.

Chance has been kinder to the cathedral than to the other churches, preserving more of the picturesqueness of the old life that sprang up under its shadow, and arranging the streets to frame in, as if built for the purpose, now one of the towers, and now a transept door, while from Bon Secours, or the other neighboring heights, it is seen commanding the tower and dwarfing even the spires of St. Ouen and St. Maclou.

The rich warm white, with which time has colored the stone of these churches, is richest and warmest and most wonderful on the walls of the cathedral. You do not know how beautiful the west front is until you see it emerge, white and glowing, from the grayness of the passing shower on a summer evening, or fade into a pale phantom in the starlight. For this reason, I dread the moment when the scaffolding that now conceals part of it must be pulled down. The scaffolding is pictorial in its way, and at certain hours it even deepens the mystery of the shadows. But the restorer is never satisfied until he has smoothed and scraped from the old stone the color and quality which it took centuries of wind and storm, of sun and smoke, to give it. His work complete, the façade will appear with the crudeness of youth by day, and by night will no longer hang white and vague between town and sky, like a ghost from out the past of which it was the crowning glory.

CHAPTER XVI

WHERE KINGS WERE CROWNED: RHEIMS

CHAPTER XVI

WHERE KINGS WERE CROWNED: RHEIMS

I

NOTRE-DAME of Rheims looks the royal part that fell to it among the cathedrals of France. From the first moment you see it springing up from the blur of houses in the plain, it makes "a great figure," as even Arthur Young, whose eyes were usually keener for turnips than cathedrals, was startled into admitting. His first view of Rheims, from the top of the hill "which separates the narrow Vale of Epernay from the great plain of Rheims," some four miles away, was magnificent, he said, and this is the first view you can have to-day, if you journey to Rheims by road, as you will if you are wise.

If you must keep to the train, you cannot entirely escape the magnificence. Notre-Dame is the biggest thing, the most beautiful thing in as dull and ugly a plain as you can find in France: to a great sphinx brooding over the Champagne and always gazing out to the west, it has been compared by Mr. Belloc. But it is in no need of comparison. It is its own standard of greatness and of mystery. It can suggest nothing more marvelous than itself towering there, as triumphant above the commercial town of unlovely factories and tall bare chimneys, as of old above the town consecrated to kings and ruled by bishops hardly less royal than they. It wears its honors with the

WEST FRONT AND TOWERS OF RHEIMS CATHEDRAL

stateliness and sumptuousness they impose, and holds its own even with the cathedral that at near Laon is set so royally upon its lofty hill.

II

It happened that, for me, this distant view was reserved until I had become familiar with the cathedral from many others.

On the first of my several visits, I got to Rheims so late in the evening, there was time only for a hurried, vague impression of clustered pinnacles and mammoth buttresses before I went to bed. It was the next morning—a hot, blazing August morning—that I first really saw the cathedral, and then it was not more than a stone's throw from my hotel window. It is in character with everything else that the cathedral, seeming to

THE NORTH SIDE OF RHEIMS CATHEDRAL

accept its responsibility as a world-renowned sight, has arranged to be overlooked as if from two stage boxes by two hotels, one to the west and one to the north. The *place* where it stands is far too closely shut in by small and insignificant houses. But the strongest light, the meanest surroundings could not lessen the marvel of so marvelous a church, and magnificent is the word that occurs to you on the threshold, as to Arthur Young on the distant hilltop, as, for that matter, to so

THE THREE PORTALS OF THE WEST FRONT OF RHEIMS CATHEDRAL

responsible an authority as Parker. There is no cathedral in France that can equal it in wealth, in extravagance, in gorgeousness of ornament. The façade of Notre-Dame of Paris, something like it in general design, is of Puritan simplicity beside the façade of Notre-Dame of Rheims. No other west doors, not even at Rouen, are more deeply recessed, more richly

RHEIMS. WEST DOOR INSIDE

charged with sculpture, row upon row, tier upon tier, some statues as unexpectedly Greek in character as others are Gothic; no other sculptures are on so large and imposing a scale. No other gables over the doors soar upward in such high acute angles, no others show such an entanglement of figures and traceries. And the great tall windows above, and the rose between, are so beset with ornament that hardly an inch of bare stone remains around them. And in the gallery of kings, the statues stand under carven canopies, intricate, delicate, lace-like in their elaboration. And the tall central gable, fretted and flamboyant, reaches up still higher, and on either side of it the towers, with the long lines of their arches and windows, add to the "soaring aspect" which is so marked in the design, and seem bent on carrying the glory of it all to the very heights of heaven.

Nor were architect and sculptor less lavish when they turned from the west front. Everywhere it is the same. The but-

RHEIMS GARGOYLES

tresses stand firmly, a mass of arcades, and niches sheltering wide-winged angels, and tall pinnacles, or they go flying across the aisles in as light and graceful and ornate a flight as if beauty were its only object: the most beautiful buttresses in France Fergusson says, the grandest pinnacles Professor Moore declares, and both are right. The transepts are but new spaces for new ornament, the apse but a new motive for a new arrangement of buttresses and pinnacles. The gargoyles, somehow, seem more monstrous in size than those that look down from other cathedral walls, and round the top of the apse, perched on a high balustrade, are grotesques—owls, mermaids, griffins, unicorns—strange beings that come of the same family as the Devils of Notre-Dame in Paris; only, the grotesques of Rheims are not so hauntingly evil, and they are placed where they can be seen from below and where they serve in the decorative scheme, for they break the horizontal lines of the balustrade, with the effect of still another row of pinnacles. I have wandered for days round the cathedral without coming to the end of its inexhaustible detail. It is almost incredible that one church could be so covered with ornament, that its walls could bear upon their surface such a rhythmical confusion of sculptured stone.

Indeed, there are people who think the exterior of Rheims overdone, barbaric in its profusion. The ornament, they say,

THE CHOIR OR EAST END

is out of scale, the statues too large, the pinnacled buttresses too high, the sculptures too liberally scattered: the cathedral cannot be seen because of the decoration. But I have never felt this. The cathedral remains grand and impressive for all

RHEIMS. GREEK FIGURES, CENTRAL DOORWAY

its detail. No loss of repose is the price of its richness, no loss of grace the price of its complexity. The proportions are so fine that the intricate sculptures only add to the dignity of the façade, where the insistence upon ascending lines—in the gables, in the windows, in the towers—emphasizes, even exaggerates, the height; the pinnacles and buttresses, the balustrades and beasts are only in keeping with the splendid scale upon which the building was planned.

Stern simplicity would be as out of place here as florid redundancy at Chartres. The sculptor was working in perfect accord with the architect through the long years that Rheims took in the building.

The miracle is that unity should have been maintained, not despite multitudinous detail, but despite the fact that this building spread over more than one period, as periods go in architecture. The cathedral was begun just a little later than Paris and Chartres—1211 or 1212 is the date, to be exact—and though, before fifty years had passed, it had been carried far enough for consecration, it was not finished in its complete royal splendor until the early part of the fifteenth century. Perhaps the real, the great, miracle of

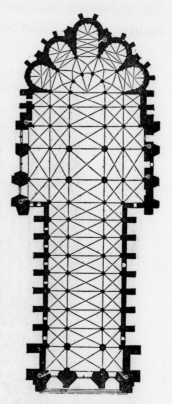

PLAN OF THE CATHEDRAL
OF RHEIMS

FROM VIOLLET-LE-DUC'S "DICTIONNAIRE
DE L'ARCHITECTURE"

all was its ever getting on so far and so quickly as it did. For the century when the builders were most active was the very century—the thirteenth—when cathedral and town were at daggers drawn, when the archbishops fought their flock from fortified castles, loaded them with chains, put them to torture, and the flock defied their archbishops from behind barricades made of stones just brought from the quarries for the new cathedral. In later ages, the revolt of the people has usually been a signal for the pulling down or the dishonoring of great churches. You can see only too plainly what the Revolution did for Rheims. But in those incomprehensible days—incomprehensible to us—popular agitation apparently was an incentive to putting them up in their beauty. In Laon and Soissons and more than one other French

A GLIMPSE OF THE CHOIR FROM THE TRANSEPT

town, church and commune grew and prospered together, even while one seemed trying so hard to destroy the other. At Rheims, the fight was a stiff one, for the archbishops, mostly, had the King behind them, and, in consequence, the delays were more frequent. The work did not go with a frenzy of zeal, as at Chartres for instance. Between the beginning and the ending of the cathedral, there was time for styles and standards in architecture to change.   But never did the delays, never did the change bring about picturesque discord as at Le Mans,

THE NORTH TRANSEPT

never did it mean a long interval when the church was left standing, a melancholy fragment, as at Clermont-Ferrand. The cathedral was completed as the thirteenth-century architect designed it.   If anything, it gained for not having been rushed through by the medieval builders, who, when left to themselves and not too much distracted by politics, were "hustlers," before the American invented the word.   The Gothic architect, as time went on, grew more confident, readier to let himself go, and therefore the splendor of Rheims only expanded with the years, and the ever-increasing flamboyancy of ornament spread over just those visible portions of the cathedral where it belongs by rights.   But, if it did not belong there, if the cathedral bore its burden of decoration less nobly, I would not have that burden lightened by as much as one figure, one bit of tracery. The church where the Kings of France were crowned could not be too rich, too extravagant, too gorgeous.   Other churches might be built for prayer, Rheims was made for princes and for princely rites.

There is no disappointment, no anti-climax when you go in the cathedral.   The interior also, though it may not have struck Arthur Young "like that of Amiens," has the regal air.   It also is royal in its stateliness and sumptuousness.   It may not have the power of impressing, as Pater wrote, if the impression you seek is one of fervor and devotion.   I cannot imagine anybody "praying well" at Rheims.   But then who would ever think of it as a church to pray in?   The surprise there would be to come upon the miraculous shrine, or the rich treasure of holy relics, or the crypt-like chapel.   If it seems formal, if it seems even spectacular, that is what you expect of it as the stage for the highest ceremonial in a land of ceremony and spectacle. And the formality is of such fine perfection, the spectacle of such noble stateliness, that the effect is produced before you stop to ask why.   You feel the interior to be immense, without searching the guide-book for actual figures of length and height.   One curious fact, to which attention was first called even at Rheims by Mr. W. H. Goodyear of the Brooklyn Museum, an unsuspected divergence of the piers above the capitals toward the exterior, has been explained by the official architect of the cathedral as a deliberate effort to increase the effects of grandeur, and, he adds, it was an effort wholly to the advantage of the edifice. This is an excellent example and shows how ready the builders were to avail themselves of any device, or trick some might call it, to produce the impression they were striving for. It proves how far they were from accepting

RHEIMS. AMBULATORY

Ruskin's definition of their artistic honesty. They gained their ends by the Jesuitical policy of adopting whatever means promised to be most effectual, and who would find fault with them for that? You realize no less the splendor of the interior without looking at the detail of the pillars with their gilded capitals, at the lofty vaulting of the roof and the choir so spacious within its simple grille, at the windows burning with royal fires lit in the thirteenth century, when stained glass reached its fullest beauty, and the tapestries glowing even in their faded glory.

THE NORTH AISLE LOOKING EAST

These tapestries always seemed to me the distinctive feature of Rheims, the last touch of magnificence to a cathedral already so magnificent. They hang all along the aisles on either side the nave: Gobelins tapestries, Perpersack tapestries, tapestries rarely seen anywhere nowadays save safely stored in museums.

It is like the sumptuousness of Rheims to display them as if they were as entirely a part of itself as the sculptures of the façade, the angels and monsters of the apse. In old castles and palaces you have too often to imagine the hangings that once covered and softened walls now empty. But at Rheims you see the hangings in their place and find them more decorative far than in your imagining. The medieval architect never meant to leave the interior of his church bare and gray. In Italy he almost always called in the painter. Sometimes even in France he relied upon paint to get the color he was not afraid of. But if the result then was as crude and restless as in the French churches modern restorers have painted according to their idea of what medieval decoration in France ought to have been, I am thankful the last traces and flakes of blues and reds and greens and yellows have faded and peeled from the gray stones. It may be we would have thought the tapestries crude in their first brilliance. But I doubt it, just as I doubt whether a Viollet-le-Duc-painted chapel looks in the least as the medieval decorator left it. As it is, though dim shadows of themselves, the tapestries of Rheims have not lost the gorgeousness so in harmony with the royal pageant for which they were the background.

How gorgeous they are, you do not quite know until you see, as I have seen, them the background for the church pageant, the ceremonial the cathedral continues to conduct with more than common state and dignity, even when only a few old women and a few tourists make up the congregation. Ordinary occasions call for more solemnity than elsewhere, and on feast-days there is great pomp, and elaborate music, and gorgeous vestments. The procession through the nave of canons in scarlet and purple, the scarlet no canons save those of Rheims are privileged to wear, and priests in glittering robes, and acolytes in white surplices, amid incense and solemn chants and flaming candles, awakens for you all your old associations with Rheims, as nothing else in the cathedral can. You seem then to be watching that larger procession: the procession of kings, one after the other, journeying from Paris to be crowned, as later they were to journey to St. Denis to be buried; and in this old pageant banners float and

RHEIMS. IN THE NAVE

wave through the clouds of incense, the clang of armor breaks upon the sacred chant as the kings and queens, the knights and ladies of the court pass, everywhere gold gleams and silks shine in the lights from the burning windows above and the flaming candles below. It is the irony of history that in this spectacle of royalty at Rheims, this review of kings from Clovis to the last crowned Bourbon, not one figure to-day stands out so vividly as that of the little peasant girl, Joan of Arc, when, knowing that her work was done, she begged the *Roi de Bourges,* whom she had made King of France, to permit her to lay aside her armor and go back in peace to her flocks and pastures. They seem to have felt this at Rheims, for hers is the statue they have set up in front of the cathedral, where all men can see it, while the kings stand meekly in a row, well out of the way, under the niches of their high gallery below the towers.

III

As a rule, I neither climb cathedral towers nor follow cathedral guides, unless they alone have the key to doors kept locked. But at Rheims, as at Paris, you miss something if you do not mount to the roof at least, and let the guide lead you where he will, and can. You get a curiously intimate impression of the cathedral up there, it is like being taken behind the scenes, you see the wheels go round and the wires dangle as you wander in the lofty regions between the vaulting and the roof, along the outer walls, in among the strange beasts and birds, with, now and again, a wide outlook over the town and the plain, and an unexpected, almost indiscreet, command of the Archbishop's Palace. You see a good deal that the builder did not mean you to see from below, where the people who went to church in his time were supposed to stay. But you lose no illusions behind the cathedral scenes. Wheels go round and wires dangle to such dramatic purpose that you are only more impressed than ever with the sumptuously colossal scale upon which the great building was designed. A big church could be stowed away in what is practically the cathedral attic, with room to spare for the priest's house beside it. You feel a pygmy among the beasts and birds watching from the cathedral peaks and peering down over the cathedral precipices; you are put to shame as an idler before the enthusiasm of the artist who never shirked his work, even where its beauty was but the most minute, an almost invisible detail, in a great decorative whole. Other cathedrals are as elaborate in parts as Rheims, but not one I know is as magnificently elaborate everywhere.

All the impressions you have of the cathedral, no matter where you may go for them, bring you back to this sense of its magnificence. I almost believed sometimes that the town, once celebrated for its grandeur, had been allowed to grow ugly and shabby purposely to set it off. *Une cité glorieuse,* Rheims may have been in St. Bernard's day; but there is nothing glorious about it now. A town with "streets almost all broad, straight, and well built, equal in that respect to any I have seen," it was at the end of the eighteenth century when Arthur Young visited it. And in appearance it may not altogether have lost the importance for which it was always noted; why, the bottles and biscuits in endless shop-windows would tell you, if you needed to be told. But it is important without the picturesqueness age retains in towns like Troyes and Le Puy, without the pretentiousness modern prosperity brings to others like Lille or Lyons. In whatever direction I might walk, after I had seen the remains of its Roman grandeur; after I had been to the old church of St. Remi, which from a distance "terminated the town proudly" for Arthur Young, and which for me, sitting in the nave, seemed rather like something out of Edgar Allan Poe as I watched the legion of rats playing in both nave and choir; after I had searched for and found a few timbered houses here and there; after I had lingered in the market square and the *Place Royale,* elegant in its eighteenth-century way; I had exhausted all that Rheims can show, except streets of second-hand shops and boulevards of houses that, at the best, are a poor reëcho of the Paris least worth reëchoing. Had they gone about it deliberately, the people of Rheims could not have given greater distinction to the cathedral than it owes to the chance that reduced the town to colorless commonplace. It is only with the sudden view of Notre-Dame, now of the east end above the gay flower market and now of the towers at the turning of a mean street, that the town becomes beautiful. Pictorially, the cathedral still rules Rheims as, politically, it did during so many hundred years from the remote days when St. Remi baptized

RHEIMS. EAST END FROM FLOWER MARKET

Clovis there, and the dove flew down from heaven with the oil by which kings were to be anointed as long as there were kings in France.

If the people of Rheims rejoiced when this political supremacy was over, they were hardly to be blamed: it was no light matter for them when their spiritual shepherd was their temporal lord, more at home with sword and armor than with cope and crozier. But, rather than that the cathedral should lose by an inch, by a touch, the beauty created under the rule of the archbishops, I would prefer to see them again the powerful, cruel lords they were, defying the people from their strong castle, sending out a blight upon the land with their interdicts and sentences of excommunication. This, however, is entirely a matter of personal prejudice, which is not shared, for the moment, anyway, by the French government. As things are now, it is far more likely that there will be no archbishop at all when next I go to Rheims. The cathedral will remain because cathedrals are National Monuments, though in what condition eventually, I do not like to think, when I remember the restorations already completed and the scaffolding I saw on the southern tower and over a part of the north transept. That scaffolding is prominent in all my memories of the French cathedrals, as relentless as Fate in Greek tragedy. It pursued me from town to town, a warning, in the midst of my pleasure, of the catastrophe that no regret of mine, nor any protest, could prevent or even delay. But fortunately the old architect at Rheims did his work so well that it will take many Revolutions and many restorers to destroy Notre-Dame altogether. For generations yet to come, the cathedral will rise, royally magnificent, above the unlovely factories and tall bare chimneys of the town, the rich tapestry of the sculptor's figures and traceries spread over its walls without, the rich tapestry of Gobelins and Perpersack hanging on its walls within.

CHAPTER XVII

A MAGNIFICENT FRAGMENT: BEAUVAIS

CHAPTER XVII

A MAGNIFICENT FRAGMENT: BEAUVAIS

I

AT Chartres, the cathedral-builders raised to heaven two spires that none who came after could hope to rival. At Amiens, they planned a nave never to be surpassed, for it touched perfection. Symmetry could yield no statelier beauty than they forced from it at Paris, nor ornament blossom into more royal magnificence than under their hands at Rheims. When the ambitious moment came to Beauvais, as it came to all the great cathedrals, and architects sought the splendor that would make of it a marvel among the marvelous churches of northern France, nothing was left but to light the "Lamp of Power" and to conquer by sheer sublimity of size. Their cathedral should reach to a majestic height hitherto unapproached, undreamed of. This was their ambition, and in it they succeeded. The new cathedral they designed to take the place of the old was never finished, it was never carried beyond apse and transepts, it remains a fragment. And yet, nowhere is the beauty, the mystery to be suggested by great height and size so overwhelming. The first impression Beauvais gives, the last impression brought from Beauvais, the impression dominating every memory of the town and strengthened with every return to it, is of this size, this height, unbelievable, intolerable almost. "There are few rocks, even among the Alps, that have

23   403

a clear vertical fall as high as the choir of Beauvais," Ruskin wrote of it. There is no rock among the Alps, he should have added, where this fall is so amazing, due, as it is, not to blind chance, but to the genius of the architect who designed the placing of stone upon stone and made each beautiful in itself. So the cliffs of the St. Gothard, the peak of the Matterhorn, might look were they wrought into a network of tracery and pinnacles, were a carven surface created to clothe their nakedness.

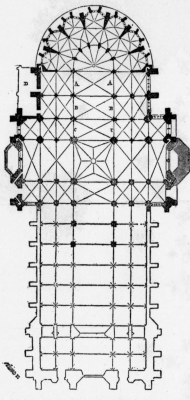

PLAN OF CATHEDRAL OF BEAUVAIS

FROM VIOLLET-LE-DUC'S "DICTIONNAIRE DE L'ARCHITECTURE"

Whenever I have been in Beauvais it has seemed to me as if the town existed solely to honor this great marvel sprung up in its midst. I would have known from Baedeker, had I not already, of the factories that have made Beauvais to the outside world far more famous for its tapestries than any glory of architecture. I soon learned from the statue of Jeanne Hachette in the great *place* that Beauvais has a history with one of my own sex for most heroic figure, and so should be of special interest to me as a woman. I am sure if it were to see only so fine a church at St. Etienne, I would journey any distance to any town. As I look back to my walks through the quiet streets, I can recall not one that did not lead to fine old houses and picturesque corners, to gables and turrets, to gardens with lilac and laburnum overhanging the gray walls in the springtime, to poplared roads and meadows all yellow with

BEAUVAIS. THE MARKET-PLACE

buttercups.   But all these things, so delightful in themselves, had to me an air of being deliberately arranged as a foil to the cathedral, as a foreground, or to give the scale.   Even at the hotel in the *place,* where I stayed on my last visit, I could have believed that the windows turned from the cathedral—to my disappointment—simply to add to the effect of the moment when, sauntering out from the long covered passage that is the hotel entrance, my breath was taken away on the threshold by my first view, across the white square, of the buttressed apse towering massively above the gabled houses.   It seemed impossible that the chief *café* of the town set out its little tables on the pavement there, close to the hotel, for any other reason except for the finer enjoyment of that stupendous view.   And nothing would have convinced me that the market was held in the *place* for any more practical purpose than its value in the composition.   If the narrow streets wound between old houses, it was only that, of a sudden, they might frame in for me one or the other of the lofty portals, and show me, as I could see them from nowhere else, the mighty flying buttresses spread like great wings to lift the transept heavenward.   If after wandering through a long unlovely suburb, or up the hills that shut in Beauvais as in a cup, or by the shaded canals across country green as in England, the great gray monster vanished for a while out of sight, it was only that with the next glimpse it might impress, overpower, me anew.   The town, the hills, the canals, the meadows were but a stage for the drama of the cathedral's beauty.

I found it wonderful always from the distance, the distant view giving the best idea of its size in proportion to the town, and also of its architectural incompleteness, for not far away St. Etienne, with long nave and western tower, rises above the house roofs, the model of what a Gothic church ought to be. The cathedral was wonderful still when my wanderings in and about the town brought me back to the little *place* of St. Pierre, with its tiny grove of horse-chestnuts all white and gay in the May sunshine, where I stood immediately below the buttressed, pinnacled, statued walls, and grew dizzy as my eyes tried to climb the inaccessible heights.   In the clear sunlight of the warm French spring the wonder and the mystery never grew less.   But it is more wonderful, perhaps, as William Morris thought, in the hour between night and day: "Seen by twilight," he wrote once to a friend, "its size gives one an impression almost of terror; one can scarcely believe in it."   And it is most wonderful of all, as the Abbé Pihan, reëchoing Scott at Melrose, insists in his guide-book, when, through the darkness, a great moon comes sailing up in the sky, and washes in with white and silver the broad spaces between the impenetrable shadows, and models the solid Gothic fabric into a church of dreams and visions, transfigured in the miracle of the moon-drenched night.

When you see it thus, you are almost tempted never to see it by daylight, never to mount its steps nor enter its wide portal, fearful lest when it grows into something more substantial than a dream, into mere stone and mortar, a place where Mass is said and Benediction given, the wonder of it will grow less. But though Beauvais may be more beautiful at some hours, its beauty never fades, and the coming of day cannot strip it of its wonder and its glory.

II

If great height makes Beauvais one of the wonders of the world, as William Morris said it was—as, fortunately, Beauvais not being on a main railroad line, the world has not yet found out—the first builders had no such ambition for it. The first Christian builders everywhere could congratulate themselves if they provided a safe roof over the heads of the faithful. At Beauvais, a lowly Romanesque nave, founded on an

BEAUVAIS CATHEDRAL SEEN AT NIGHT FROM THE MARKET-PLACE

earlier, some assert, a pagan temple, remains as proof of the
centuries that passed before the architects' imagination began
to take bolder flights.   Mean and undecorated without, insignificant within save for two beautiful strips of old embroidery
always hanging there, it leans against the vast stretch of brick
wall to the west of the later church, and dwindles into nothing-
ness by the comparison, as if bent on justifying its name of
Basse-Œuvre.   It was never incorporated into the new building, never became a part of it, as in the case of the far more important Romanesque nave at Le Mans.   That it survives at all
is the merest accident.

Beauvais did not escape the fires inevitable in the building of every medieval church, fires as frequent and disastrous as they are supposed to be in the newest American town, and for precisely the same reason: because so
much wood was used.   Some sort of rebuilding was at times
imperative, and the surprising thing is that it did not always
mean complete rebuilding.   The old nave at Beauvais escaped
as if by miracle, and there would have been no suggestion of
getting rid of it if Gothic architects had not been Vandals in
their way, quite without sentiment for the work of their pre-
decessors, firm in their belief in the finer qualities of their own.
The destruction of all that survived of the primitive church was
therefore decided upon when the thirteenth century, awakening
in all northern France the desire of free citizens in their
new communes for great buildings as their meeting-place, and
the power of the architect to build these for them, inspired
besides at Beauvais that vision of great height which Beauvais
never could shake off.   The little old church was a pygmy even
among Romanesque churches and had no place in the scheme
of giants.   But if the vision in its fulfilment brought beauty
to Beauvais, it brought disaster also, and the moment of destruction never came for the Romanesque nave, just as the moment of
completion never came for the great Gothic church.   Insig-

nificant survival, magnificent fragment, both are reminders of the architect's ambition, which, in its fruition and in its failure, is the beginning and end of the story of the cathedral—the central fact which you can never forget while you are at Beauvais.

It is said that Eudes de Montreuil, architect to St. Louis, designed the new building. Whether he, or another, the design was approved by the bishop who was temporal, as well as spiritual, lord of Beauvais: how powerful you may see in the old episcopal palace, now converted into law courts by the people who have made National Monuments of their churches. But the towered, turreted gateway remains, eloquent of days when for the Bishop of Beauvais life as often meant battle as for the Bishop of Rheims, or Laon. The cathedral was begun in the first half of the century that saw one after another glorious church spring out of the soil of northern France, and some twenty-five years after Robert de Luzarches had got to work in near Amiens. The building went on vigorously, the builders warmed by the ardor of the faithful, the architect— whether Eudes de Montreuil or no—seeking ever after the marvel of height, sure of immortality for it, even should his own name be forgotten. In less than thirty years (in 1272) the choir was finished.

It was the fashion at one time to praise the old builders for their piety, and to account by their faith for the perfection of their work. They may have been as pious as the modern sentimentalist would have them, but their work, technically, was far from perfect. Their virtue was that they were not bound hand and foot by rule and convention, that they were not afraid to experiment, to run risks. Sometimes their courage, their daring, brought them through triumphantly; sometimes it betrayed them into hopeless blundering, as many a spireless tower, many a jumble of styles, many an architectural patchwork in the same Gothic building, is the witness. And they

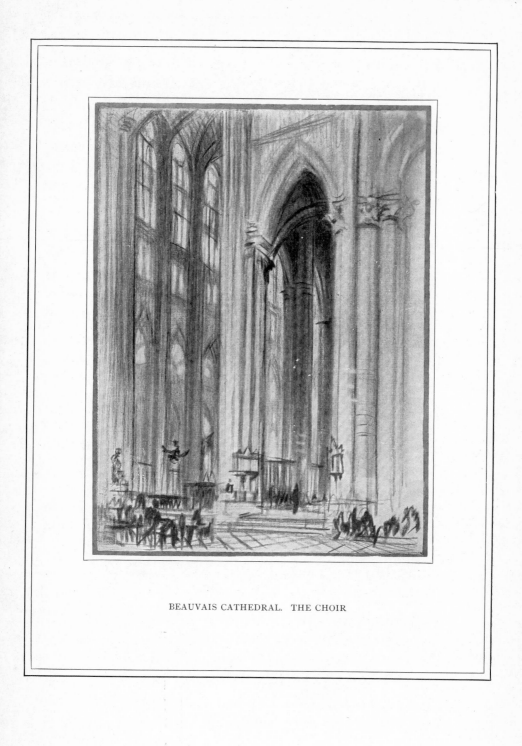

BEAUVAIS CATHEDRAL. THE CHOIR

blundered at Beauvais. Pillars reaching up after unaccustomed heights were weakened for their more immediate duty as supports. For twelve years the choir stood there in its gigantic beauty. Then the great roof fell in, and for forty years the bishop had his throne, the people their meeting-place, in the *Basse-Œuvre,* spared until then—spared until now —in all its insignificance, awaiting the day, which it is safe to say will never come, when it will be pulled down to make way for the greater nave designed to take its place. The failure was as gigantic as the scheme, and this really is the story of Beauvais throughout the centuries that followed: the story of splendid ideals, with partial achievement, partial ruin, as the sequel.

Ambition flared up again early in the fourteenth century, and, with it, the right architect again appeared, his name too —Enguerrand le Riche—remembered or doubted by tradition. But sad days had come for France, her own people warring one against another, English armies in possession, and battle making a more peremptory call on patriotism than beauty. The architect's work already done was defaced by the enemy, his plans for work to be done had to wait for the time and money to carry them out. The sixteenth century was almost a year old before the first stone of the transepts was laid: the cathedral in the building, like many another architectural monument of France, could claim Francis I as a patron. Nothing, however, crushed or lessened the striving after height by which the builders at Beauvais sought glory and distinction for their cathedral. Transepts were cast in the same mammoth mold as the apse, and then the builders grew impatient, who can now say how urged and goaded on by even more impatient citizens? They finished one bay of the nave, but could wait no longer to see the hopes of centuries realized, and, at once, on the four great pillars where nave and transepts meet, they set up a spire that dwarfed the highest in France, the highest anywhere.   From the summit, proud citizens could see on the horizon the roofs of Paris, the capital where there was no such lofty watch-tower to boast of, and Jean Vast, the architect, acclaimed himself as greater than Michelangelo, boasting that the dome of St. Peter's at Rome had been humbled by the spire of St. Peter's at Beauvais.

During five years Beauvais rejoiced.   But Gothic architecture, as the modern critic defines it, is a system of thrusts and balances.   It needed more than one bay of the nave to withstand the thrust of that heaven-searching spire.   With the fifth year—it was one Ascension Day, and priest and congregation had just left the cathedral to walk in solemn procession through the town—the spire came crashing down, filling choir and transepts with chaotic ruin, and ending once and forever the hope Beauvais had clung to for ages.

For the great days of cathedral-building had passed.   The inspiration had gone with the need.   The money set aside for the nave was spent in rebuilding choir and transepts.   There were new plans, but never the money nor the enthusiasm.   A rough wall was built up where the nave should have begun, and Beauvais was left the fragment we know, with the strange sky-line that makes it look from afar like a citadel rather than a church.   The *Basse-Œuvre* is too small to count in the arrangement of lines and masses, and appears to have no use whatever, as it props itself up against the huge wall, except to point a moral for those in search of one.

There was a time when the architectural authority was ready to seize upon this, or any, moral, and allowed himself to see in the beautiful crippled giant that rules it over the town only the text for a sermon.   "An example of the vaulting ambition that o'erleaps itself," is Fergusson's description of Beauvais, an "extraordinary masonic *tour-de-force*" to astonish the "gaping vulgar."   Professor Charles H. Moore, of a more liberal generation, regrets the ill proportions of the choir even as he

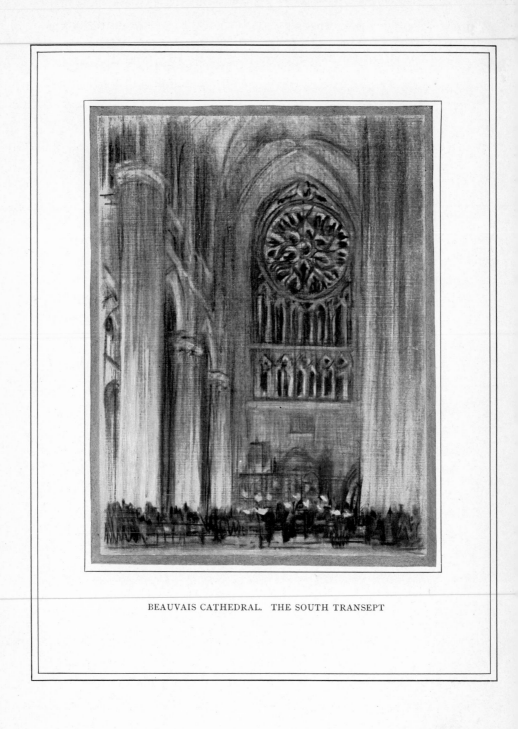

BEAUVAIS CATHEDRAL. THE SOUTH TRANSEPT

pronounces it "magnificent." But for me the magnificence overshadows every defect, every shortcoming. What the architects of Beauvais set out to do, they accomplished, though their work was never completed. They achieved, even in the fragment, the sublimity at which they aimed. In choir and transepts, beneath the buttresses and pinnacles of the outer walls, the ascending lines carry the eyes upward, and ever upward, as if in an attempt to climb to the very throne of the Most High. I could never go to the cathedral that this impression of height did not take hold of me, absorb me. It did more of old for the faithful, since, there above the walls and piers and arches, up which they sent their eyes wandering, was actually their Paradise, the goal of the one supreme climb for which life was given then. They, like Burne-Jones, saw no ambition o'erleaping itself, but only "holy beauty" within the walls of Beauvais. In no other cathedral do you understand so well what Huysmans meant when he wrote that in the Gothic church, eyes, always lowered under Romanesque roofs, are lifted.

William Morris, admitting his terror before Beauvais in the twilight, added, "But when you see the detail, it is so beautiful that the beauty impresses you more than the size." There may not be as much ornament as in many another French church, the architects having subordinated everything to the one great effect they sought, and Beauvais having suffered its share from the bad taste of the eighteenth century and the brutality of the Revolution. I have a vivid recollection of the bit of old chapter-house, now forming part of the Museum of the town, where there is an array of dishonored sculptures from the cathedral which make it at all times a melancholy record of the sacrilege of centuries. It was the more melancholy when last I was there because of the blooming of new life in the lilac-trees and the golden narcissus starring the grass of the little garden—which of old was inclosed on all four sides by the now ruined cloisters, the life from them gone beyond the reach of spring or summer forever more. The sacrilege has spared the town as little as the cathedral. I remember my regret before a bas-relief of the Four Sons of Aymon, because of old it had decorated the house that was pulled down to give way to my very modern hotel in the *place* with the beautiful view. But not this, nor any of the other waifs and strays from the past, was to me as sad a sight as the broken sculptures from the cathedral, for they show only too well of how much it has been robbed. However, enough detail has been spared to make it easy to forget for a time, with William Morris, the beauty of which it is a lesser, though an essential, part. The interior of Beauvais will never seem cold and bare so long as the eye, in its upward flight, reaches windows, fewer in number it may be, but burning and glowing with the same warmth and splendor as at Chartres; so long as the lovely old tapestries, faded and mellowed into new loveliness, cover the huge stretch of western wall that should open upon a vista of noble piers and arches. I never found a suggestion of emptiness at Beauvais; Amiens, or Laon, is emptier; and I have been to services there when the atmosphere seemed charged with something of the same spirit, the same devoutness, that makes of Chartres the House of Prayer. Nor can I understand why Fergusson should have regretted the meagerness and attenuation of the exterior, where I saw, instead, almost extravagance in the elaboration of buttresses and fretted pinnacles, in the carven loveliness of the two great portals. The southern portal, as if warmed by the sun into more luxuriant life of blossom and flower, is the richer of the two in the ornament that stretches to the topmost peak of the high transept gable; above the northern portal the Tree of Jesse spreads out in lines and curves and spaces almost frigid in their beautiful severity, as if chilled into restraint in the colder light. But both portals are set about with traceried,

BEAUVAIS CATHEDRAL. THE SOUTH PORTAL

pinnacled niches where saints once stood in rows; both have a wealth of carving on perhaps the most splendid doors in France. The realism of the choir screen at Amiens is all but outdone by the rendering here of battle scenes filled with a wealth of incident, the subject only too grimly appropriate to the doors of a French cathedral. I can imagine nothing less meager. Altogether, if Beauvais can terrify by its size, it can charm by its detail, and, in the end, make itself loved by those who, coming often, become more and more familiar with it in its every aspect and every phase.

III

THE cathedral is dedicated to St. Peter, the rock upon which Christ built his church and against which the gates of hell were not to prevail. The great Mother Church at Rome, which Jean Vast thought he had humbled, does not wear the name with better grace nor more appropriately. The cathedral of Beauvais looks rock-like; it proved so in the town's troubled days. There seemed no chance for it when the red cap of Liberty flamed through its desecrated aisles and crowned the Infant Jesus in his Mother's arms, and the Mother, the Blessed Virgin, was transformed into a new Goddess of Reason whose worshipers, to show their reasonableness, destroyed the beauty built up by centuries and massacred those whose charge was to guard it. It was then the statues were hurled from their niches at the cathedral doors and priests were murdered. Up in the Seminary of St. Jean on the hill all were slain save one, and he, struggling as he could down the steep descent, hiding among boulders and bushes, at last fell, breaking both his legs and so adding to the list of martyrs. A young *curé* I met one spring morning near the place told me this and other tales of terror that became very real as I looked down upon the huge choir, and I could realize only too well that, to those who watched, waiting their turn, it must have appeared, in truth, as if the gates of hell had prevailed and the last day dawned upon St. Peter's Church.

But the wave of Liberty, Equality, and Fraternity swept past and away, the Infant Jesus wove his own crown again, the Goddess of Reason was once more the Blessed Mother, and only the empty niches spoke of the danger that had threatened. Worse days came with new revelations of Reason—days when the restorer was let loose, when France seized upon the cathedral as an Historical Monument, when the Bishop's Palace was taken from him and given to the lawyers. And these troubles too were survived, as most probably the still worse troubles of our own time will be. But even if, in the struggle with the State, the cathedral of Beauvais is lost to the Church, is emptied and stripped bare and handed over a prey to the tourist, like the abbey of St. Michel on its windy mount, the beauty will remain. Art is the rock upon which the cathedral of St. Peter in the gray North is as firmly set as the Pyramids of the Egyptian desert, or the broken stones of the Parthenon under the sunlit skies of Greece.